The Syntax of Argument Structure

Linguistische Arbeiten

Edited by
Klaus von Heusinger, Agnes Jäger,
Gereon Müller, Ingo Plag,
Elisabeth Stark and Richard Wiese

Volume 581

The Syntax of Argument Structure

Empirical Advancements and Theoretical Relevance

Edited by
Artemis Alexiadou and
Elisabeth Sophia Maria Verhoeven

DE GRUYTER

ISBN 978-3-11-127848-3
e-ISBN (PDF) 978-3-11-075725-5
e-ISBN (EPUB) 978-3-11-075734-7
ISSN 0344-6727

Library of Congress Control Number: 2021942370

Bibliographic information published by the Deutsche Nationalbibliothek
The Deutsche Nationalbibliothek lists this publication in the Deutsche Nationalbibliografie;
detailed bibliographic data are available on the Internet at http://dnb.dnb.de.

© 2023 Walter de Gruyter GmbH, Berlin/Boston
This volume is text- and page-identical with the hardback published in 2021.
Typesetting: Integra Software Services Pvt. Ltd.
Printing and binding: CPI books GmbH, Leck

www.degruyter.com

Contents

Artemis Alexiadou, Elisabeth Sophia Maria Verhoeven
The syntax of argument structure —— 1

Patrick Brandt, Petra B. Schumacher
Too strong argument structures and (un-)prepared repair —— 13

Michael Baumann, Sandra Pappert, Thomas Pechmann
Evidence against lexicalist or configurational approaches to structural encoding in sentence production —— 33

Anna Czypionka, Carsten Eulitz
Case marking affects the processing of animacy with simple verbs, but not particle verbs —— 69

Helen de Hoop, Peter de Swart
Unexpected (in)animate argument marking —— 105

Jeannique Darby, Artemis Alexiadou, Giorgos Spathas, Michael Walsh
Interpretability, aspectual coercion, and event structure in Object-Experiencer verbs: An acceptability study —— 137

Patricia Irwin
Discourse and unaccusativity —— 181

Index —— 203

Artemis Alexiadou, Elisabeth Sophia Maria Verhoeven
The syntax of argument structure
Empirical advancements and theoretical relevance

Abstract: In recent years, enormous progress has been made in the development and availability of empirical techniques in language research. They have been fruitfully integrated into the discussion of theoretical models at all linguistic layers. The present article sets out this background and identifies relevant questions and challenges that arise from these novel empirical data for the study of the syntax of argument structure. It presents the articles collected in this volume in their contribution to progress in the field.

Keywords: argument structure, empirical methods, theoretical modelling

1 Introduction

Bridging theoretical modelling and advanced empirical techniques is a central aim of current linguistic research (e.g. Featherston & Sternefeld eds. 2007; Stolterfoht & Featherston eds. 2012). The progress in empirical methods contributes to the precise estimation of the properties of linguistic data and promises new ways for justifying theoretical models and testing their implications (Fanselow et al. eds. 2006). The syntax of argument structure has been the focus of numerous studies following this line of research, investigating phenomena such as the causative alternation (Fadlon 2014), unaccusativity (Keller & Sorace 2003; Hirsch & Wagner 2011; Irwin 2012; Verhoeven & Kügler 2014; Momma et al. 2018), ergativity (Longenbaugh & Polinsky 2017), argument structures of unergatives and transitives (Olta-Massuet et al. 2017), argument hierarchies and argument realization (Bornkessel et al. 2005; Lamers & de Swart eds. 2012), psych predicates (Lamers & de Hoop 2014; Verhoeven 2014, 2015), the dative alternation (Bresnan et al. 2007), inherent vs. structural case (Bayer et al. 2001).

Artemis Alexiadou, Humboldt-Universität zu Berlin, Institut für Anglistik und Amerikanistik, Unter den Linden 6, 10099 Berlin, Germany & Leibniz-Zentrum Allgemeine Sprachwissenschaft (ZAS), Schützenstr. 18, 10117 Berlin, Germany, e-mail: artemis.alexiadou@hu-berlin.de
Elisabeth Sophia Maria Verhoeven, Humboldt-Universität zu Berlin, Institut für deutsche Sprache und Linguistik, Dorotheenstraße 24, 10117 Berlin, Germany, e-mail: elisabeth.verhoeven@hu.berlin.de

Such studies provide interesting but potentially controversial contributions to linguistic theory: some discover gradience in the verbal lexicon that can only be precisely measured with quantitative methods (see e.g. Keller & Sorace 2003); others claim that properties attributed to verbal syntax are an epiphenomenon of other layers of grammar (see e.g. Hirsch & Wagner 2011). Furthermore, new empirical methods also come with the challenge to disentangle the effects of grammar from the effects of further sources of variation, e.g. processing (Fanselow & Frisch 2006). Studies such as e.g. Polinsky et al. (2012) show reflexes of core properties of verbal syntax in the processing of ergativity.

The present collective volume takes up the line of research represented in such studies. It originates from a workshop addressing the interplay between new empirical advancements and theoretical perspectives in the investigation of argument structure held on the occasion of the 38th annual meeting of the German Linguistic Society at the University of Konstanz. The volume contains six studies on the syntax of argument structure combining empirical and theoretical perspectives. The main focus lies on the relevance of empirical results achieved through up-to-date methodology for the theoretical analysis and modelling of argument-structure. The contributions tackle issues of argument structure from different perspectives addressing questions related to diverse verb types (unaccusative and unergative verbs, (di)transitive verbs, psychological verbs), morpho-syntactic operations (prefixation, simple vs. particle verbs), case distinctions (dative vs. accusative, case vs. prepositions), argument and voice alternations (dative vs. benefactive alternation, active vs. passive), word order alternations (object preposing) and the impact of animacy, agentivity, and eventivity on argument structure. They report data obtained through a variety of methods such as psycho- and neurolinguistics experiments, corpus studies and acceptability judgments.

2 Bridging theory and empirical methods

It is by now commonly acknowledged that linguistic theories need to stand the test of the rapidly growing possibilities of objectivized quantitative empirical testing in order to be legitimate. The last decade has seen the rise of fields such as experimental syntax or experimental semantics and pragmatics, employing methods originating from psycho- and neurolinguistics such as acceptability judgments, reaction or reading time measurements, priming tasks, eye tracking, or event-related potential (ERP). The relevance of these new fields is visible in recent and upcoming book publications (Goodall ed. to appear; Sprouse ed. to appear; Noveck 2018; Cummins & Katsos eds. 2018; Meibauer & Steinbach eds. 2011; etc.) or larger research endeavors such as XPrag.de – New Pragmatic Theories based on Experimental Evidence (https://www.xprag.de/). These research directions involve a change in the focus of interest originally associated with experimental methods in linguistics. While from a psycho-linguistic and neurolinguistic perspective the subject of interest lies on processes of language production and processing, here the focus shifts to questions of the adequacy of grammar theories and their predictions.

Another constantly growing field of empirical research in linguistics includes corpus linguistics, which provides the tools and techniques for analyzing ever larger amounts of data from natural language production. Coupled with a rapid development of statistical methods, as witnessed in recent years, these methods provide a powerful tool for the study of language in general and the testing of grammatical theories in particular. At the same time, the constantly expanding empirical methods not only make it possible to test predictions inherent in a theory or compare competing assumptions of alternative theories, but also create new types of data that demand corresponding theoretical developments that have the potential to lead to new, e.g. cognitively more adequate, linguistic theories (cf. Phillips to appear).

What are the challenges resulting from advanced empirical methods as employed in psycho- and neurolinguistics or corpus linguistics for theoretical modeling? Does the investigation of argument structure come with special prerequisites when it comes to empirical testing? How does empirical testing feed linguistic theory? We want to elaborate on two such challenges inherent in quantitative studies of argument structure: (a) gradience resulting from gradient acceptability or frequencies in observation data and forced choice acceptability studies; (b) disentangling effects of grammar and effects of processing.

The nature of the observed gradience immanent in quantitative data depends on the scale of the data. We obtain different numeric values for a given phenomenon, depending on the selected scale, e.g. in analyzing the proportions of aggregated data (by several speakers and/or several lexical items) or in calculating the central values of gradient acceptability judgments. A crucial question/controversy that has been addressed by many scholars using quantitative methods is the relation between gradience in experimental or corpus results and the nature of grammatical categories (e.g. Keller 2000; Keller & Sorace 2003; Sprouse 2007, 2015). Does gradience in empirical measurement (necessarily) imply a gradient nature of grammatical categories? How can gradient measurements be reconciled with a categorical understanding of grammar? Studies in experimental syntax typically test syntactic structures or operations with various lexical items. The reasoning for this is the aim to test the generalizability of a syntactic hypothesis across lexical realizations. Variation is expected in any type of repeated observations and it is taken for granted that different lexical realizations will not render the same result, even if the syntactic structure or operation at issue does not depend on the lexical realization. This is not evidence that the grammar itself is gradient, it is rather the null hypothesis in observing gradient data like proportions, time intervals, or acceptability values in a scale. At the same time, gradience in lexical categories may well reflect the residual of our understanding of grammar. The lexical items that we use in order to test the acceptability of a syntactic construction are not just idiosyncratic entries in a lexicon but finally multidimensional entities that can be further decomposed in semantic/syntactic features. Hence, suspecting lexical variation opens the challenge to identify and (empirically) establish the relevant semantic/syntactic features that may contribute to reduce the residual variation in the data.

Argument structure by its very nature seems to be more susceptible to or dependent on lexical variation since the lexical items themselves constitute argument structure classes. Quantitative studies on argument structure are commonly based on testing several lexical instantiations of a given class (as also evidenced in most studies of the present volume), e.g. they examine a number of verbs as representing a verb class. Here, gradience at the lexical level is particularly relevant since it is a major source of indeterminacy in establishing boundaries between verb classes. For instance, certain readings may not be categorically excluded for a verb or a class of verbs but may be possible in an appropriate context (see e.g. Darby et al. this volume on gradient agentivity and eventivity with psych verbs and a proposal of coercion being at play for a subclass of psych verbs). Furthermore, certain lexico-semantic properties of verbs may be less stable than others. For instance, Keller & Sorace (2003) show that lability or underspecification of aspectual properties or argument roles produce gradience in the acceptability of auxiliary selection and impersonal passivization with certain unaccusative and unergative verbs. Moreover, gradience may arise from the fact that syntactic properties are determined by the interplay of various lexical factors, whose mutual interactions are indeterminate (Sorace 2004).

A crucial question is again whether the empirically observed gradience reflects gradience in grammar or can be reconciled with a categorical or binary view of the involved grammatical categories. One possible empirically based answer to this question is exemplified in Verhoeven (2017) where the impact of gradient agentivity with psych verbs on word order choice in natural language production is measured. If we assume a binary notion of agentivity this involves a binary classification of psych-verbs: a subset of psych verbs allows for agentive readings and another subset of verbs does not do so. Non-agentive verbs such as *concern* exclude an agentive interpretation in which the subject has conscious control over the event whereas verbs like *bother* are compatible with agentive or non-agentive readings. Such a binary distinction is expected to lead to a straightforward classification of every verb in one or the other class. As a diagnostic for this distinction we expect that the respective verbs are (in)compatible with a propositional content that entails an agentive contribution of the subject constituent, as exemplified in (1) and (2).

(1) a. John concerned the teacher on purpose.
    b. John bothered the teacher on purpose.

(2) a. John decided to concern the teacher.
    b. John decided to bother the teacher.

However, applying these diagnostics in an experimental setting reveals gradience: most psych verbs are not unambiguously compatible or incompatible with such contexts, but they are judged to be compatible to a certain extent. The crucial question is whether this gradience is grammatically relevant. This is tested with gradient and categorical models of agentivity as predictors for corpus frequencies of word order with the respective verbs. The results show that a binary notion of agentivity reaches the maximal fit in explaining the respective frequencies in the corpus. Such results have implications for theories of argument structure in general and psych verbs in particular, see the discussion in Darby et al. (this volume).

Advanced experimental methods also present the challenge of dissociating the effects of grammar from the effects of further sources of variation, e.g. processing (Fanselow & Frisch 2006; Phillips et al. to appear). One well-known effect in acceptability measurements relates to grammatical illusions, i.e. putatively ungrammatical sentences are judged as acceptable due to a mismatch between the grammar and the parser (cf. for instance subject verb agreement mismatches due to agreement attraction with an intervening DP as in *the key to the cabinets are rusty*, see Wagers et al. 2009; Phillips et al. to appear). In speeded judgment experiments such structures reached better acceptability values than structures without an intervening DP that can be responsible for agreement attraction (i.e. *the key to the cabinet are rusty*). However, in careful judgment tasks this difference is less clear. This points to the significance of the type of measurement applied as well as the cognitive mechanisms involved in the judgment process. As demonstrated and advocated in Phillips et al. (to appear), the use of sophisticated empirical testing needs to come along with a better understanding of which cognitive processes are involved in the different measurements and how the grammatical system and the cognitive system are linked more specifically.

While it is true that disentangling the effects related to the grammar from effects related to processing is a prerequisite for a fruitful application of experimental methods in the study of grammar theory, progress has been made in this endeavour by systematically integrating typological variation in experimental studies. Such studies allow for testing competing hypotheses on the role of grammatical properties such as for instance the relation between linear and hierarchical structure (cf. e.g. animate-first vs. animate-high in Prat-Sala & Branigan 2000) or reflexes of core properties of verbal syntax in the processing of relative clauses (Polinsky et al. 2012). The latter issue relates to effects of differences in alignment systems (accusative vs. ergative) on (universal) assumptions about the subject function and the role of morphological coding of intransitive and transitive subjects (and objects) (Polinsky to appear). Traditionally, most studies investigating processing effects of different grammatical functions examine (well-researched) accusative-aligned languages such as English, German, Japanese or Korean. That means that the attested subject-preference in the processing of relative clauses (i.e. the processing advantage for subject gaps over object gaps) is potentially dependent on the specific properties of this type of languages. The inclusion of ergative-aligned languages in this family of studies (e.g. Carreiras et al. 2010 on Basque; Polinsky et al. 2012 on Avar; Longenbaugh & Polinsky 2017 on Niuean; Clemens et al. 2015 on Ch'ol and Q'anjob'al) allowed for a more comprehensive view of the subject preference, integrating not only the syntactic properties of ergative languages but also the role of morphological case and agreement marking in accusative and ergative languages for relative clause processing. The results so far show that the subject preference is basically independent of alignment type and also holds for the mentioned ergative languages. At the same time morphological marking of the dependent case (i.e. accusative or ergative, respectively) facilitates processing of the gaps corresponding to the DPs with independent cases (i.e. nominative or absolutive, respectively) resulting in processing differences between ergative and accusative languages.

3 Contributions to the present volume

The articles gathered in this volume all respond in one way or another to the questions raised in the previous section. They present data using a wide range of methods such as psycho- and neuro-linguistic experiments, corpus studies and acceptability judgement in order to further the analysis of well-known issues in the analysis of argument structure.

In their article, entitled *Too strong argument structures and (un)prepared repair: The case of* zu-*excessives* **Patrick Brandt** and **Petra Schumacher** study structures with *zu* (*zu groß* 'too big') as comparatives. They propose an analysis which involves an intermediate step of reflexivization, where the two arguments of the underlying comparative are identified, leading to a contradiction which needs to be repaired. The results from two ERP studies are taken as evidence for this analysis. They demonstrate that *zu*-excessives show processing patterns similar to other structures which also have been shown to involve contradictory semantics such as structures with privative adjectives (*a fake diamond*). The ERP results from the *zu*-excessives reveal additional processing costs which are analysed as indicating a repair mechanism enforced by the contradiction in the semantic representation. The authors take the results as evidence supporting compositional approaches to syntax and semantics, which assume interface operations that repair conflicting structures and result in hidden meaning.

The study *Evidence against lexicalist or configurational approaches to structural encoding in sentence production* by **Michael Baumann**, **Sandra Pappert**, and **Thomas Pechmann** tests the hypothesis of strict incrementality in sentence production against lexicalist approaches of a mapping of thematic roles onto syntactic functions or configurational accounts assuming functional heads for the integration of arguments in syntactic structure. The series of priming experiments presented takes dative and benefactive alternation structures, which are assumed to differ in their argument structure both in lexicalist and configurational analyses, as testing ground. The experiments reveal significant priming across structures, which was not modulated by the specific alternation type. Hence the results do not provide evidence for the relevance of lexicalist or configurational assumptions of argument structure in sentence production. Rather the experimental results are argued to be in line with a strictly incremental conception of structural encoding which relies on conceptual notions such as proto-roles.

The contribution by **Anna Czypionka** and **Carsten Eulitz** entitled *Case marking affects the processing of animacy with simple verbs, but not particle verbs* reports the results of two ERP studies on German sentence comprehension with respect to argument processing. In two separate experiments, this study tests simple verbs and particle verbs while manipulating object case (accusative vs. dative) and object animacy (animate vs. inanimate). The experiment testing simple verbs revealed increased processing costs for sentences with animate accusative objects in comparison to the three other conditions (inanimate accusatives, animate datives, inanimate datives). In contrast, the parallel experiment with particle verbs showed increased processing costs for sentences with animate objects across case values. The results are interpreted as supporting syntactic accounts that assume a more complex structure for simple nominative-dative assigning verbs but not for simple nominative-accusative assigning verbs. According to these authors, the fact that particle verbs only show animacy effects but no case effects rules out an alternative semantic (i.e. non case-based) account.

Helen de Hoop and **Peter de Swart** explore constraints on object fronting and passivization structures in relation to animacy properties of the arguments in their article *Unexpected marking of (in)animate arguments*. The structures discussed include word order freezing in Kinyarwanda which occurs when objects are equal to or outrank subjects in animacy, or constraints on passivization in Biak where only inanimate patients can be subjects in a passive construction. Furthermore, the frequency patterns of object preposing and passivization in unaccusative vs. causative object-experiencer structures in Dutch are analyzed. Assuming a bidirectional optimality-theoretic approach the authors show that the respective patterns in the typologically diverse languages (Dutch, Kinyarwanda, and Biak) can be explained as a competition between a subject-first preference and a topic-first preference. The model takes into account both the speaker's and the hearer's assumptions about their interlocutor's perspectives in production and interpretation, respectively.

In a large-scale acceptability study **Jeannique Darby**, **Artemis Alexiadou**, **Giorgos Spathas**, and **Michael Walsh** investigate English Object-Experiencer verbs, testing their behaviour with respect to agentivity and eventivity and comparing them to canonical agentive/eventive verbs and experiencer subject verbs. They highlight the role of processing effects in acceptability studies and explain their results in the light of aspectual coercion. In contrast to Grafmiller (2013), they interpret the gradient acceptability results as being due to differences in aspectual coercion and reach the conclusion that the tested Object-Experiencer verbs belong to two different event-structural classes, a subclass with members that more easily receive agentive/eventive readings and a subclass consisting of verbs denoting causative states that may be coerced into agentive/eventive readings. The involved type of additive coercion functions as a repair mechanism, which involves processing difficulties reflected in decreased acceptability found with the stative Object-Experiencer verbs when occurring in agentive/eventive contexts. Hence this study supports theoretical approaches to Object-Experiencer verbs that assume the existence of a subclass of causative states.

In her article *Discourse and unaccusativity: quantitative effects of a structural phenomenon* **Patricia Irwin** argues for a common syntactic analysis of a subset of unaccusative verb phrases (containing motion or manner of motion verbs such as *arrive, walk in*) and existential BE verbs which predicts their occurrence with indefinite (discourse-new) subjects due to their function of establishing new discourse referents. The establishment of the new discourse referent is proposed to be due to the function INSTANTIATE as part of the VP's denotation. This contrasts with VP structures of unergative verbs (*laugh*) and change of state unaccusatives (*break*). This prediction is tested and corroborated in a corpus study based on the Corpus of Contemporary American English (COCA). It is shown that the so-called existential unaccusatives occur significantly more frequently with indefinite subjects than unergatives do. Based on this study, Irwin discusses the significance of natural production data as provided in corpora for syntactic theory but also highlights their limits when arguing for specific theoretical analyses.

In summary, the present collection of articles takes up current theoretical questions on the syntax of argument structure and advances their investigation by adding insights from various empirical paradigms. It thus demonstrates the fruitfulness of an approach that tests theoretical assumptions with current empirical methods.

References

Bayer, Josef, Markus Bader & Michael Meng. 2001. Morphological underspecification meets oblique case: Syntactic and processing effects in German. *Lingua* 111(4–7). 465–514. https://doi.org/10.1016/S0024-3841(00)00041-3.

Bornkessel, Ina, Stefan Zysset, Angela D. Friederici, D. Yves von Cramon & Matthias Schlesewsky. 2005. Who did what to whom? The neural basis of argument hierarchies during language comprehension. *NeuroImage* 26(1). 221–233. https://doi.org/10.1016/j.neuroimage.2005.01.032.

Bresnan, Joan, Anna Cueni, Tatiana Nikitina & R. Harald Baayen. 2007. Predicting the dative alternation. In Gerlof Boume, Irene Kraemer & Joost Zwarts (eds.), *Cognitive Foundations of Interpretation*, 69–94. Amsterdam: Royal Netherlands Academy of Science.

Carreiras, Manuel, Jon Andoni Duñabeitia, Marta Vergara, Irene de la Cruz-Pavía & Itziar Laka. 2010. Subject relative clauses are not universally easier to process: Evidence from Basque. *Cognition* 115(1). 79–92. https://doi.org/10.1016/j.cognition.2009.11.012

Clemens, Lauren, Jessica Coon, Pedro Mateo Pedro, Adam Milton Morgan, Maria Polinsky, Gabrielle Tandet & Matthew Wagers. 2015. Ergativity and the complexity of extraction: A view from Mayan. *Natural Language and Linguistic Theory* 33. 417–467. https://doi.org/10.1007/s11049-014-9260-x.

Cummins, Chris & Napoleon Katsos (eds.). 2018. *The Oxford Handbook of Experimental Semantics and Pragmatics*. Oxford: Oxford University Press.

Fadlon, Julie. 2014. *The psycho-linguistics of verbal diathesis: The transitive–unaccusative alternation*. Tel Aviv: Tel Aviv University dissertation.

Fanselow, Gisbert & Stefan Frisch. 2006. Effects of processing difficulty on judgements of acceptability. In Gisbert Fanselow, Caroline Féry, Ralf Vogel & Matthias Schlesewsky (eds.), *Gradience in Grammar: Generative Perspectives*. Oxford: Oxford University Press. https://doi.org/10.1093/acprof:oso/9780199274796.003.0015.

Fanselow, Gisbert, Caroline Féry, Ralf Vogel & Matthias Schlesewsky (eds.). 2006. *Gradience in Grammar: Generative Perspectives*. Oxford: Oxford University Press. https://doi.org/10.1093/acprof:oso/9780199274796.001.0001.

Featherston, Sam & Wolfgang Sternefeld (eds.). 2007. *Roots. Linguistics in Search of its Evidential Basis*. Berlin & New York: De Gruyter. https://doi.org/10.1515/9783110198621.

Goodall, Grant (ed.). to appear. *The Cambridge Handbook of Experimental Syntax*. Cambridge: Cambridge University Press.

Grafmiller, Jason. 2013. *The semantics of syntactic choice: an analysis of English emotion verbs*. PhD dissertation, Stanford University.

Hirsch, Aron & Michael Wagner. 2011. Patterns of prosodic prominence in English intransitive sentences. Paper presented at GLOW 34.

Irwin, Patricia. 2012. *Unaccusativity at the interfaces*. New York, NY: New York University dissertation.

Keller, Frank & Antonella Sorace. 2003. Gradient auxiliary selection and impersonal passivization in German: An experimental investigation. *Journal of Linguistics* 39(1). 57–108. https://doi.org/10.1017/S0022226702001676.

Keller, Frank. 2000. *Gradience in Grammar: Experimental and computational aspects of degrees of grammaticality*. Edinburgh: University of Edinburgh dissertation.

Lamers, Monique & Helen de Hoop. 2014. Animate object fronting in Dutch: A production study. In Brian MacWhinney, Andrej L. Malchukov & Edith A. Moravcsik (eds.), *Competing motivations in grammar and usage*, 42–53. Oxford: Oxford University Press.

Lamers, Monique & Peter de Swart (eds.). 2012. *Case, word order and Prominence: Interacting cues in language production and comprehension*. Dordrecht: Springer.

Longenbaugh, Nicholas & Maria Polinsky. 2017. Experimental approaches to ergative languages. In Jessica Coon, Diane Massam & Lisa Demena Travis (eds.), *The Oxford Handbook of Ergativity*, 709–732. Oxford: Oxford University Press. https://doi.org/10.1093/oxfordhb/9780198739371.013.29.

Meibauer, Jörg & Markus Steinbach (eds.). 2011. *Experimental Pragmatics/Semantics*. Amsterdam: Benjamins.

Momma, Shota, L. Robert Slevc & Colin Phillips. 2018. Unaccusativity in sentence production, *Linguistic Inquiry* 49(1). 181–194. https://doi.org/10.1162/LING_a_00271.

Noveck, Ira A. 2018. *Experimental Pragmatics. The Making of a Cognitive Science*. Cambridge: Cambridge University Press.

Olta-Massuet, Isabel, Victoria Sharpe, Kyriaki Neophytou & Alec Marantz. 2017. Syntactic Priming as a test of argument structure: A self-paced reading experiment. *Frontiers in Psychology* 8:1311. https://doi.org/103389/fpsych.2017.01311.

Phillips, Colin, Phoebe Gaston, Nick Huang & Hanna Muller. To appear. Theories all the way down: Remarks on "theoretical" and "experimental" linguistics. In Grant Grand (ed.), *The Cambridge Handbook of Experimental Syntax*. Cambridge: Cambridge University Press.

Polinsky, Maria, Carlos Gómez Gallo, Peter Graff & Ekaterina Kravtchenco. 2012. Subject preference and ergativity. *Lingua* 122. 267–277. https://doi.org/10.1016/j.lingua.2011.11.004.

Polinsky, Maria. to appear. Experimental syntax and linguistic fieldwork. In Jon Sprouse (ed.), *Oxford Handbook of Experimental Syntax*. Oxford: Oxford University Press.

Prat-Sala, Mercè & Holly P. Branigan. 2000. Discourse constraints on syntactic processing in language production: A cross-linguistic study in English and Spanish. *Journal of Memory and Language* 42. 168–182. https://doi.org/10.1006/jmla.1999.2668.

Sorace, Antonella. 2004. Gradience at the lexicon-syntax interface: Evidence from auxiliary selection and implications for unaccusativity. In Artemis Alexiadou, Elena Anagnostopoulou & Martin Everaert (eds.), *The Unaccusativity Puzzle*, 243–268. Oxford: Oxford University Press.

Sprouse, Jon (ed.). to appear. *Oxford Handbook of Experimental Syntax*. Oxford University Press.

Sprouse, Jon. 2007. Continuous acceptability, categorical grammaticality, and experimental syntax. *Biolinguistics* 1. 123–134.

Sprouse, Jon. 2015. Three open questions in experimental syntax. *Linguistics Vanguard* 1(1). 89–100. https://doi.org/10.1515/lingvan-2014-1012.

Stolterfoht, Britta & Sam Featherston (eds.). 2012. *Empirical approaches to linguistic theory: Studies in meaning and structure*. Berlin & Boston: De Gruyter.

Verhoeven, Elisabeth & Frank Kügler. 2014. Accentual preferences and predictability: An acceptability study on split intransitivity in German. *Lingua* 165(Part B). 298–315, https://doi.org/10.1016/j.lingua.2014.09.013.

Verhoeven, Elisabeth. 2014. Thematic prominence and animacy asymmetries: Evidence from a cross-linguistic production study, *Lingua* 143. 129–161. https://doi.org/10.1016/j.lingua.2014.02.002.

Verhoeven, Elisabeth. 2015. Thematic asymmetries do matter! A corpus study of German word order. *Journal of Germanic Linguistics* 27(1). 45–104. https://doi.org/10.1017/S147054271400021X.

Verhoeven, Elisabeth. 2017. Scales or features in verb meaning? Verb classes as predictors of syntactic behavior. *Belgian Journal of Linguistics* 31(1). 164–193. https://doi.org/10.1075/bjl.00007.ver.

Wagers, Matthew W., Ellen F. Lau & Colin Phillips. 2009. Agreement attraction in comprehension: Representations and processes. *Journal of Memory and Language* 61. 206–237. https://doi.org/10.1016/j.jml.2009.04.002.

Patrick Brandt, Petra B. Schumacher
Too strong argument structures and (un-)prepared repair
The case of *zu*-excessives

Abstract: We present *zu*-excessive structures like *Otto ist zu schwer* 'Otto is too heavy' as instantiations of comparatives that have been reflexivized. Comparatives express asymmetric relations between distinguished referents, but reflexivization identifies argument places (or reduces two argument places to one), leading to a symmetric relation. Reflexivization is thus in conflict with the asymmetry property of comparatives and leads to an intermediate semantic representation that is contradictory. Two experiments substantiate that *zu*-excessives share this property with privative adjective and animal-for-statue constructions that similarly give rise to contradictory semantics. The processing of any of the constructions mentioned yields a positivity in the event-related-potential signature characteristic of conceptual reorganization; however, the observed positivity occurs earlier in the case of *zu*-excessives than in the other cases. We propose this difference is due to *zu* signalling the mandatory preparation for an ensuing repair rather than reflecting the repair operation itself that involves manipulating the standard of comparison, coded elsewhere in the string (if at all).

Keywords: compositionality, repair, standard, excessive, comprehension

1 Hidden meaning and compositionality

Over the last few years, rule- and derivation-based conceptions of the syntax and semantics of the argument structure of natural languages have come under fire from approaches questioning the central role of compositionality, i.e. the idea that

---

Acknowledgements: This research was supported by a grant from the German Research Foundation (DFG) to PBS (SCHU 2517/6-1). We would also like to thank Eric Fuß for helpful discussion and Claudia Kilter, Hanna Weiland-Breckle and Filiz Özden for their assistance during data preparation and recording.

Patrick Brandt, Leibniz Institut für Deutsche Sprache, R5 6-13, 68161 Mannheim, Germany, e-mail: brandt@ids-mannheim.de
Petra B. Schumacher, Universität zu Köln, Institut für deutsche Sprache und Literatur I, Sprachwissenschaft, Albertus-Magnus-Platz, 50923 Cologne, Germany, e-mail: petra.schumacher@uni-koeln.de

the meanings of complex expressions derive from the meanings of their parts and the way these parts are put together structurally. Construction grammar (Goldberg 1995) holds that the syntax-semantics interface really consists in a taxonomy of constructions, which are more or less complex meanings that are irreducibly linked to more or less complex syntactic structures. In contrast, compositional approaches hold that hidden meaning may be the result of interface operations that repair otherwise conflicting structures (Brandt 2016, 2019; Jackendoff 1997; Reinhart 2006). With this contribution, we want to shed more light on this debate by examining a particular case of hidden meaning – namely the excessive construction in German. Excessive constructions like (1) that are formed with the degree particle *zu* ('too') can occur without explicit information that is necessary for interpretation, such as being too heavy *for something*. This standard of comparison can be overtly realized (2) but can also remain unarticulated. In the latter case, the missing information must be recovered from context.

(1) Otto ist zu schwer.
    Otto is too heavy

(2) Otto ist zu schwer für einen Jockey.
    Otto is too heavy for a jockey

In the following, we propose an analysis of excessive constructions as comparatives, the two arguments of which are identified by reflexivization. This is in conflict with the asymmetry property of comparatives, reflected by the intuitive oddity of locutions like *Otto is heavier than himself*. The conflicting semantic information is repaired much akin to repair mechanisms described for so-called privative adjectives (as in *fake diamond*) that require the negation of properties of their head noun or material expressions that when combined with an animate noun give rise to a statue reading (as in *the stone lion*) and similarly necessitate the negation of certain properties of the head noun.

In section 2, we present these cases of syntax-semantics mismatches that strengthen the analysis of syntax-semantics interface repair operations before turning to a more in-depth discussion of excessive structures in section 3. Subsequently, we present a series of real-time comprehension experiments on excessive constructions in section 4, which reveal similar processing patterns as previously observed for constructions involving privative and material adjectives. These data show that processing excessive structures is computationally demanding (compared to structures containing the particle *so* 'so' that does not trigger repair mechanisms) and reflect a mechanism that has previously been associated with updating processes following mismatches in argument structure. Section 5 indicates directions for future research.

2 Privative predicates and weakening

One of the most basic principles of syntactic-semantic composition is the head principle, stating that the syntactic head of a phrase determines the overall meaning of that phrase as much as it determines its overall category. The head primacy principle of Kamp & Partee (1995) guarantees that adjectival modification of nominals delivers nominals again which due to the modification have a more specific meaning.[1] For instance, [[German jockey]] denotes a subset of what [[jockey]] denotes, namely, the intersection of the sets denoting things that are German and things that are jockeys. Somewhat more involved than this simple case of so-called intersective modification, [[skillful Jockey]] denotes a subset of the things that are jockeys, where what this set contains exactly is also a matter of what the relevant standards regarding skillfulness in the domain of jockeys are. Regardless of the question of how such standards are determined (cf. below sections 3 and 5), the head primacy principle assures that a skillful jockey is a jockey just as much as a German jockey is a jockey. More abstractly, the principle guarantees that we can be sure to find the referent(s) (if any) of [[A N]] among the referents (if any) of [[N]] but do not have to look beyond the meaning of [[N]], which arguably is an important asset when the meaning of complex noun phrases is to be determined.

Against the background of the head primacy principle, so-called privative adjectives – among them English *fake*, *false*, or *forged* as well as German *falsch*, *gefälscht*, *unecht* – present a puzzle in that interpreting noun phrases that contain privative adjectives involves moving outside the denotation of the noun that functions as the phrasal head indeed. A *fake diamond* is not a diamond and *forged evidence* is not evidence, crucially, even if the denotata of the complex noun phrases bear obvious traits of the denotata of the nominal heads of the construction. The meaning of noun phrases that involve modification by privative adjectives appears to be characterized by an extra operation that is not overtly coded in syntax. The case of privative adjectives suggests itself for

---

[1] Kamp and Partee's (1995: 161) "Head Primacy Principle" is given in (i):
(i) The Head primacy principle (HPP): In a modifier-head structure, the head is interpreted relative to the context of the whole constituent, and the modifier is interpreted relative to the local context created from the former context by the interpretation of the head.

an analysis in terms of a repair mechanism to resolve conflicting information; quite intuitively, privative predicates give rise to a contradiction that is due to the predication of both the presence and the absence of a certain property (being a diamond, constituting evidence) of one and the same referent and thus violate the basic semantic requirement of non-contradictoriness. The derivation of the hidden quantificational meaning in terms of redressing an intermediate contradictory and hence semantically "illegal" meaning representation can be sketched as in (3).

(3) This is a fake diamond.
     This is a diamond and this is not a diamond.
     In some sense this is a diamond and in some sense it is not.

In (3), the "in some sense it is not" is really the negative (absent property) meaning mentioned above that is moved from the level of ordinary objects to a higher structural level that achieves the encoding and quantification of indexical information, i.e. the "coordinates" with respect to which propositional meanings are evaluated such as times, possible worlds and thresholds (viz. standards of comparison) as laid out in Brandt (2016, 2019). Privative predicates are genuinely contradiction-inducing according to this analysis, and the hidden quantificational meaning of the structures involving them is the effect of redressing the interpretive problem that this poses.

Experimentally investigating modification by means of privative adjectives in an event-related potential (ERP) study,[2] Schumacher et al. (2018) find in association with the processing of this particular type of construction a positive ERP component that is also characteristic of certain types of referential shift or reconceptualization (Schumacher 2013, 2014), which is attributed to the updating of mental representations due to syntax-semantics mismatches. Specifically, reading *a fake diamond* vs. *an impure diamond* yielded late positive-going ERP effects relative to the onset of the adjective and the noun, with an onset latency around 600–700 ms each. Schumacher et al. (2018) submit that the observed positivities for the privative construction reflect the repair mechanism sketched above that redresses a semantic contradiction which arises from the negation

---

2 ERPs reflect the neuronal activity triggered by cognitive, sensory and motor events. They provide a high temporal resolution of the underlying activity and help to tease apart discrete processes as they are for instance involved in the resolution of syntax-semantics mismatches. Importantly, the underlying processes are identified by contrasting the relative difference of the ERP signal between a critical construction and a minimally differing control construction.

encoded lexically for the privative adjective. Support for the idea that suspending the local realization of certain meaning aspects leads to processing difficulties reflected in a Late Positivity comes from Schumacher's (2013) investigation of the productive animal-for-statue alternation, shown in (4a), compared to the unproblematic combination of material adjective and artefact in (4b).

(4)   a. The wooden dove was on the table.
       b. The wooden trunk was next to the bed.

Quite obviously, the interpretation of animal-for-statue constructions involves negating or ignoring certain properties of the head noun (like animacy), such that it fits the semantics of the modifying adjective. In particular, the semantic features of the noun (here being animate) are too strong to be combinable with the adjective (that requires an artifact-denoting entity) without giving rise to contradiction.[3] To note, animal-for-statue constructions and constructions involving nouns modified by privative adjectives bear one and the same ERP signature characterized by a Late Positivity. Other types of adjective-noun combinations that do not involve contradictory meanings do not show such processing costs, e.g. the signature produced by processing adjectives with a highlighting function (*echter Diamant* 'real diamond') that might be expected to require pragmatic adjustments during the highlighting of a particular property of the head noun does not significantly differ from that of ordinary adjectives (*weißer Diamant* 'white diamond') that were used in a control condition.

The next section presents a parallel case that involves a functional formative for which we argue that it triggers a contradiction. By "functional formative" we refer to a bound or free morpheme that serves to relate content elements structurally or marks certain paradigmatic grammatical operations like comparison, pluralization or reflexivization.

3 The formative *zu*

The grammatical formative *zu* 'too' shows a wide range of functions; from the categorial perspective, it includes at least the word classes preposition, adjective, adverb, infinitive marker and degree particle. Especially in the latter two quasi-

---

3 Partee (2010) presents an analysis according to which privative adjectives suspend the head primacy principle such that the nominal head is interpreted with respect to the adjective. Furthermore, she submits that the head noun receives a weaker interpretation in the scope of privative adjectives.

inflectional uses, *zu* appears to systematically bring about modal interpretations, cf. Holl (2010) and references therein for infinitival *zu*, as well as the remarks around (2) above. We focus here on *zu* in its use as a degree particle in so-called excessive constructions like (5).

(5) Otto ist zu schwer.
     Otto is too heavy

Excessive constructions are a kind of comparative structure; *zu* 'too' appears to fill the same structural position as the comparative morpheme *-er* (already Bresnan 1973 for English *too*). One of the basic traits of comparatives is that they are asymmetric: if x is A-*er* than y, then it follows that y is not A-*er* than x. This asymmetry entails that comparatives are genuinely two-place constructions syntactically and semantically that call for two well-distinguishable individuals. In particular, on the "A not A" approach to comparatives going back to Ross (1969) and Lewis (1972) (cf. as well Klein 1980 and Schwarzschild 2008, among many others), a comparative codes the predication of a gradable predicate of the first individual and the negation of that gradable predicate of the second individual, such that (6a) becomes (6b), where "d" is short for a certain degree of instantiation of the relevant property.

(6) a. Otto is heavier than Ede.
     b. Otto is d-heavy and Ede is not d-heavy.

(6) entails that Ede is less heavy than Otto; in fact, negation comes out meaning 'less' in gradable domains, such that *not heavy* conveys the same as *less than heavy*.[4] Now, however, excessive structures allow for only one ordinary individual argument in their structure, at least superficially. If the semantics associated with the two argument places of regular comparatives are predicated of one single individual, that individual will end up being ascribed contradictory properties, namely, being both d-heavy and not d-heavy at the same time. Indeed, we can observe that structures belonging to the comparative realm behave corruptly if semantically only one individual is available. For example, all of the following sentences with positive or superlative adjectival predicates are true and rather acceptable when addressing one's only son:

---

[4] Jespersen (1924: 325) writes concerning the matter: "*Not* means 'less than', or in other words 'between the terms qualified and nothing'. Thus *not good* means 'inferior', but does not comprise 'excellent'."

(7) You are my big son.
You are my little son.
You are my biggest son.
You are my smallest son.

In contrast, the corresponding pairs of *bona fide* comparative structures are rather odd, indicating that regular comparatives strictly require the semantic presence of at least two distinguishable individuals.

(8) # You are my bigger/smaller son.

We submit that excessive structures are reflexivized comparatives (Brandt 2016, 2019), i.e. that the structure underlying them codes that "something is more A than itself". Let us briefly illustrate how this intuitively odd semantics reduces to a contradiction similar to what we observe with privative predicates or animal-for-statue constructions as discussed in the last section.

Under the "A not A" approach to the semantics of comparatives just mentioned, x is A-*er* than y yields (9).

(9) x is A and y is not A

For example, *Otto is heavier than Ede* corresponds to a situation in which Otto is d-heavy and Ede is not d-heavy. Assuming now that excessive structures are reflexivized comparatives and further assuming that reflexivization corresponds to the identification of the two argument places of a transitive structure (cf. Steinbach 2001 for German), we have:

(10) x is A and y is not A   (regular comparative semantics)
x = y   (reflexivization)
x is A and x is not A   (resulting contradiction)

The first line expresses the asymmetry of the two arguments related in a comparative with respect to the instantiation of a certain property: the degree to which x instantiates the property in question is higher than the degree to which y instantiates the property. The second line represents the result of reflexivization that we take here to correspond to the identification of the argument places. Alternatively, reflexivization would reduce one argument place by "bundling" the properties associated with the respective semantic roles (Reinhart & Siloni 2005). Either way, one argument will end up being ascribed a certain property as well as its negation, as expressed in the plain contradiction in the third line in (10).[5] Let us now see how the underlying contradictoriness of the excessive structure could be the reason for the modal interpretation not transparently marked but intuitively present in excessive structures; a comparative structure that contains an existential modal in the *than*-clause acting as the standard of comparison thus gives a fair paraphrase of the *zu*-excessive as in (11).

(11) Otto is too heavy.
'Otto is heavier than he may be (regarding a certain standard).'

The norm or standard relevant for the interpretation of the excessive depends on or presupposes a purpose or comparison class, much like a regular comparative construction depends on a standard of comparison, coded in the *than* clause in English or the *als* clause in German. Indeed, the purpose clause or phrase coding the comparison class in *zu*-excessives appears to fill the same slot that the standard of comparison in regular comparatives fills. In the absence of an agentive verbal predicate, it is thus impossible to add a purpose clause to a regular adjectival comparative construction, contrast the excessive in (12a) and the comparative in (12b).

(12) a. Otto is too big to be a jockey / for a jockey.
  b. *Otto is bigger (than Ede) (in order) to be a basketball player / for a basketball player.

Suggestively from a syntactic point of view, it is possible to code the purpose clause in an excessive structure specifically with typically comparative means in German, namely, as an *als* clause that is ordinarily used to mark the standard of comparison.[6]

(13) Otto ist zu gross als dass er Jockey sein könnte.
  Otto is too big as that he jockey be could
  'Otto is too big to be a jockey.'

---

[5] Indeed, reflexivization is a suspicious operation independently also in the ordinary individual domain to the extent that one individual (or two individuals that are identical to each other) come to realize differing semantic role information, in particular, properties of the agent as well as the patient role that are more often than not taken to be incompatible. A way out of the dilemma consists in assuming that patient arguments are in fact not restricted at all or so weakly so that their semantics includes (is entailed by) agentive semantics as well; already when we say that patients are non-agents (the result of) reflexivization becomes problematic.
[6] Eric Fuß (p.c.) has reminded us of this supportive fact.

Other properties of purpose clauses in excessives like the licensing of negative polarity items similarly point to the kinship between purpose clauses in *zu*-excessives and *than*-clauses in regular comparative structures (pace Bylinina 2014: chapter 3). In light of these facts, we suggest that excessive structures are fundamentally two place relations like other comparatives, the difference being that in excessives, the second argument place is not filled by the *than* clause as in a regular comparative but by the purpose clause instead. At a more general level, both types of clause play the central role in determining the standard relevant for the comparison. We will therefore henceforth collectively refer to them as "standardizers".[7] Less surprisingly given the common function as standardizer, we propose that in the excessive construction, the purpose clause substitutes for the 'regular comparative' standard of comparison, essentially. More precisely, the negative predication that is the hallmark of the standard of comparison in the regular comparative under the "A not A" approach is "moved" to the purpose clause that comes with excessive structures (even if it remains silent) in reaction to the intermediately derived contradiction. The negative meaning "not: P(x)" (Otto is not d-heavy) is ignored with regard to the main predication (i.e. in terms of the regular standard of comparison as coded by a *than*-clause) and realized with regard to the predicate provided by the purpose clause. The syntax derives a structure that as such would receive a contradictory semantic representation; the interface reacts by suspending the interpretation of the offending negation, effectively "moving" it to the purpose clause that takes the place of the standard. The basic derivation is sketched with a concrete example in (14), where "d" stands for "degree" again.

(14) a. Otto is too heavy (to be a jockey).
    b. Otto is d-heavy and Otto is not d-heavy (and Otto is a Jockey)
    c. Otto is d-heavy (and Otto is d-heavy) and Otto is not a Jockey

---

[7] This perspective may help solve a long-standing puzzle in the realm of comparatives, namely, the fact that so-called absolute comparatives appear to code a meaning that is weaker than the meaning coded by the positive counterparts. Thus, *jüngerer Professor* 'younger professor' does not entail that the professor in question is young. If the standardizer is not articulated but implicitly corresponding to something like "someone is less heavy", then the absolute comparative comes out meaning "more A than not A", i.e., in the case at hand, "younger than not young (or less than young)", which is pretty much what the absolute comparative seems to mean. See footnote 4 above.

We contend that the last line corresponds to the basic semantics of the excessive construction.[8] More elaborately, Brandt (2016, 2019) assumes that the infinitival purpose clause codes possibility (Otto is possibly a Jockey),[9] which becomes impossibility after accommodation of the negative meaning. More superficial pragmatic mechanisms drawing on rhetorical relations ensure that Otto's weight is taken to be the reason for this impossibility (Asher 2007), entailing that if Otto had a different weight, it might be possible for him to be a jockey. What is crucial for our purposes is that the state of affairs coded in the purpose clause is essential for constructing the "original" standard of comparison as much as its manipulation by means of the repair proposed here leads to a new standard of comparison (which can be modelled as a world where the requirements regarding the weight of jockeys are different). The standard of comparison or purpose clause, collected here under "standardizer" thus mark the beginning and the end result of the syntactic-semantic derivation of the excessive structure which eventually receives an interpretation along the lines of (15).

---

8 An anonymous reviewer suggested that the locution expressed by "Otto is not a jockey" does not belong to semantics proper but has the status of an implicature. Flanked by a small survey conducted with native speakers, the authors' intuitions with respect to German reveal that cancellation is hard already in the case of expressing the standard by means of a prepositional phrase (a), harder in the case of infinitival expression of the standard (b) and quite impossible in the case of introducing the standard by a finite sentence (c); special marking by discourse particles like *doch* ('still'/'anyway') is needed in any case:

(i) (a) Otto ist zu schwer für einen Jockey, ?#aber er ist doch ein Jockey.
 (b) Otto ist zu schwer, um Jockey zu sein, #aber er ist doch ein Jockey.
 (c) Otto ist zu schwer, als dass er Jockey sein könnte, #aber er ist doch ein Jockey.

It has been argued prominently that patterns originating as implicatures may get hard-wired and become presuppositions (non-negatable entailments), compare for instance Levinson's (2000) analysis of Principle B effects. More generally, there is an acknowledged path of grammaticalization from particularized to generalized implicatures up to conventionalized implicatures and presuppositions, such that there "soft presuppositions" and "hard implicatures" arise (Romoli & Schwarz 2015). On our analysis, the target of the "movement" of the negation is not *a priori* determined but a matter of the structural options available. In comparatives, the "second" argument place is predestined to host it as it is the "negatively defined" argument place to start, cf. as well the discussion around (10) above. In sum, we do not agree that the less than crystal-clear status of the standardizer with respect to the notoriously problematic semantics-pragmatics divide is challenging specifically for our approach.

9 Cf. for discussion of the modal interpretation of infinitives in terms of anchoring propositional meanings to possible worlds Reis (2003).

(15) Otto has a certain weight, and (therefore) he is not a jockey.

Turning again to the empirical side of our investigation, the next section presents evidence from an ERP study that processing excessive structures may give rise to a positivity in a similar way as in the case of animal-for-statue alternations or privative predicates. This suggests that the three constructions may indeed be unified by a derivation in terms of redressing a contradictory meaning representation.

4 Processing of excessives

In two ERP studies, we compared excessive structures containing the particle *zu* 'too' (16a) to equative structures containing the particle *so* 'so' (16b), the latter not giving rise to a contradiction at the syntax-semantics interface by hypothesis. In light of the link to the processing of privative predicates and animal-for-statue alternations, we predicted a positive-going potential for the (a) over the (b) structures. We further tested whether context exerts a facilitating advantage in providing a standard for comparison. To this end, we compared excessive and control structures without context (experiment 1) to those preceded by a context sentence (experiment 2).

(16) a. (Jockeys dürfen höchstens 55 kg wiegen.) Peter ist zu schwer für einen guten Jockey.
(jockeys may after most 55 kg weigh) Peter is too heavy for a good jockey
'(Jockeys may weight at most 55 kg.) Peter is too heavy to be a good jockey.'
'(Jockeys may weight at most 55 kg.) Peter is too heavy to be a good jockey.'
b. (Ringer müssen mindestens 70 kg wiegen.) Simon ist so schwer wie ein echter Ringer.
(wrestlers must at.least 70 kg weigh) Simon is as heavy as a real wrestler
'(Wrestlers must weigh at least 70 kg.) Simon is as heavy as a real wrester.'

4.1 Participants

Forty-eight monolingual native speakers of German, all of whom were students at the University of Cologne, participated in the investigation. All participants were right-handed and reported normal or corrected-to-normal vision and no history of neurological disorder. Twenty-four participants were recorded in each experiment. In experiment 1 (no context), data from 20 participants were included in the analysis after artifact screening (18 women, 2 men; mean age: 23.2 years; range: 19–31 years). In experiment 2 (prior context), we were able to analyze data from 22 participants (10 men and 12 women; mean age: 23.3 years; range: 19–30 years of age).

4.2 Materials

Forty pairs of stimuli were constructed that included either an excessive *zu* or an equative/positive *so* before an adjective. They were interspersed with 400 fillers in experiment 1 and 160 fillers in experiment 2. All items were pseudo-randomized and presented in three different orders across participants. To assure that participants attended to the stimuli, each test item was followed by a word recognition task (50 % with a correct word probe and 50 % with an incorrect word probe).

4.3 Procedure

After giving written informed consent, the participants were prepared for the recording of the electroencephalogram (EEG). They were then seated in front of a computer monitor in a sound-proof booth and performed a practice session to get accustomed to the experimental setup and task before the experimental session started. The written experimental items were presented word by word in the middle of the monitor in off-white letters against a black background. Each trial started with a fixation star that was displayed for 500 ms in the center of the screen and followed by a 150 ms blank screen. Each word was displayed for 450 ms with a 150 ms blank screen between words. Each experimental item ended with a 1000 ms blank screen, followed by three question marks that served as signals for the upcoming word recognition task and the presentation of a probe word. The maximum response time to the word recognition task was set to 3000 ms. Participants were asked to decide whether the probe word had occurred in the previous stimulus or not. They used a gamepad controller to mark their response. True and false answer buttons were counterbalanced across participants.

4.4 EEG recording

The EEG was recorded from 24 Ag/AgCl scalp electrodes (ground: AFz), which were referenced to the left mastoid and re-referenced offline to linked mastoids. To monitor for artifacts due to blinks and other ocular movements, two sets of electrode pairs were placed around the participants' eyes. Electrode impedances were kept below 5 kΩ and all channels were amplified with a *BrainAmp* DC amplifier (Munich, Germany) and digitized at 500 Hz.

4.5 EEG preprocessing

After recording, the EEG data were filtered offline with a 0.3–20 Hz band pass filter to correct for slow signal drifts prior to the target words. Automatic (±40 μV for the eye electrodes) and manual rejections were performed to exclude trials containing artifacts from ocular movements or amplifier saturation. Trials with time-outs and incorrect responses in the behavioral task were also removed prior to statistical testing. Average ERPs were time-locked to particle onset and computed from 200 ms before until 2000 ms after the onset of the particle.

4.6 Data analysis

Statistical analyses were carried out on the basis of the mean amplitude values per condition in time windows determined by visual inspection. A repeated measures analysis of variance (ANOVA) was performed with the factors CONDITION (excessive vs. control) and the topographical factor REGION OF INTEREST (ROI, with two levels: anterior vs. posterior). The channels were grouped by their anterior-posterior distribution across the scalp and entered the analysis as anterior (F3, F4, F7, F8, Fz, FC1, FC2, FC5, FC6, FCz, C3, C4, Cz) or posterior sites (T7, T8, CP1, CP2, CP5, CP6, CPz, P3, P4, P7, P8, Pz, POz). The analyses were carried out using the *ez*-package (Lawrence 2013) in R (R Core Team 2015).

4.7 Results

For experiment 1 (no context), Figure 1 presents the averaged ERPs for excessive structures (solid line) compared to the *so*-control structures (dotted line). The plotted ERPs span from the onset of the particle (onset at 0 ms) across the adjective (onset at 600 ms) and the spill over region representing the beginning of the purpose clause (onset at 1200 ms, as indicated by vertical bars in the figure's scale). The ERPs show an early positivity between 150–300 ms following the particle *zu* and a later negative deflection between 1550–1700 ms (350–500 ms after onset of spill over segment). No other differences reached statistical significance. The analysis of variance in the window from 150–300 ms registered an interaction of CONDITION x ROI ($F(1,19)=7.13$, $p<0.02$), which when resolved by region showed an effect over posterior electrode sites ($F(1,19)=6.30$, $p<0.03$). It further revealed a main effect of CONDITION between 1550–1700 ms ($F(1,19)=6.85$, $p<.02$).

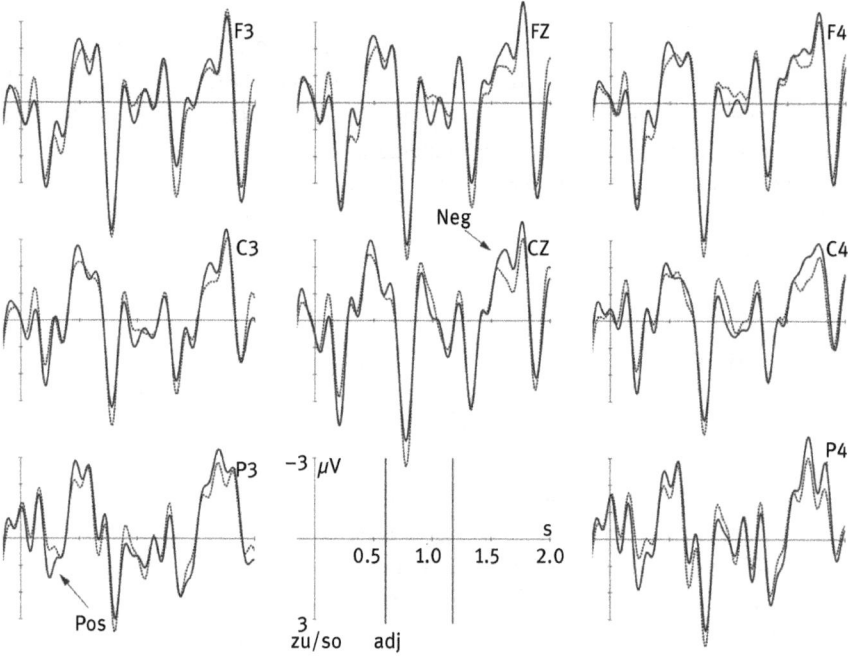

Figure 1: Effects of excessives in experiment 1 (solid line; the dotted line represents the control condition): Posterior positivity (between 150–300 ms) time-locked to particle onset and negativity relative to onset of spill over segment (350–500 ms).

For experiment 2 (prior context), the averaged ERPs for excessive structures (solid line) and the *so*-control construction (dotted line) following supporting context sentences are illustrated in Figure 2. The plot shows the same range as in experiment 1. The figure indicates again an early positivity between 200–350 ms relative to the onset of the excessive particle *zu* and a negative deflection further downstream between 1550–1700 ms (350–500 ms after onset of spill over segment). The ANOVA for the window from 200–350 ms revealed an interaction of CONDITION x ROI ($F(1,21)=11.76$, $p<0.01$). The resolution of this interaction showed a marginal difference in the posterior ROI ($F(1,21)=4.18$, $p<0.054$). The analysis of the window from 1550–1700 ms brought forth an interaction of CONDITION x ROI ($F(1,21)=17.13$, $p<.01$), which was reflected in an effect of CONDITION over the anterior electrodes ($F(1,21)=9.46$, $p<.01$).

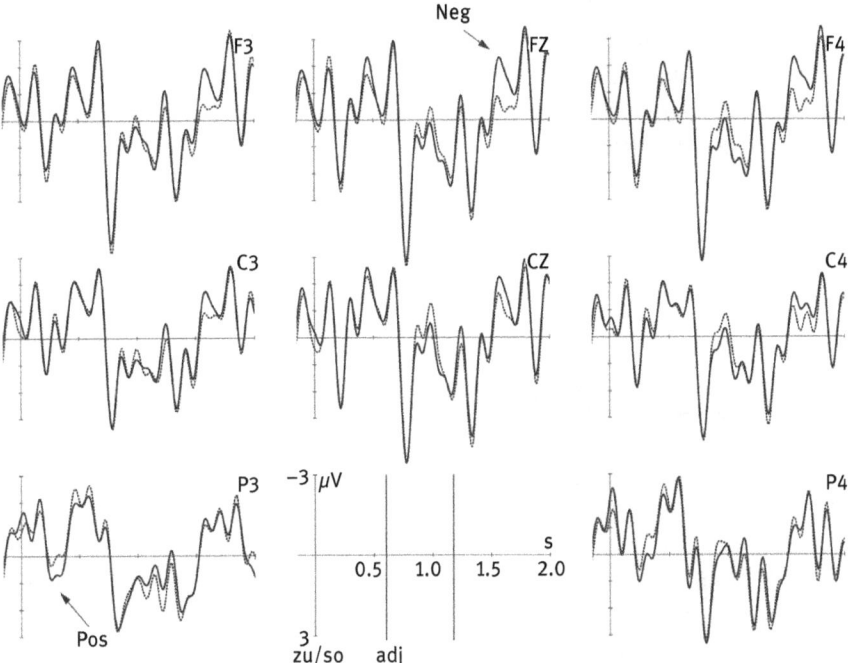

Figure 2: Effects of excessives in experiment 2 (solid line) vs. equative controls (dotted line): Posterior positivity (between 200–350 ms) time-locked to particle onset and anterior negativity relative to onset of spill over segment (350–500 ms).

The findings from the two experiments indicate that the processing of excessive structures is costly. In particular, encountering the excessive particle immediately exerts computational demands, reflected in a positive ERP signature. This positivity occurs very early and given the parallel construction of the experimental material, it can only be triggered by the occurrence of the particle *zu* 'too', which signals to the reader the presence of an excessive structure and hence the upcoming need to redress a literally coded contradictory meaning along the lines of the repair sketched above. Intuitively, the repair consists in manipulating the standard of comparison, the coding of which is a matter of heated discussion in the current syntax-semantics-pragmatics literature (cf. Bylinina 2014, for a recent overview and discussion). Our results so far suggest that when a standardizer is encountered (i.e. the first segment following the adjective in our experimental material, like *für* 'for' in the example stimulus above), its processing exerts additional costs reflected in a negative deflection. However, the contextual manipulation in our experimental setup was not aimed at differentiating among standardizers; as a consequence, eventual processing differences between different types of standardizers could not be interpreted systematically as a function of differences regarding the presentation and construction of the standard of comparison. As this appears to be a promising strategy to approach empirically the question of how standards of comparison are actually built up, we discuss in the next section potentially important differences in the test material as leading to distinct predictions regarding processing.

5 (Un-)prepared repair

We have seen experimental evidence suggesting that the degree particle *zu* acts as a kind of warning sign, indicating that a repair operation will have to be carried out promptly that involves manipulation of the standard of comparison – given its promptness, the observed positivity does not seem to reflect the repair operation itself (as the standard to be manipulated is not coded by *zu*), but rather flags the problem and in its train the preparation for the repair, so to speak. There is some agreement that construing a standard involves at least a person acting as a "judge" regarding the instantiation by an object of some gradable property that is often relative to a comparison class as well as to a purpose (Bylinina 2014). These ingredients may be distributed over the linguistic expression in different ways, such that properly controlling for how it is contributed might help improve our understanding not only of the linguistic coding of standards of comparison but also more general properties of the relation between syntax, semantics, and processing. Crucially, constructions with privative adjectives also registered an early sign of a repair: the positivity emerged as early as on the privative adjective. This indicates that the repair is already lexically encoded in the privative adjective, respectively the degree particle.

In light of what we know about incremental language processing, we might expect that from a processing perspective, getting relevant information about the to-be-manipulated standard of comparison in advance of the actual manipulation is preferable to getting it late – technically under the analysis here entertained, the problem is that there is a meaning component that cannot be directly accommodated locally and has to be accommodated on the standardizer. We would expect that it matters whether the standard of comparison has been established when the problem occurs so that it can be promptly redressed, rather than that the interface has to "wait" for the information that is needed for the repair and keep the problematic material active in the meantime. Most tellingly in this regard, the experimental material contained (some) examples where the standardizer appears before the critical excessive particle *zu* and (many) examples where it occurred after *zu*. Future experiments should care about a differentiation between and a balanced distribution of "standard first" and "standard last" examples, provisionally exemplified in the used test sentences in (17) (repeated from above) and (18) respectively.

(17) a. (Jockeys dürfen höchstens 55 kg wiegen.) Peter ist zu schwer für einen guten Jockey.
(jockeys may at.most 55 kg weigh) Peter is too heavy for a good jockey
'(Jockeys may weigh at most 55kg.) Peter is too heavy to be a good jockey.'
b. (Ringer müssen mindestens 70 kg wiegen.) Simon ist so schwer wie ein echter Ringer.
(wrestlers must at.least 70 kg weigh) Simon is as heavy as a real wrestler
'(Wrestlers must weigh at least 70 kg.) Simon is as heavy as a real wrestler.'

(18) a. Die Schwimmer gingen wieder nach Hause. Das Wasser war zu kalt für einen Wettkampf.
the swimmers went again to home the water was too cold for a competition
'The swimmers went home again. The water was too cold for a competition.'

b. Die Schwimmer gingen wieder nach Hause. Das Wasser war so kalt dass es beinahe fror.
the swimmers went again to home the water was so cold that it nearly froze
'The swimmers went home again. The water was so cold that it nearly froze.'

Clearly, (17) and (18) are not quite minimal pairs – while a judge remains implicit in both examples, the standardizer in (17) is a prepositional phrase denoting a comparison class, but a prepositional phrase denoting a purpose in (18); a putatively relevant cutoff point is given in (17), but not in (18). Obviously, comparison classes as well as purposes may be coded by other categories (like adverbs or infinitival clauses), as well as remain implicit or be deduced from independently present material in other functions, and so on. Teasing apart and systematizing the relevant distinctions and properly testing them experimentally surely makes for a noble and time-consuming task. One of our aims here has been to suggest that it may be worthwhile as well.

References

Asher, Nicholas. 2007. A large view of semantic content. *Pragmatics and Cognition* 15. 17–39.
Brandt, Patrick. 2016. Fehlkonstruktion und Reparatur in der Bedeutungskomposition. *Linguistische Berichte* 248. 395–433.
Brandt, Patrick. 2019. *Discomposition redressed. Hidden change, modality, and comparison in German*. Tübingen: Narr.
Bresnan, Joan. 1973. Syntax of the comparative clause construction in English. *Linguistic Inquiry* 4(3). 275–343. https://www.jstor.org/stable/4177775.
Bylinina, Lisa. 2014. The grammar of standards: Judge-dependence, purpose-relativity, and comparison classes in degree constructions. Utrecht: LOT.
Carston, Robyn. 1997. Enrichment and loosening: Complementary processes in deriving the proposition expressed. *Linguistische Berichte* 8. 103–127.
Dowty, David. 1991. Thematic proto-roles and argument selection. *Language* 67(3). 547–619. https://doi.org/10.2307/415037.
Eisenberg, Peter. 2013. *Grundriss der deutschen Grammatik*. vol. 2: *Der Satz*. Stuttgart: Metzler.
Goldberg, Adele. 1995. *Constructions. A construction grammar approach to argument structure*. Chicago, IL: University of Chicago Press.
Holl, Daniel. 2010. *Modale Infinitive und dispositionelle Modalität im Deutschen*. Berlin: Akademie Verlag.
Jackendoff, Ray. 1997. *The architecture of the language faculty*. Cambridge, MA: MIT Press.
Jespersen, Otto. 1924. *The philosophy of grammar*. London: Allen and Unwin.

Kamp, Hans & Barbara Partee. 1995. Prototype theory and compositionality. *Cognition* 57(2). 129–191. https://doi.org/10.1016/0010-0277(94)00659-9.
Klein, Ewan. 1980. A semantics for positive and comparative adjectives. *Linguistics and Philosophy* 4(1). 1–45. https://doi.org/10.1007/BF00351812.
Lawrence, Michael A. 2013. *ez: Easy Analysis and Visualization of Factorial Experiments*. R Package Version 4.2-2. Available at: http://CRAN.R-project.org/package=ez. (2021-04-13)
Levinson, Steven C. 2000. *Presumptive Meaning*. Cambridge, MA: MIT Press.
Lewis, David. 1972. General semantics. In Donald Davidson & Gilbert Harman (eds.), *Semantics of Natural Language*, 169–218. Dordrecht: Reidel.
Miller, George A. 1956. The magical number seven plus or minus two: Some limits on our capacity for processing information. *The Psychological Review* 63(2), 81–97. https://doi.org/10.1037/h0043158.
Partee, Barbara. 2010. Privative adjectives: Subsective plus coercion. In Rainer Bäuerle, Thomas Ede Zimmermann & Uwe Reyle (eds.), *Presuppositions and Discourse: Essays offered to Hans Kamp*, 273–285. Bingley, UK: Emerald.
Primus, Beatrice. 1999. *Cases and thematic roles: Ergative, accusative and active*. Tübingen: Niemeyer.
R Core Team 2015. *R: A language and environment for statistical computing*. Vienna: R Foundation for Statistical Computing.
Reinhart, Tanya. 2006. *Interface strategies*. Cambridge, MA: MIT Press.
Reinhart, Tanya & Tali Siloni. 2005. The lexicon-syntax parameter: Reflexivization and other arity operations. *Linguistic Inquiry* 36(3), 389–436. https://www.jstor.org/stable/4179330.
Reis, Marga. 2003. On the form and interpretation of German *wh*-infinitives. *Journal of Germanic Linguistics* 15(2). 155–201. https://doi.org/10.1017/S147054270300028X.
Romoli, Jacopo & Florian Schwarz. 2015. An experimental comparison between presuppositions and indirect scalar implicatures. In Florian Schwarz (ed.), *Experimental perspectives on presuppositions*, 215–240. Dordrecht: Springer.
Ross, John Robert. 1969. The deep structure of comparatives. Paper presented at The First and Last Annual Harvard Spring Semantics Festival.
Schumacher, Petra B. 2013. When combinatorial processing results in reconceptualization: Towards a new approach of compositionality. *Frontiers in Psychology* 4. https://doi.org/10.3389/fpsyg.2013.00677
Schumacher, Petra B. 2014. Content and context in incremental processing: "the ham sandwich" revisited. *Philosophical Studies* 168(1). 151–165. https://doi.org/10.1007/s11098-013-0179-6.
Schumacher, Petra B., Patrick Brandt & Hannah Weiland-Breckle. 2018. Online processing of "real" and "fake": The cost of being too strong. In Elena Castroviejo Miró, Louise McNally & Galit Weidmann Sassoon (eds.), *The semantics of gradability, vagueness, and scale structure: Experimental perspectives*, 93–111. Basel: Springer.
Schwarzschild, Roger. 2008. The semantics of comparatives and other degree constructions. *Language and Linguistics Compass* 2(2). 308–331. https://doi.org/10.1111/j.1749-818X.2007.00049.x.
Steinbach, Markus. 2002. *Middle Voice: A comparative study of the syntax-semantics interface of German*. Amsterdam: Benjamins.

Michael Baumann, Sandra Pappert, Thomas Pechmann
Evidence against lexicalist or configurational approaches to structural encoding in sentence production

Abstract: Psycholinguistic accounts of sentence production differ in the role they attribute to lexically represented information as, e.g. the argument structure of verbs. According to lexicalist approaches, argument structure information triggers the mapping of thematic roles onto syntactic functions. In contrast, the hypothesis of radical incrementality claims that conceptual factors are the main determinants of linguistic encoding. Models further differ in whether they assume one or two stages of grammatical encoding. Despite its ubiquity in parsing theory, a configurational account of sentence production has not been proposed explicitly (but see Shin & Christianson 2009). The finding that priming of the dative alternation (DA) is boosted by verb repetition (Pickering & Branigan 1998) is in line with a lexicalist account. Experiments on German showed structural priming between DA and benefactive alternation (BA) sentences, the latter including verbs of creation and preparation (Pappert & Pechmann 2013). Since DA and BA structures were both semantically and syntactically similar (cf. Hole 2014; Kittilä 2005; Pylkkänen 2008) the evidence was not conclusive. A recent experiment to be reported here combined DA primes and BA primes (the latter now without reference to an event of transfer, e.g. *Der Schüler wischt dem Lehrer die Tafel / die Tafel für den Lehrer*, 'The pupil wipes *the teacher the blackboard / the blackboard for the teacher') with DA targets. There was significant priming across structures. Even though DA and BA structures in this experiment are suggested to differ in semantics, argument structure and syntactic configuration, the priming effect was not modulated by alternation type. This outcome speaks against both a lexicalist and

---

Acknowledgements: The authors wish to thank two anonymous reviewers for their insightful comments on an earlier version of the paper. The research reported was supported by a grant from the Deutsche Forschungsgemeinschaft [PA 1519/2] to the second and to the third author.

Michael Baumann, Universität Bielefeld, Universitätsstr. 25, 33615 Bielefeld, Germany, e-mail: michael.baumann@uni-bielefeld.de
Sandra Pappert, Universität Heidelberg, Institut für Deutsch als Fremdsprachenphilologie, Plöck 55, 69117 Heidelberg, Germany, e-mail: pappert@idf.uni-heidelberg.de
Thomas Pechmann, Universität Leipzig, Institut für Linguistik, Beethovenstr. 15, 04107 Leipzig, Germany, e-mail: pechmann@rz.uni-leipzig.de

a configurational account in terms of low vs. high applicatives in German DA and BA structures (cf. Pylkkänen 2008). It favours an incremental approach to structural encoding that makes reference to proto-roles (proto-recipients comprising beneficiaries). Whether or not such an approach generalizes across languages is a matter of debate (cf. Chang, Baumann, Pappert & Fitz 2015; Pappert & Pechmann 2014).

Keywords: sentence production, lexicalist accounts, radical incrementality, structural priming, benefactive alternation, dative alternation

1 Introduction

Currently, there are at least two competing hypotheses on the main driving force of structural encoding. The lexicalist hypothesis holds that syntactic information stored with word entries in the mental lexicon, especially the argument structure of verbs, guides the mapping from thoughts to linguistic forms. Most proponents of this account assume weak incrementality, i.e. that the subject may be encoded independently from access to argument structure information which the encoding of additional constituents has to await (Kempen & Hoenkamp 1987; Levelt 1989; Pechmann 1989). In contrast, advocates of radical incrementality (cf. Ferreira & Swets 2002) assume that conceptual accessibility guides structural encoding and that all nominal constituents may be encoded irrespective of structural constraints imposed by a verb, allowing a late selection of the verb (Hwang & Kaiser 2014; Momma, Slevc & Phillips 2016). Such a view might be consistent with configurational accounts of syntax that assume, e.g. functional heads that accomplish the integration of constituents in the syntactic tree (cf. Pylkkänen 2008).

The aim of the experiment presented here is to shed light on the contribution of argument structure and syntactic structure to the degree of incrementality in sentence production. It made use of the *syntactic priming* technique (Bock 1986b) based on the observation that speakers tend to persist in the use of previously processed constructions. It allows for the manipulation of factors that affect grammatical encoding. Since it is far from obvious that the processes involved in syntactic persistence are purely syntactic and not, e.g. semantic or lexical, we commit to the term *structural priming*. The last decades saw an increase of studies investigating sentence production with variants of this method, looking at different languages, constructions, and populations (cf. Mahowald, James, Futrell & Gibson 2016, for a recent meta-study) and thereby contributing significantly to the refinement of existing models (Branigan & Pickering 2017).

The present contribution is devoted to the evaluation of lexicalist and configurational approaches to sentence production that differ in their commitment to incrementality. Firstly, an outline of a consensus model of sentence production is given that focuses on the process of grammatical encoding. Subsequently, the competing accounts of structural encoding are introduced. Then, evidence from structural priming experiments is reviewed that supports or undermines the respective approaches. This section begins with an explication of the phenomenon of structural priming as well as of the evidence from the corresponding experimental paradigm, also covering cross-constructional priming. The following section presents linguistic analyses of benefactive alternation constructions before our study on cross-constructional priming between dative and benefactive alternation structures is reported that tests the predictions of the competing approaches to structural encoding. Finally, the implications of the results for models of sentence production are discussed.

2 Overview of the production model

The investigation of structural priming effects at different levels of linguistic encoding requires a theory of sentence production that specifies relevant notions for each of the assumed processing levels. We adopt the consensus model of grammatical encoding as identified by Ferreira & Slevc (2007). It is called a 'consensus' model because it represents those hypotheses that are shared by most researchers in the field. The evidence it is based on stems from various sources such as speech error corpora and experiments. Nonetheless, we will see in the course of this chapter that architectural details are still under debate. The model subdivides the process of sentence production in three subprocesses: conceptualization, grammatical encoding, and articulation.

Information transfer is supposed to proceed from one stage to the next in either a serial or a weakly interactive manner. The first stage takes the meaning the speaker wants to express and forms a preverbal message that specifies a proposition and the intended speech act (e.g. a question or an assertion). A message is commonly conceived as an event involving inter alia thematic roles. For example, in an event of a dog chasing a cat, two participants are involved – a cat and a dog. The referents are related by means of the event and, thus, are assigned appropriate thematic roles: The dog as the chaser is the agent and the cat as the chased entity is the patient. The preverbal message thus contains the information about 'who does what to whom'. Additionally, the perspective to be expressed is grounded. Concepts of information structure theory like *topic and comment* or *given and new information* are applicable here (Gundel, Hedberg & Zacharski 1993; Prince 1981). If the dog was already mentioned in the discourse and the cat is new information, the message may be encoded in active voice (*The dog chases the cat*). But if the discourse statuses were reversed, the message might be encoded in passive voice instead (*The cat is chased by the dog*). The tendency to place given before new information was amongst others suggested by Gundel (1988). Bock (1977) yielded experimental evidence for it in a question-answering task.

The preverbal message is handed over to the stage of grammatical encoding. Grammatical encoding is assumed to proceed in two steps (cf. Garrett 1975). In a first step, thematic roles are mapped onto syntactic functions. Garrett (1975) termed the resulting structure a *functional representation* and, inspired by Chomsky (e.g. Chomsky 1965), assumed that the functional representation is hierarchically organized, resembling a linguistic tree. Since there was no evidence for this view (but see Shin & Christianson 2009), an alternative proposal claimed that the functional structure is flat instead of hierarchically organized (Levelt 1989). Irrespective of its internal organization, the functional structure is assumed to play an important role in the computation of agreement because it identifies the controller, namely the superficial subject in languages like English and German (Bock, Eberhard, Cutting, Meyer & Schriefers 2001). In the chase event (*The dog chases the cat*), the agent (*the dog*) is assigned the subject function and identified as the controller of the verb whereas the patient (*the cat*) is assigned the function of the direct object. In a second step, the constituents are assembled and the phrase structure is specified. This is the moment where distinctions are made, e.g. between noun phrases and prepositional phrases and noun phrases are marked for definiteness, number and case. Function words and affixes are assumed to be stored separately from content words and different mechanisms are suggested for their insertion in the syntactic structure. This idea traces back to an observation made by Merrill Garrett (1975, 1980): In word exchanges, inflectional affixes tend to strand in their original positions (e.g. *It just sound__ed__ to start* instead of . . . *started to sound*).

Word order is traditionally assumed to be specified during constituent assembly, an idea that led to the designation of the resulting structure as a *positional representation* (Garrett 1975). However, this idea has been questioned. The radically incremental view of sentence production holds that participants are encoded in the order they become available at the conceptual level (Ferreira & Swets 2002; Prat-Sala & Branigan 2000). In a language with rigid word order, structural rules constrain this order during constituent assembly whereas in a language with relatively free word order, structural preferences may just modulate the order of thematic roles (Pappert 2016). This view receives independent support from structural priming data showing that the order of thematic roles persists irrespective of their phrase structural realization (Chang, Bock & Goldberg 2003; Pappert & Pechmann 2014). Since there is some doubt that the linearization of phrases (as opposed to phrase-internal word order) is determined at the so-called positional level, the term *phrase structural representation* might be a better choice.

Two steps of syntactic encoding parallel the idea of twofold lexical access on syntactic (*lemma*) representations and morpho-phonological (*word form*) representations (cf. section 3.1). Lemma information like a verb's argument structure has been suggested to guide syntactic encoding (cf. Kempen & Hoenkamp 1987). According to this view, the subject is the only constituent that may be encoded before the verb is selected. The lexicalist approach was adopted by Levelt (1989) and influenced theories of structural persistence as the combinatorial nodes account (Pickering & Branigan 1998; cf. section 4.1).

Alternative proposals do not explicitly assume a lexical involvement in syntactic encoding (Garrett 1975) or they even deny a necessary interaction of lexical and syntactic information (Chang, Dell & Bock 2006; Chang, Baumann, Pappert & Fitz 2015). Formulation is then guided by conceptual information including an event structure that specifies information about the situation and the involved participants as, e.g. their thematic roles. Encoding proceeds as participants become available and the verb is selected such that it fits the syntactic structure built so far. This conception is compatible with radical incremental encoding that allows that all nominal constituents are encoded before verb information is accessed – an idea highly relevant for grammatical encoding in verb-final languages (cf. Hwang & Kaiser 2014 for Korean; Momma et al. 2016 for Japanese).

In any case, phrase structural encoding yields a representation that is handed over to phonological and phonetic encoding. The representation resulting thereof in turn activates articulatory motor programs (Levelt 1989). The details of these processes are beyond the scope of this chapter.

3 Approaches to sentence production

Psycholinguistic theories of sentence production unanimously distinguish conceptualization, formulation, and articulation (for overviews see Bock & Levelt 1994; Ferreira & Slevc 2007). However, they differ both in the emphasis they put on the factors that constrain linguistic encoding (conceptual, lexical and/or syntactic factors; cf. Melinger, Pechmann & Pappert 2009) and in the assumption of sub-stages (e.g. one vs. two levels of syntactic encoding). We will shortly outline the lexicalist view and the notion of incrementality before discussing the extent to which sentence production might rely on configurational representations.

3.1 Lexicalist encoding

Lexicalist approaches to sentence production claim that the argument structure of a verb guides the mapping from meaning to form at least for those participants that are not realized as subject (as for the specific status of the subject see section 3.2). The argument structure thus has the potential to license (or exclude) certain structural options. Lexicalist theories differ in the impact attributed to lexical information on structural encoding. Moderately lexicalist theories assume that several factors guide encoding as, e.g. information structure, thematic role hierarchies, and syntactic patterns or rules, but that the argument structure of the verb is a particularly important one (Bock & Levelt 1994; Ferreira 2000). By contrast, strictly lexicalist theories propose that conceptual information has its impact on lexical selection but that solely lemma information triggers syntactic encoding (Kempen & Hoenkamp 1987; Levelt 1989). In the following, we will concentrate on the latter view.

Sentence production begins with the encoding of an event. The concept activates a lexical concept that signals the availability of a corresponding verb in the language (cf. Bierwisch & Schreuder 1992). The lexical concept then calls the lemma which informs about the syntactic category and relevant syntactic properties of the lexical item. In the case of verbs, these relevant syntactic properties correspond to abstract categories that determine morphological details as, e.g. tense, person, and number and to the argument structure (Levelt 1989; Levelt, Roelofs & Meyer 1999; Pickering & Branigan 1998). In accordance with linguistic theories (cf. Levin & Rappaport Hovav 2005 for an overview) the argument structure is suggested to list the number and type of constituents to be realized with the verb. It guides the mapping of conceptually specified thematic roles onto syntactic functions. These call their own procedures that initiate phrasal encoding (Kempen & Hoenkamp 1987). In the case of a dative alternation verb such as *hand*, two argument structures are represented that guide the realization of the theme as direct object in both cases whereas the recipient is realized either as a prepositional object (e.g. *The girl hands the flowers to the minister*) or as an additional direct object (e.g. *The girl hands the minister the flowers*; cf. Pickering & Branigan 1998). Again, lexical concepts mediate between referents at the conceptual level and the corresponding lemmas (e.g. nouns; Bierwisch & Schreuder 1992; Levelt et al. 1999). The lemmas further activate word forms that fill the slots provided by the phrase structure. It has been proposed that function words are stored in a separate lexicon and that they are activated only after constituent assembly, thus not guiding phrasal encoding (Bradley, Garrett & Zurif 1980).

Lexicalist theories of sentence production are very influential in the explanation of structural persistence (cf. section 4.1) and lexical manipulations are pervasive in related experimental research (cf. Mahowald et al. 2016). Nevertheless, it is very likely that lexicalist models are especially apt to account for sentence production in SVO languages whereas there is some doubt that early verb activation is effective in the production of SOV sentences as well (cf. section 3.2).

3.2 Incrementality

Theories of incremental sentence production focus on the time course of structural encoding. Starting from the observation that we often begin with the articulation of an utterance without having planned it to its end, Kempen and Hoenkamp (1987) proposed that some units of the sentence may already be articulated meanwhile other units are encoded and still others are conceptualized. This phenomenon was termed *incremental sentence production*. Experimental evidence demonstrates that conceptualization, formulation and articulation can indeed interleave (Brown-Schmidt & Konopka 2015; Ferreira & Swets 2002; Konopka & Meyer 2014).

However, the conditions of incremental sentence production are far from settled. Most authors adopt a weak version of incrementality, stating that the most accessible participant may be encoded as subject before the verb lemma is activated (Bock, Irwin & Davidson 2004; Christianson & Ferreira 2005; Ferreira & Swets 2002; Kempen & Hoenkamp 1987; Levelt 1989). Studies that investigate the timing of noun phrase encoding mostly focus on structures that do not speak to the role of verb-specific information as, e.g. complex or coordinated noun phrases as well as simple locatives like *De pijl staat naast de tas* ('The arrow is next to the bag'; Meyer 1996; Wagner, Jescheniak & Schriefers 2010). There are some studies on more complex sentences but these focus on sentence-initial constituents and confirm early encoding of the subject (Griffin 2001; Konopka & Meyer 2014). A mechanism that guarantees early encoding of the subject is efficient in SVO languages since it allows the constituent preceding the verb to be realized before verb-specific information is accessed. In contrast, the encoding of post-verbal constituents can wait until structural constraints imposed by the verb are available. Thus, weak incrementality is compatible with a lexicalist account of sentence production.

But weak incrementality should be less effective in an SOV language. Experimental evidence is equivocal, indicating that the verb is encoded late in German and Korean SOV sentences as well as in Japanese SV sentences whereas it seems to be encoded early in Japanese OV sentences that display subject pro drop (Hwang & Kaiser 2014; Momma et al. 2016; Schriefers, Teruel & Meinshausen 1998). Late verb selection would favour the counterpart of weak incrementality. Radical incrementality holds that conceptual accessibility alone drives the relative order in which constituents are encoded (cf. Ferreira & Swets 2002; Melinger et al. 2009). Future research is needed to ascertain the conditions under which late verb selection occurs in SOV languages. We suggest that late verb selection has to be supported by an array of alternative argument structures provided by verbs and their diatheses. Otherwise, the incidence of reformulations will be higher in these languages than in SVO languages.

If structural encoding does not rely on argument structure information, other factors may come into play, i.e. the relative accessibility of concepts and lexical items. Conceptual accessibility refers to the availability of a participant in the discourse context. It has been shown to influence both structural choices and word order (Christianson & Ferreira 2005; Osgood & Bock 1977; Prat-Sala & Branigan 2000) and to cause divergences from the default order of encoding imposed by the hierarchy of thematic roles (Chang et al. 2006). Moreover, lexical access to nouns may be easier or harder and affect the relative position of the respective noun phrase (Bock 1986a). Finally, structural persistence may exert its impact on encoding (Bock 1986b). Since the experiment reported here used a structural priming paradigm, structural persistence will be discussed in more detail below (cf. section 4).

Incremental sentence production may result in structural alternations that are licensed by the verb. During the conceptualization of, e.g. a transfer, the availability of the theme may exceed that of the recipient. As a consequence, the theme will be realized as the direct object and the recipient will be assigned the complementary function of the prepositional object. If, by contrast, the recipient is more prominent than the theme, the recipient will first be encoded as the direct object and then the theme will be encoded as the second object.

Eventually, the degree of incrementality applied to structural encoding may vary with task demands and articulatory pressure (Ferreira & Swets 2002; Schriefers 1993). Thus, the production system might not be either weakly or radically incremental but it might flexibly adapt to the needs of real life conversations (Konopka & Meyer 2014).

3.3 Configurational representations?

The consensus model of sentence production introduced above (section 2) postulates two levels of syntactic encoding, thereby following classical serial models (Garrett 1975; Kempen & Hoenkamp 1987; Levelt 1989). According to this view, thematic relations are first mapped onto syntactic functions and thereafter the corresponding constituent structure is assembled. With all due caution, the functional representation might be interpreted as a syntactic configuration in the sense of generative grammar or its successors even if models of grammar should not be confounded with models of processing. As far as we know, there is actually no theory of sentence production that adopts an explicitly configurational account. But some central claims concerning sentence production resemble at least vaguely proposals that are discussed in theoretical linguistics. For example, the idea of incremental mapping of conceptual representations onto syntactic structures (cf. section 3.2) might evoke theories that posit a strong semantics-syntax interface (e.g. Levin & Rappaport Hovav 2005). Moreover, lexicalist accounts of structural encoding postulate lexical procedures that build hierarchical syntactic representations (Kempen & Hoenkamp 1987; Levelt 1989). These accounts were explicitly inspired by Lexical Functional Grammar (Bresnan 1982) but might probably also adapt more recent ideas like, e.g. the integration of lexical roots into syntactic representations (Marantz 2013; a recent lexicalist account of sentence production rather relies on unifications; Kempen 2014). Merely syntactic accounts are less prominent in psycholinguistic theorizing maybe because they do not help to model the flow of information from conceptualization to articulation. There is one study on structural alternations that refers to differences in branching directions within the VP (Shin & Christianson 2009). However, incremental encoding of the subject receives independent support from linguistic analyses that treat the subject different from the object(s) as an external argument (Kratzer 1996). Beyond research related to argument structure, hypotheses on the computation of agreement tend to have a richer notion of syntactic theories, e.g. with respect to mechanisms involved in feature checking (e.g. Franck, Lassi, Frauenfelder & Rizzi 2006).

There are alternative accounts that refuse the assumption of two levels of syntactic encoding. One group of authors assumes that thematic roles and relations are directly mapped onto a flat syntactic structure (Pickering, Branigan & McLean 2002; Cai, Pickering & Branigan 2012; Köhne, Pickering & Branigan 2014). Another group refers explicitly to the notion of constructions in a series of experiments (Chang et al. 2003; Hare & Goldberg 1999) but does not base the model of sentence production on it (Chang et al. 2006).

To summarize, there are much fewer accounts of structural encoding that are inspired by theories of syntax than there are in sentence comprehension research (see Pickering & van Gompel 2006, for an overview). A main reason for this might be that the input to sentence production is not syntactic and that its output is less susceptible to experimental control than the input to sentence comprehension. Nevertheless, actual developments in linguistic theories might be inspiring for future sentence production research.

4 Evidence from structural priming

Structural priming refers to the tendency of speakers to reuse previously processed syntactic structures despite available meaning equivalent alternatives (Bock 1986b; see Pickering & Ferreira 2008 for an overview). Structural alternations with the same truth conditional meaning (like grammatical voice or the dative alternation) constitute the test case. Experimental and corpus studies have shown that persistence does not hinge on the use of a structure by the speaker herself (Gries 2005; Tooley & Bock 2014). Findings also evidence that persistence emerges irrespective of lexical overlap between structures but that the repetition of lexical material, especially that of verbs, enhances the priming effect (Cleland & Pickering 2003; Pickering & Branigan 1998; Scheepers, Raffray & Myachykov 2017).

4.1 Within-construction priming

In the corresponding experimental paradigm, participants are presented with prime sentences whose properties are systematically manipulated and consecutively generate target sentences. If participants utter more frequently construction A after exposure to construction A than after exposure to construction B then it can be concluded that (some aspects of) the constructions have their own representational equivalents in the production system. Thus, the manipulation of primes allows for the dissociation of factors that drive structural persistence. This in turn permits inferences on the representations and mechanisms that are involved in sentence production.

Early systematic research on structural repetitions dates back to Levelt and Kelter (1982). In a question-answering study, they interrogated Dutch shopkeepers via telephone about their closing time (*(Om) hoe laat gaat uw winkel dicht?*, (at) how late goes your shop closed, 'At what time does your shop close?') and found a tendency in answers to retain the initial preposition when it was present in the question or to leave it out when it was not (*(Om) vijf uur*, '(at) five o'clock'). This behavior was attributed to a mechanism that supports syntactic planning and thus contributes to fluent speech production. Shortly thereafter, Weiner and Labov (1983) independently advocated a syntactic source. In an analysis of the factors that drive speakers to choose a passive over an active construction in interviews, they found that the probability of a passive (vs. active) construction was above chance if a passive structure preceded the actual sentence within a range of up to five clauses. Inspired by Weiner and Labov, Estival (1985) explicitly studied passive persistence in a speech corpus and reported convergent evidence.

The first experiments in a laboratory setting that addressed structural persistence were conducted by Kathryn Bock (1986b). In her experiments, participants heard and repeated sentences (the primes) either in passive (*The file was dropped by a clerk into the wastebasket*) or in active voice (*A clerk dropped the file into the wastebasket*). The relative proportion of active and passive responses was counted in a subsequent picture description task. To isolate conceptual from syntactic sources she manipulated the animacy of the agent referents in the target pictures. In line with the observational corpus data, she found a significant effect of persistence from passives to passives in participants' responses. She also showed that dative alternation constructions behaved comparably: The probability of a double object (DO) response increased after a DO prime sentence (*The corrupt inspector offered the bar owner a deal*) relative to that after a prepositional object (PO) prime (*The corrupt inspector offered a deal to the bar owner*). The findings were ascribed to persistence at the level of functional syntactic representations since the priming effect occurred independently from message level factors (agent animacy manipulation in passive priming).

In another study, Bock et al. (1992) tried to disentangle conceptual and syntactic factors in structural persistence. They systematically varied the animacy of the subject and the object in active and passive prime sentences and let participants describe pictures that depicted inanimate agents and animate patients. This time, inanimate subjects in primes promoted inanimate subjects in targets irrespective of a structural match between primes and targets. This independent effect of animacy was interpreted in favour of the hypothesis that syntactic function assignment is strongly influenced by conceptual features (see also Osgood & Bock 1977).

A drawback of the studies was that animacy features were confounded with thematic roles. Therefore, the results were inconclusive as to whether the mapping of animacy to syntactic functions or that of thematic roles was primed. Chang et al. (2003) further investigated how semantic and syntactic constraints in the production process are linked. They conducted an experiment on the

English locative alternation. Results showed persistence of the location-before-theme construction (*The farmer loaded the wagon with hay*) compared with the theme-before-location alternative (*The farmer loaded hay onto the wagon*). Since the alternatives match in their syntactic properties (NP V NP PP) but diverge in the linear order of the location and the theme, Chang et al. inferred that the mapping of the thematic role array (such as agent/theme/location) to equivalent syntactic forms (in terms of argument structure constructions; cf. Goldberg 2002) was primed. An account that assumes priming of basic conceptual features such as animacy (Bock 1986b; Bock et al. 1992) as primary factor could be ruled out because both the theme and the goal were inanimate. Consequently, they concluded that the processor is sensitive to categories that can be captured in terms of thematic roles.

Evidence for the enhancement of structural persistence by verb overlap between primes and target utterances favours a lexicalist account of structural encoding, though. Pickering and Branigan (1998) demonstrated that verb repetition leads to an effect called the *lexical boost* in priming. In a written sentence completion task, they found a pronounced tendency to a PO (vs. DO) completion when the target fragment contained the same verb as the prime fragment did compared with a different verb condition. The results speak in favour of a lexicalist approach. Specifically, Pickering and Branigan suggested that so-called combinatorial nodes that encode syntactic rules (e.g. VP → V NP PP; Chomsky 1965) and are linked with verb lemmas at the lemma layer of the lexicon (Levelt 1989; Levelt et al. 1999) guide grammatical encoding. These nodes retain residual activation after the processing of a corresponding prime structure (Branigan, Pickering & Cleland 1999). For this reason, the (re-)access of a primed node is facilitated relative to that of its competitor node(s) and this leads to lexically-independent structural persistence. In the case of verb repetition priming is boosted because of additional pre-activation of the link between a specific verb lemma and a combinatorial node.

Nonetheless, the finding of similarly enhanced persistence by noun repetition (Cleland & Pickering 2003; Scheepers et al. 2017) questions this interpretation because it is not easy to plausibly accommodate this in the model proposed by Pickering and Branigan (1998) for verb representations (but see Cleland & Pickering 2003 for an attempt). Furthermore, the results of a primed dialogue experiment by Hartsuiker, Bernolet, Schoonbaert, Speybroeck, and Vanderelst (2008) show that the boost is relatively short-lived (Branigan et al. 1999). The boost effect did not survive the separation of primes and targets by six filler trials whereas the verb-independent effect still showed up. Hence, an alternative explanation for the lexical boost has been proposed by Bock and Griffin (2000) and put forward by others (Chang et al. 2006; Chang, Dell, Bock & Griffin 2000; Chang, Janciauskas & Fitz 2012). They attribute the boost to traces in the episodic memory that act as a kind of cue to encoding. Hartsuiker et al.'s (2008) arguments support this notion. They speak in favour of a separation of a lexically-based short-term mechanism from that of priming abstract mapping procedures (see also Bernolet, Collina & Hartsuiker 2016). Based on their findings, Scheepers et al. (2017: 113) concluded that "the lexical boost to structural priming should not be regarded as being diagnostic of lexically-specific syntactic representations".

Nevertheless, alternating verbs exhibit specific preferences for one structure over the other and these were shown to modulate the persistence effect. Priming experiments that included verb bias as a variable found stronger effects if verbs occurred in a low bias prime structure than if they occurred in a high bias prime structure compared with a baseline condition (Bernolet & Hartsuiker 2010; Jaeger & Snider 2007; Segaert, Weber, Cladder-Micus & Hagoort 2014). These findings are accounted for in terms of surprisal theory (cf. Hale 2001). The theory predicts a positive correlation of the input surprisal (the prime-verb mis/match) and the strength of the behavioral adjustment – in our case, the weighting of meaning-to-structure correspondence that leads to priming. Prime surprisal is compatible both with an implicit learning account of structural persistence that is augmented by a mechanism for the tracking of verb-structure links (Chang et al. 2000; Chang et al. 2006) and with a lemma-based account that locates preference information in the lexical argument structure (Malhotra, Pickering, Branigan & Bednar 2008; Segaert et al. 2014). Thus, both accounts presume at least a potential lexical involvement in sentence production.

To summarize, within-construction priming studies indicate that several factors unfold their potential to guide the sentence production process. In this sense, sentence production itself can be characterized as multi-factorial. The mapping from meaning to linguistic structure seems to hinge on the relation between units that can be characterized in terms of thematic roles on the one hand and functional syntactic representations on the other hand. Nonetheless, many details remain to be settled. For example, the grain size of thematic roles at the conceptual level is not yet ascertained. In addition, the evidence concerning the involvement of lexical argument structure in the mapping procedure is inconclusive. Thus further research is required to test the competing predictions of lexicalist accounts, radical incrementality, and configurational representations.

4.2 Cross-constructional priming

The preceding paragraphs reported effects of structural persistence that were attributed to different levels of linguistic encoding. A means to isolate effects on a certain level is to present primes that pertain to some constructional variants and to elicit responses that pertain to other (slightly different) constructional variants (cf. seminal studies by Bock & Loebell 1990; Chang et al. 2006). The incidence of structural priming is then taken as evidence for an effect on a level where the structures resemble each other. If constructions for which priming was found are for example semantically similar but syntactically distinct, this may mean that priming is semantically based. If there is, by contrast, priming between constructions that are syntactically similar but differ in semantics, priming might be syntactic. However, the picture tends to be more complicated. Usually, constructions resemble each other in some semantic and syntactic features but differ in others. In such a case, a series of experiments with different constructions may be needed to ascertain the location of the effects. The absence of a priming effect, by contrast, should not be interpreted but with the utmost caution. The null effect might be due to differences between structures or to methodological issues. If a null effect is predicted in the critical conditions, a design including control conditions that are expected to produce a difference may warrant the interpretability of results.

Cross-constructional priming has the potential to shed more light on the levels of structural encoding. We will focus here on priming between benefactive and dative alternation structures that resemble each other in some aspects but differ in others. Classical examples are given in (1)–(4).

(1) The secretary gives a cake to her boss.

(2) The secretary gives her boss a cake.

(3) The secretary bakes a cake for her boss

(4) The secretary bakes her boss a cake.

As we will see, these structures show rough parallels on the conceptual level and on the phrase structural level. They differ with respect to both the events involved (transfer vs. creation and preparation) and the thematic roles filled by the third participant (recipient vs. beneficiary), in terms of argument structure (ditransitive vs. transitive verb), and with respect to the prepositions used in the prepositional object variants of the alternations (*to* vs. *for*). Whether or not their functional structure is assumed to be parallel or not depends on the theoretical framework the analyses are based on (see section 5).

The first study that tested structural persistence between dative and benefactive alternation primes and dative alternation targets in English focused on the different prepositions *for* and *to* (Bock 1989). Participants repeated a prime presented auditorily and then described a picture showing a situation in which a transfer would probably occur. Two experiments revealed a significant effect of structural priming not only from dative alternation conditions to dative alternation responses but also from benefactive alternation conditions to dative alternation responses. The type of alternation did not modulate the priming effect. The author concluded that overlap of function words between primes and targets is not a necessary condition for structural persistence to arise. Additional conclusions might concern the events and the thematic roles involved, the argument structure and maybe the syntactic configuration. Since the verbs used in the responses were not documented, interpretations as to whether the effects might have arisen on the one or the other level of encoding remain speculative.

A second investigation of cross-constructional priming from dative alternation structures to benefactive alternation structures and vice versa in English focused on phrase structural as opposed to thematic role effects (Chang et al. 2003). During a prime trial, participants read a double object or a prepositional object structure of one alternation type, performed a distractor task, and then recalled the previously read structure and repeated it aloud. In target trials, participants performed the same series of tasks, but now they saw a double object construction of the alternation type not seen in the prime trial. The proportion of erroneous prepositional object recalls was found to vary as a function of the phrase structural realization of the prime. The authors assumed that the dative and the benefactive alternation differ in the involved thematic role (recipient vs. beneficiary), but, abstracting from prepositions, display parallel phrase structure, alternating between the double object construction (NP NP) and a prepositional object construction (NP PP). Results revealed evidence for structural persistence that was taken as a phrase structural effect. Since data were collapsed across alternation conditions, we do not know whether priming was stronger in one direction than in the other. Moreover, the suggested interpretation ignores the similarity of the roles. In a later publication, the authors acknowledge this and assume a hierarchy of thematic roles (XYZ) that does not differentiate between recipients and beneficiaries (Chang et al. 2006).

A third study examined priming between the dative and the benefactive alternation in German (Pappert & Pechmann 2013). German differs from English in having no double object construction but an indirect object construction (dative before accusative; cf. (6) and (8) as examples for dative and benefactive alternation constructions, respectively) that contrasts with the prepositional object construction (accusative before prepositional phrase; cf. (5) and (7); as for the analysis of both constructions as indirect object constructions cf. Malchukov, Haspelmath & Comrie 2010).

(5) Die   Sekretärin überreicht einen   Kuchen an   ihren   Chef.
    the.NOM secretary   hands   a.ACC   cake   to   her.ACC boss

(6) Die   Sekretärin überreicht ihrem   Chef   einen   Kuchen.
    the.NOM secretary   hands   her.DAT boss   a.ACC   cake
    'The secretary hands a cake to her boss/her boss a cake.'

(7) Die   Sekretärin backt einen   Kuchen für   ihren   Chef.
    the.NOM secretary   bakes a.ACC   cake   for   her.ACC boss

(8) Die   Sekretärin backt ihrem   Chef   einen   Kuchen.
    the.NOM secretary   bakes her.DAT boss   a.ACC   cake
    'The secretary bakes a cake for her boss/her boss a cake.'

Participants first heard a prime sentence and repeated it. Subsequently, they saw a word list that served as input for a sentence generation task (cf. Ferreira 1994; Verhoeven 2014). The word list included either a ditransitive transfer verb or a transitive verb of creation or preparation that was to be used in the response. In addition, three nouns were presented that referred to a potential agent, theme, and recipient or beneficiary. Responses showed significant effects of cross-constructional priming in both directions: Participants produced more benefactive indirect object responses (8) after dative indirect object primes (6) than after dative prepositional object primes (5); and more dative indirect object responses (cf. (6)) after benefactive indirect object primes (cf. (8)) than after benefactive prepositional object primes (cf. (7)). The authors suggest that this cross-constructional priming might be due to parallels in, e.g. broadly defined thematic roles or phrase structure. It encompasses events of transfer and of creation and preparation, recipients and beneficiaries, ditransitive and monotransitive verbs, obligatory and optional constituents or arguments and adjuncts, *an-* ('to') and *für-* ('for') phrases. This evidence suggests that these linguistic differences need not necessarily be distinct categories for the sentence production system. In the next section, we will take a closer look at how the constructions are treated in different linguistic accounts.

5 Semantic and syntactic characteristics of benefactive alternation constructions

Pappert and Pechmann (2013) tested priming between dative and benefactive alternation constructions that differ with respect to the described events, the involved thematic roles, the argument structure of the verbs, the syntactic status of the critical constituents and the prepositions used. However, a review of linguistic accounts of benefactive alternation constructions of the *baking*-type (*The secretary bakes her boss a cake/a cake for her boss*) reveals that these constructions are quite similar to the corresponding dative alternation constructions both in terms of semantics and syntax. For example, the described event does not only entail a preparation, but also an event of transfer (Shibatani 1996), and thus, the beneficiary is better conceived as a participant that is also a recipient (Kittilä 2005). Consequently, there are syntactic approaches that assume a parallel syntactic configuration of both dative alternation structures and benefactive alternation structures that refer to a transfer event (Pylkkänen 2008).

But there are alternative benefactive constructions that are claimed to differ more from so-called dative constructions than those that describe a transfer. Even though not all authors do discuss these subtypes (e.g. Goldberg 1995, 2002), it is a rather uncontroversial issue that there are some differences in meaning. Van Valin and LaPolla (1997) distinguish three types of beneficiaries (they call them *benefactives*): (a) recipient beneficiaries who benefit from an action of the *baking* type by receiving the product or affectee, (b) plain beneficiaries who just benefit from an action that does not involve a transfer (e.g. *The mother sings for her child*), and (c) deputative beneficiaries who benefit from an action by not having to perform it on their own (*instead of*-relation, e.g. *She stood in the line for him*). A change of possession is intended in actions of transfer and might be so in actions of creation or preparing, whereas alternative actions that affect the theme as for example improvements and impairments rather do not imply a transfer (*dativus commodi* and *dativus incommodi*; Wegener 1985). It should be noted that both recipient beneficiaries and plain beneficiaries are potentially ambiguous and might alternatively be interpreted as deputative beneficiaries at least in English and German. Without knowledge of the context, it may be not obvious whether (the speaker assumes that) the beneficiary of an action would also have performed the action and, e.g. have baked a cake on his own. For independent reasons, Hole (2014) stresses the shared properties of beneficiaries and treats them alike but distinguishes them from recipients.

In English, all three types of beneficiaries may be realized as *for*-phrases. The realization as a "dative" (i.e. an object in a double object construction) seems to be more restricted. Only the realization of the recipient beneficiary in a double object construction is motivated because there is an implication of transfer (cf. Goldberg 1995) whereas the realization of the plain beneficiary and the deputative beneficiary is not. However, there is evidence for some language-internal variation as to whether these beneficiaries alternate as well (Shibatani 1996). Corpus data reveal soft constraints on the use of the double object construction with plain beneficiaries in English (Fellbaum 2005).

In German, the realization of a beneficiary as a dative-marked constituent varies rather freely with its realization as a *für*-phrase. Lehmann (2005) assumes that datives may be used to refer to plain beneficiaries if there is a theme referent encoded in the sentence (*indirectus*). This does not seem to require a specific engagement by the beneficiary (e.g. *Der Junge mäht seinem Opa den Rasen*, the. NOM boy mows his.DAT grandpa the.ACC lawn, 'The boy mows the lawn for his grandpa') as observed for Korean (Song 2010). Nonetheless, some examples seem highly marked (e.g. ?*Das Mädchen singt seinem Vater ein Lied*, the.NOM girl sings its.DAT father a.ACC song, 'The girls sings a song for her father'), pointing towards verb meaning constraints on the use of the dative (Wegener 1985). If a beneficiary may be realized either as a dative or as a *für*-phrase, the alternating structures show verb-specific differences in production frequency (cf. Colleman & Bernolet 2012). Moreover, German *für*-phrases may display an ambiguity between so-called VP- and NP-attachment that is not necessarily resolved prosodically (cf. Zschernitz, Pappert & Pechmann 2010). Since the ways of encoding the recipient beneficiary do not differ from those of encoding the plain beneficiary, German may be considered as a beneficiary-prominent language (cf. Kittilä 2005).

Whereas there is relatively broad consensus on the semantics and the syntactic surface realization of dative and benefactive alternation items, the syntactic configuration of these structures is a much more controversial issue. Since they are non-core arguments, it has been proposed that beneficiaries are introduced into the syntactic structure either by prepositions or via applicative procedures (Pylkkänen 2008). Whereas the original account of applicatives refers to argument structure changing operations that are associated with the affixation of the verb (Bresnan & Moshi 1990), the proposal made by Pylkkänen holds that there are applicative heads (Appl) in the syntactic configuration that introduce additional arguments. Pylkkänen (2008) assumes two applicative positions, a high applicative and a low applicative. If there is a possessive relation between the applicative referent and the referent of the direct object, the applicative is low and enters the configuration within the VP. This analysis treats recipients and recipient beneficiaries alike. If, however, there is a thematic relation between the beneficiary and the event described by the verb, as, e.g. in plain beneficiaries and deputative beneficiaries, the applicative is high and enters the configuration in a position above the VP. These high and low applicatives are predicted to be superficially similar, e.g. when realized as datives, but there should be asymmetries in syntactic behaviour. Such asymmetries were not found in German (Colleman 2010). To test if the account applies nonetheless to German, Pappert and Pechmann (2013) presented two types of low applicatives, such that cross-constructional priming might also be due to parallels in the syntactic configuration.

The evaluation of cross-constructional priming is further complicated by the fact that the German dative is subject to many competing analyses. The traditional view holds that there are indirect objects that are arguments as well as so-called *free datives* that are adjuncts. Free datives were proposed to be more restricted in word order than dative arguments (Lenerz 1977; but see Müller 2016). This view is questioned by an account that analyses all datives as free datives that can adjoin anywhere in the syntactic tree, just obeying semantic constraints (Vogel & Steinbach 1998). This view of free positioning contrasts with proposals that at least all datives with animate referents have their base position above the direct object (McIntyre 2006), that all datives are base-generated below the direct object (Müller 1999), or that their base position is either flexible, or above, or below the direct object, depending on the verb (Haider 2000). Very similarly, the mechanisms of dative case assignment are a controversial issue, ranging from the assumption that dative is a structural case (McFadden 2006; Wegener 1991) to the assumption that the dative is a lexical case (Haider 2010). A third view holds that the dative is both a structural and a lexical case (Fanselow 2000). Finally, it has been proposed that datives are prepositional phrases without a preposition (Bayer, Bader & Meng 2001). These controversial issues about the German dative will not be explicitly addressed in the experiment to be reported below, but we should keep them in mind for the discussion of the results.

The current experiment was designed to further investigate the parallels or differences between dative and benefactive alternation structures, now focusing on plain or deputative beneficiaries and henceforth collapsed under the label *beneficiary* (cf. Kittilä 2005) that are less similar to recipients than recipient beneficiaries. It takes advantage of the fact that beneficiaries alternate more freely in German than in English. These benefactive alternation constructions differ from the dative alternation constructions in various aspects, as, e.g. their argument structure. This holds for the constructions presented by Pappert and Pechmann (2013) as well. In addition, they differ in semantic aspects since the dative alternation constructions refer to a transfer event involving a recipient whereas the benefactive alternation constructions involving a beneficiary do not. According to the account by Pylkkänen (2008), they further differ in the syntactic configuration, i.e. the recipient is integrated as a low applicative whereas the beneficiary is integrated as a high applicative. If these semantic and configurational differences matter for the speaker, there should be no cross-constructional priming between the dative and the benefactive alternation structures in this experiment. If, however, these differences are irrelevant, and the similarities in terms of the proto-recipient role (Primus 1999) as well as of the surface phrase structure are important, there should be cross-constructional priming.

6 Experiment

The current study aimed at a further dissociation of confounds that were present in cross-constructional priming between benefactive alternation and dative alternation constructions (Pappert & Pechmann 2013). Since the conceptual similarity of recipients and recipient beneficiaries might have favoured cross-constructional priming, we increased the contrast between the competing roles now. To achieve this, we paired benefactive alternation primes with dative alternation targets. As explained above, benefactive constructions referred to benefactive actions that did not entail a transfer. If the semantic differences between events of transfer involving a recipient and events of improvement or impairment involving a beneficiary are substantial to the sentence production system, there should be no or weaker priming between these benefactive alternation items and the dative alternation targets. Moreover, the semantic differences might even have syntactic consequences. Since the beneficiary does not enter a possessive relation with the theme (as the recipient does) but relates to the event of, e.g. improvement itself, it is suggested to merge as high applicative above the VP (Pylkkänen 2008). In consequence, these beneficiary constructions are assumed to be integrated differently than recipient beneficiaries (and recipients) into the syntactic configuration because they map to different positions in the syntactic tree. Thus, if persistence reported by Pappert & Pechmann (2013) was due to parallels in the syntactic configuration we would not expect to find priming in the actual experiment. However, if the priming mechanism is not sensitive to differences in semantics, syntactic configuration and argument structure, we should replicate the effect reported by Pappert & Pechmann (2013) and find cross-constructional priming. This would likewise suggest the independence of the mapping procedure from lexical information and in turn speak for an account of sentence production where participants can be passed on to syntactic function assignment incrementally.

6.1 Method

We conducted a sentence production experiment in the structural priming paradigm. The experimental method closely resembled that adopted by Pappert & Pechmann (2013).

6.1.1 Participants

Forty-eight participants (38 female) who were native speakers of German were recruited at the University of Leipzig. Their mean age was 25 years, ranging from 18 to 38 years. They did not report visual or auditory problems that might have hindered them from solving the experimental task. They got a monetary compensation for their engagement.

6.1.2 Materials

As prime sentences we selected 20 monotransitive verbs that undergo the benefactive alternation and paired them with 20 dative alternation verbs taken from the materials of Pappert & Pechmann (2013). Monotransitive verbs were restricted to the criterion of denoting benefaction events without an entailment of transfer, thus licensing beneficiaries in the sense of Kittilä (2005; plain or deputative beneficiaries, Van Valin & LaPolla 1997). The beneficiary benefitted from the action himself and an interpretation as a caused transfer of the theme into the direction and/or possession of the benefitting participant was unlikely as ascertained by the authors and two independent judges. The described events implied improvements from the perspective of the beneficiary, as, e.g. *schrubben* ('to clean'), *anschieben* ('to push-start'), *wischen* ('to wipe'), and *betanken* ('to fuel'). In German, the benefactive alternation comprises a construction with the theme realized as a direct object in accusative case before the beneficiary realized as a prepositional phrase (AccPP, cf. (9)), and the counterpart with the beneficiary as a dative constituent preceding the theme participant realized as a direct object in accusative case (DatAcc, cf. (10)). The German dative alternation varies between a construction with the theme realized as the direct object in accusative case preceding the recipient participant realized as a prepositional object (AccPP, cf. (11)) and an alternative construction with the recipient realized as an indirect object in dative case before the theme realized as a direct object in accusative case (DatAcc, cf. (12)). Consequently, the benefactive and the dative alternation constructions are identical in phrase structure but can be analyzed to differ in the entailed thematic roles (beneficiary vs. recipient; Kittilä 2005) and underlying syntactic configuration (high vs. low applicative; Pylkkänen 2008).

We used the same nouns to construct the benefactive and dative prime sentences of a pair to keep the variation due to nouns low among alternations. The preposition in the dative alternation AccPP primes was always *an* ('to') whereas the preposition heading the PP in the benefactive constructions was always *für* ('for'). The prime sentences were spoken by a native speaker of German and recorded for auditory presentation.

For the targets of an item we made up word lists of a dative alternation verb together with nouns that could plausibly be used as the agent, the theme and the recipient of the event denoted by the verb. In the item set, these verbs were presented twice, once in primes and once in targets. But primes were combined with targets so that dative alternation prime and target verbs of a resulting pair were always different. Nonetheless, dative alternation verbs occurred twice as often in the experiment than the verbs used in benefactive prime constructions. If any, the dative alternation verb repetition should boost priming by dative alternation structures as compared to benefactive alternation structures. Additionally, no noun was repeated in the whole item set. An item then consisted of two benefactive alternation primes (cf. (9) and (10)), two dative alternation primes (cf. (11) and (12)) and a dative alternation target (cf. (13)).

(9) benefactive alternation, accusative before prepositional phrase (AccPP)
Der Schiffsjunge schrubbt den alten Kahn für
the.NOM cabin.boy cleans the.ACC old boat for
den Fischer.
the.ACC fisher
'The cabin boy cleans the old boat for the fisher.'

(10) benefactive alternation, dative before accusative (DatAcc)
Der Schiffsjunge schrubbt dem Fischer den alten Kahn.
the.NOM cabin.boy cleans the.DAT fisher the.ACC old boat
'The cabin boy cleans the old boat for the fisher.'

(11) dative alternation, accusative before prepositional phrase (AccPP)
Der Schiffsjunge vermittelt den alten Kahn an
the.NOM cabin.boy offers the.ACC old boat to
den Fischer.
the.ACC fisher
'The cabin boy offers the old boat to the fisher.'

(12) dative alternation, dative before accusative (DatAcc)
Der   Schiffsjunge vermittelt dem   Fischer den   alten   Kahn.
the.NOM cabin.boy   offers   the.DAT fisher   the.ACC old   boat
'The cabin boy offers the fisher the old boat.'

(13) dative alternation target
Fan ('fan') Rose ('rose') Sänger ('singer') überreichen ('to hand')

Target word lists appeared on the monitor in vertical order. They were arranged so that the agent noun always occupied the top position followed by the theme and the recipient noun. The verb always appeared at the bottom. This sequence resembles that of thematic roles in an AccPP construction. We created four experimental lists using the 2x2 Latin Square design. As a consequence, each participant saw each item only once and an equal number of items per condition. Critical trials were intermixed with 72 structurally unrelated filler primes and targets to conceal the intention of the experiment. Fillers were, e.g. intransitive sentences like *Das Licht flackert* ('The light is flickering'). We created four pseudo-randomized versions of each list. The resulting sixteen versions of the experimental lists were assigned to an equal number of participants.

6.1.3 Procedure

Participants were tested individually in a sound attenuated chamber. The experiment was run on a desktop PC using the software ERTS (Beringer 1999). They received written instructions prior to taking a seat in front of a computer monitor. Participants were instructed to listen to and to repeat prime sentences. Subsequently they should generate a sentence from the target words that they were presented with as a vertical list on the computer monitor. They were told to produce aloud a grammatical sentence using all target words.

The session started with a short practice phase of 12 trials to ensure that participants became accustomed to the task. An experimental trial proceeded as follows: An asterisk was displayed in the center of the monitor. Simultaneously, a prime sentence was played via loudspeakers and participants subsequently repeated the sentence. The experimenter confirmed the repetition with a button press. In that moment, the asterisk was substituted by the target word list that was shown centered on the screen for 1300 ms and was then replaced by an asterisk again. Target words (and asterisks) were shown in white on black background, the font was IBM 18pt. Words were presented in upper and lower case, obeying the capitalization rules of German. When the experimenter had coded the response by a button-press, the consecutive trial began. A response counted as valid dative alternation response if it displayed the canonical word order, contained all target words and was grammatical. Valid responses had the accusative object preceding a prepositional phrase (AccPP) or a dative object preceding the accusative object (DatAcc). Alternative responses were coded as Other. For example, the sentence *Der Fan überreicht die Rose an den Sänger* ('The fan hands the rose to the singer') counted as valid AccPP response whereas *Der Fan überreicht an den Sänger die Rose* ('The fan hands to the singer the rose') was coded as Other because it exhibited a scrambled word order. The sentence *Der Fan überreicht der Sänger die Rose* (the.NOM Fan hands the.NOM singer the.ACC rose) counted as Other as well because it was ungrammatical with two noun phrases marked for nominative case. Responses were recorded to allow for post-experimental checking of the codes.

After half of the trials, a short break was offered to participants. The whole experiment lasted about 30 minutes.

6.2 Results

The whole response set (N=951; nine trials had to be discarded due to technical errors) was made up of 31.9 % dative alternation AccPP, 37.4 % dative alternation DatAcc and 30.7 % invalid Other responses. Invalid responses were equally distributed over conditions. Only valid dative alternation responses entered further analyses. The valid 659 responses split up into 46.0 % AccPP and 54.0 % DatAcc responses. Frequencies and percentages of AccPP responses per condition are summarized in Table 1.

Table 1: Absolute number of dative alternation responses and percentage of AccPP responses per Alternation Type and Prime Structure.

Prime Alternation	Prime Structure	AccPP Responses	DatAcc Responses	% AccPP
Benefactive	AccPP	89	79	53.0
	DatAcc	58	108	36.0
Dative	AccPP	98	75	56.7
	DatAcc	58	99	36.9

Statistical analyses were carried out in the R software environment (R Core Team, 2014) making use of the *afex* package for factorial designs (Singmann, Bolker, Westfall & Aust 2016). We computed generalized linear mixed effect models (GLMMs) with the factors Alternation Type and Prime Structure as independent variables and the response category (dative alternation AccPP vs. DatAcc) as binary dependent variable. The likelihood ratio test method was employed. We started with the maximal model justified by the data (Barr, Levy, Scheepers & Tily 2013) and further simplified the model with ANOVA model comparisons (Matuschek, Kliegl, Vasishth, Baayen & Bates 2017). The optimizer was changed to *bobyqa* to facilitate model convergence. The final model then contained Structure (AccPP vs. DatAcc) and Alternation (benefactive vs. dative) as fixed factors, as well as their interaction. Random intercept terms for participants and items constituted the random effects part. The effects in the simple model did not diverge from those in the maximal model. The output of the simple model revealed a significant main effect of Prime Structure (*beta* = 0.58, *SE* = 0.12, *z* = 5.18, *p* < .001) which means that the overall 18.3 % difference between AccPP and DatAcc prime structures was reliable. There was no effect of Alternation type (*beta* = 0.06, *SE* = 0.11, *z* = 0.57, *p* = .57). Finally, the analysis showed no significant interaction: The priming effect was not moderated by the Alternation type (*beta* = 0.03, *SE* = 0.11, *z* = 0.23, *p* = .82). Hence, the slight increase of 3.7 % AccPP responses from benefactive alternation AccPP to dative alternation AccPP primes was not statistically reliable.

6.3 Discussion

The experiment tested cross-constructional priming between benefactive alternation primes and dative alternation targets. A previous experiment had shown that benefactive alternation constructions with recipient beneficiaries prime dative alternation targets to the same extent as dative alternation primes do (Pappert & Pechmann 2013). The current experiment aimed at a dissociation by using the same method, but presenting non-recipient beneficiaries now. The priming effect produced by benefactive alternation constructions was compared to that produced by dative alternation constructions, again. The current experiment yielded a main effect of priming that replicated previous effects, showing that accusative-PP responses were more frequent after accusative-PP primes than after dative-accusative primes. As in the predecessor experiment, there was no modulation of the priming effect by the alternation type, i.e. the effect was not stronger after dative alternation than after benefactive alternation primes. Moreover, a supplemental comparison of the response data from Pappert and

Pechmann (2013) with the present results showed that relative response proportions after recipient beneficiaries and non-recipient beneficiaries did not differ, either.

Dative and benefactive alternation constructions display linguistic similarities and dissimilarities (cf. section 5). We found a significant priming difference between structures that was not modulated by the alternation type, i.e. the assumed linguistic dissimilarities did not interfere with the strength of the priming effect. These findings indicate that the differences between dative and benefactive alternation constructions are not that relevant to the production system that they hindered priming to occur. At the conceptual level, the distinction between events of transfer on the one hand and events of improvement or impairment to the benefaction of someone on the other hand does not seem to be essential. This implies that the dissimilarities between beneficiaries, recipient beneficiaries and recipients do not matter, either. Since the results show persistence from structures with transitive verbs to structures with ditransitive verbs, the results also speak against a necessary involvement of argument structure in structural priming (against Pickering & Branigan 1998). However, they do not exclude the possibility that verb lemmas are connected with any syntactic contexts the respective verb appeared in (cf. Pickering & Branigan 1999). The experiment further tested the prediction that the syntactic configuration is relevant for persistence and that priming occurs between structures that are parallel with respect to phrases that for semantic reasons are suggested to be applied high or low (cf. Pylkkänen 2008). It turned out that priming occurred irrespective of whether there was a high or a low applicative in terms of Pylkkänen (2008). Hence, this distinction is not relevant to structural encoding, either. Finally, we replicated the finding that preposition identity (*an* 'to' vs. *für* 'for') is not a necessary condition for structural persistence to be found (cf. Bock 1989; Pappert & Pechmann 2013).

Besides these dissimilarities, there are several similarities between dative and benefactive alternation constructions, which might have contributed to structural persistence. During conceptualization, the entailment of a benefit in an event might be more relevant for encoding than a distinction in terms of a physical transfer, since all dative alternation target verbs referred to an event of positive transfer to the benefit of the target recipient. Moreover, the hierarchy of thematic roles (XYZ; cf. Wunderlich 2006; Chang et al. 2006; as for the disagreement on whether Y represents the recipient or Z represents the goal, cf. Levin & Rappaport Hovav 2005) might matter rather than role details. The findings are also in line with a proto-role account of thematic relations (Dowty 1991; Primus 1999) that subsumes recipients and beneficiaries under the role of the proto-recipient. Detailed thematic relations should be evoked during conceptualization, but in a language that does not code these roles differently, the preverbal message might just refer to proto-roles as input for uniform grammatical encoding. As an alternative to a proto-role account, the priming effect might be attributed to parallels in phrase structure and case marking (dative-accusative vs. accusative-PP). But given the finding that the order of thematic roles can be primed across different phrase structural realizations (Pappert & Pechmann 2014), an account solely in terms of phrase structure seems less likely.

To summarize, the experiment reported here helped to dissociate predictions derived from both linguistic analyses of the involved constructions as well as from psycholinguistic accounts of grammatical encoding. Nonetheless, the effects we found may still be attributed to different levels of representation.

7 Conclusions

The productivity of dative case marking in German even in constructions with beneficiaries allowed us to continue testing cross-constructional priming between dative and benefactive alternation structures. We thus arrived at the dissociation of factors that were potentially confounded in previous research on grammatical encoding. However, some confounds remain and call for further investigations.

Firstly, there is no consensus on the adequate syntactic analyses of dative and benefactive alternation sentences in German (cf. section 5). Accordingly, our results do not speak to the general relevance of syntactic configurations to grammatical encoding. Hence, we cannot decide on whether there are two levels of syntactic processing or not (cf. section 3.3). Nevertheless, the experiment indicated at least that the distinction between high and low applicatives as proposed by Pylkkänen (2008) is not relevant for the production of dative and benefactive alternation sentences in German.

Secondly, the experiment evaluated the predictions derived from lexicalist theories of sentence production. It showed that overlap in argument structure is not a necessary condition for structural persistence in German, thus questioning the pivotal role of verbs for sentence generation. As far as we can see, the lexicalist approach to sentence production resembles to some extent recent developments in Minimalist frameworks (cf. Marantz 2013, for an overview). Our findings are not compatible with such approaches. Future research will show whether this outcome can be replicated in other languages and whether verb positions in these languages are an issue. Maybe verb-specific information is less essential for grammatical encoding in a language in that speakers are used to listen to verb-final sentences.

Finally, the outcome can be reconciled with accounts that emphasize the impact of conceptual processing on sentence production. We suggest that conceptual representations will be elaborated in detail, but if it comes to the generation of a preverbal message, they will be reduced to shallow representations that include just the necessary information for grammatical encoding. Thus, accounts of sentence production have to adopt a theory of thematic roles for the preverbal message that assumes rather broad categories either in terms of protoroles or in terms of a hierarchy of thematic roles (XYZ). The absence of evidence in favour of a lexicalist approach together with some evidence that conceptual factors are relevant for grammatical encoding is most compatible with the notion of radical incrementality. Further research is needed to scrutinize the interdependence of verb positions (SVO vs. SOV) and processing types (lexicalist weakly incremental encoding vs. radically incremental encoding).

References

Barr, Dale J., Roger P. Levy, Christoph Scheepers & Harry J. Tily. 2013. Random effects structure for confirmatory hypothesis testing: Keep it maximal. *Journal of Memory and Language* 68(3). 255–278. https://doi.org/10.1016/j.jml.2012.11.001.

Bayer, Josef, Markus Bader & Michael Meng 2001. Morphological underspecification meets oblique case: Syntactic and processing effects in German. *Lingua* 111(4–7). 465–514. https://doi.org/10.1016/S0024-3841(00)00041-3.

Beringer, Jörg. 1999. *Experimental Run Time System (ERTS)*. Frankfurt a. M.: Berisoft.

Bernolet, Sarah, Simona Collina & Robert J. Hartsuiker. 2016. The persistence of syntactic priming revisited. *Journal of memory and language* 91. 99–116. Advance online publication. https://doi.org/10.1016/j.jml.2016.01.002.

Bernolet, Sarah & Robert J. Hartsuiker. 2010. Does verb bias modulate syntactic priming? *Cognition* 114(3). 455–461. https://doi.org/10.1016/j.cognition.2009.11.005.

Bierwisch, Manfred & Robert Schreuder. 1992. From concepts to lexical items. *Cognition* 42(1–3). 23–60. https://doi.org/10.1016/0010-0277(92)90039-K.

Bock, J. Kathryn. 1977. The effect of a pragmatic presupposition on syntactic structure in question answering. *Journal of Verbal Learning and Verbal Behavior* 16(6). 723–734. https://doi.org/10.1016/S0022-5371(77)80031-5.

Bock, J. Kathryn. 1986a. Meaning, sound, and syntax: Lexical priming in sentence production. *Journal of Experimental Psychology: Learning, Memory, and Cognition* 12(4). 575–586. http://doi.org/10.1037/0278-7393.12.4.575.

Bock, J. Kathryn. 1986b. Syntactic persistence in language production. *Cognitive Psychology* 18(3). 355–387. https://doi.org/10.1016/0010-0285(86)90004-6.

Bock, J. Kathryn. 1989. Closed-class immanence in sentence production. *Cognition* 31(2). 163–186. http://doi.org/10.1016/0010-0277(89)90022-X.

Bock, J. Kathryn, Helga Loebell & Randal Morey. 1992. From conceptual roles to structural relations: Bridging the syntactic cleft. *Psychological Review* 99(1), 150–171. https://doi.org/10.1037/0033-295X.99.1.150.

Bock, J. Kathryn, Kathleen M. Eberhard, J. Cooper Cutting, Antje S. Meyer & Herbert Schriefers. 2001. Some attractions of verb agreement. *Cognitive Psychology* 43. 83–128. https://doi.org/10.1006/cogp.2001.0753.

Bock, J. Kathryn & Zenzi M. Griffin. 2000. The persistence of structural priming: Transient activation or implicit learning? *Journal of Experimental Psychology: General* 129(2). 177–192. https://doi.org/10.1037/0096-3445.129.2.177.

Bock, J. Kathryn, David E. Irwin & Douglas J. Davidson. 2004. Putting first things first. In John M. Hendrson & Fernanda Ferreira (eds.), *The interface of language, vision, and action: Eye movements and the visual world*, 249–278. New York, NY: Psychology Press.

Bock, J. Kathryn & Willem J. M. Levelt. 1994. Language production: Grammatical encoding. In Morton Ann Gernsbacher (ed.), *Handbook of psycholinguistics*, 945–984. San Diego, CA: Academic Press.

Bock, J. Kathryn & Helga Loebell. 1990. Framing sentences. *Cognition* 35(1). 1–39. https://doi.org/10.1016/0010-0277(90)90035-I.

Bosse, Solveig. 2015. *Applicative arguments A syntactic and semantic investigation of German and English*. New York, NY: Lang.

Bradley, Dianne C., Merrill F. Garrett & Edgar B. Zurif. 1980. Syntactic deficits in Broca's aphasia. In David Caplan (ed.), *Biological studies of mental processes*, 269–286. Cambridge, MA: MIT Press.

Branigan, Holly P. & Martin J. Pickering. 2017. An experimental approach to linguistic representation. *Behavioral and Brain Sciences* 40, e282. https://doi.org/10.1017/S0140525X16002028.

Branigan, Holly P., Martin J. Pickering & Alexandra A. Cleland. 1999. Syntactic priming in written production: Evidence for rapid decay. *Psychonomic Bulletin & Review* 6(4). 635–640. https://doi.org/10.3758/BF03212972.

Bresnan, Joan. 1982. The passive in lexical theory. In Joan Bresnan (ed.), *The mental representation of grammatical relations*, 3–86. Cambridge, MA: MIT Press.

Bresnan, Joan & Lioba Moshi. 1990. Object asymmetries in comparative Bantu syntax. *Linguistic Inquiry* 21(2). 147–185. https://www.jstor.org/stable/4178668.

Brown-Schmidt, Sarah & Agnieszka E. Konopka. 2015. Processes of incremental message planning during conversation. *Psychonomic Bulletin & Review* 22(3). 833–843. https://doi.org/10.3758/s13423-014-0714-2.

Cai, Zhenguang G., Martin J. Pickering & Holly P. Branigan. 2012. Mapping concepts to syntax: Evidence from structural priming in Mandarin Chinese. *Journal of Memory and Language* 66(4). 833–849. https://doi.org/10.1016/j.jml.2012.03.009.

Chang, Franklin, Michael Baumann, Sandra Pappert & Hartmut Fitz. 2015. Do lemmas speak German? A verb position effect in German structural priming. *Cognitive Science* 39(5). 1113–1130. https://doi.org/10.1111/cogs.12184.

Chang, Franklin, J. Kathryn Bock & Adele E. Goldberg. 2003. Can thematic roles leave traces of their places? *Cognition* 90(1). 29–49. https://doi.org/10.1016/S0010-0277(03)00123-9.

Chang, Franklin, Gary S. Dell & J. Kathryn Bock. 2006. Becoming syntactic. *Psychological Review* 113(2). 234–272. https://doi.org/10.1037/0033-295X.113.2.234.

Chang, Franklin, Gary S. Dell, J. Kathryn Bock & Zenzi M. Griffin. 2000. Structural priming as implicit learning: A comparison of models of sentence production. *Journal of Psycholinguistic Research* 29(2). 217–229. http://doi.org/10.1023/A: 1005101313330.

Chang, Franklin, Marius Janciauskas & Hartmut Fitz. 2012. Language adaptation and learning: Getting explicit about implicit learning. *Language and Linguistics Compass* 6(5). 259–278. https://doi.org/10.1002/lnc3.337.

Chomsky, Noam 1965. *Aspects of the theory of syntax. Massachusetts Institute of Technology. Research Laboratory of Electronics. Special technical report: Vol. 11.* Cambridge, MA: MIT Press.

Christianson, Kiel & Fernanda Ferreira. 2005. Conceptual accessibility and sentence production in a free word order language (Odawa). *Cognition* 98(2). 105–135. https://doi.org/10.1016/j.cognition.2004.10.006.

Cleland, A. Alexandra & Martin J. Pickering. 2003. The use of lexical and syntactic information in language production: Evidence from the priming of noun-phrase structure. *Journal of Memory and Language* (49). 214–230. http://doi.org/10.1016/S0749-596X(03)00060-3.

Colleman, Timothy 2010. The benefactive semantic potential of 'caused reception' constructions: A case study on English, German, French, and Dutch. In Fernando Zuñiga & Seppo Kittilä (eds.), *Benefactives and malefactives: Typological perspectives and case studies*, 219–243. Amsterdam: Benjamins. https://doi.org/10.1075/tsl.92.09col.

Colleman, Timothy & Sarah Bernolet. 2012. Alternation biases in corpora vs. picture description experiments: DO-biased and PD-biased verbs in the Dutch dative alternation. In Dagmar Divjak & Stefan Th. Gries (eds.), *Frequency effects in language representation*, 87–125. Berlin & Boston: Mouton de Gruyter. https://doi.org/10.1515/9783110274073.87.

Dowty, David. 1991. Thematic proto-roles and argument selection. *Language* 67(3). 547–619. https://doi.org/10.1353/lan.1991.0021.

Estival, Dominique. 1985. Syntactic priming of the passive in English. *Text – Interdisciplinary Journal for the Study of Discourse* 5(1–2). https://doi.org/10.1515/text.1.1985.5.1-2.7.

Fanselow, Gisbert. 2000. Does constituent length predict German word order in the middle field? In Josef Bayer & Christine Römer (eds.), *Von der Philologie zur Grammatiktheorie: Peter Suchsland zum 65. Geburtstag*, 63–77. Tübingen: Niemeyer.

Fellbaum, Christiane 2005. Examining the constraints on the benefactive alternation by using the World Wide Web as a corpus. In Marga Reis & Stephan Kepser (eds.), *Evidence in linguistics: Empirical, theoretical, and computational perspectives*, 209–240. Berlin & New York: Mouton de Gruyter.

Ferreira, Fernanda. 2000. Syntax in language production: An approach using tree-adjoining grammars. In Linda R. Wheeldon (ed.), *Aspects of language production (Studies in cognition)*, 291–330. Hove: Psychology Press.

Ferreira, Fernanda & Benjamin Swets. 2002. How incremental is language production? Evidence from the production of utterances requiring the computation of arithmetic sums. *Journal of Memory and Language* 46(1). 57–84. https://doi.org/10.1006/jmla.2001.2797.

Ferreira, Victor S. & L. Robert Slevc. 2007. Grammatical encoding. In M. Gareth Gaskell (ed.), *The Oxford handbook of psycholinguistics*, 453–469. Oxford: Oxford University Press. http://doi.org/10.1093/oxfordhb/9780198568971.013.0027.

Franck, Julie, Glenda Lassi, Ulrich H. Frauenfelder & Luigi Rizzi. 2006. Agreement and movement: A syntactic analysis of attraction. *Cognition* 101(1). 173–216. https://doi.org/10.1016/j.cognition.2005.10.003.

Garrett, Merrill. 1975. The analysis of sentence production. In Gordon H. Bower (ed.), *The Psychology of Learning and Motivation*, 133–177. New York: Academic Press. https://doi.org/10.1016/S0079-7421(08)60270-4.

Garrett, Merrill. 1980. Levels of processing in sentence production. In Brian Butterworth (ed.), *Language production: Vol. 1. Speech and talk*, 177–220. London: Academic Press.

Goldberg, Adele E. 1995. *Constructions: A Construction Grammar approach to argument structure*. Chicago, IL: University of Chicago Press.

Goldberg, Aedele E. 2002. Surface generalizations: An alternative to alternations. *Cognitive Linguistics* 13(4). 327–356. https://doi.org/10.1515/cogl.2002.022.

Gries, Stefan Th. 2005. Syntactic priming: A corpus-based approach. *Journal of Psycholinguistic Research* 34(4). 365–399. https://doi.org/10.1007/s10936-005-6139-3.

Griffin, Zenzi M. 2001. Gaze durations during speech reflect word selection and phonological encoding. *Cognition* 82(1). B1–B14. https://doi.org/10.1016/S0010-0277(01)00138-X.

Gundel, Jaenette K. 1988. Universals of topic-comment structure. In Michael Hammond, Edith A. Moravcsik & Jessica Wirth (eds.), *Typological studies in language: Studies in Syntactic Typology*, 209–242. Amsterdam: Benjamins. https://doi.org/10.1075/tsl.17.16gun.

Gundel, Jaenette K., Nancy Hedberg & Ron Zacharski. 1993. Cognitive status and the form of referring expressions in discourse. *Language* 69(2). 274–307. https://doi.org/10.2307/416535.

Haider, Hubert. 2000. Branching and discharge. In Peter Coopmans, Martin Everaert & Jane Grimshaw (eds.), *Lexical specification and insertion*, 135–164. Amsterdam: Benjamins. https://doi.org/10.1075/cilt.197.08hai.

Haider, Hubert. 2010. *The syntax of German*. Cambridge, UK: Cambridge University Press.

Hale, John. 2001. A probabilistic earley parser as a psycholinguistic model. In *The North American Chapter of the Association for Computational Linguistics (NACL)* 2, 1–8. Association for Computational Linguistics. https://doi.org/10.3115/1073336.1073357.

Hare, Mary L. & Adele E. Goldberg. 1999. Structural Priming: Purely Syntactic? In Martin Hahn & Scott C. Stones (eds.), *Cognitive Science Society (CSS) 21*, 208–211. Mahwah, NJ: Erlbaum.

Hartsuiker, Robert J., Sarah Bernolet, Sofie Schoonbaert, Sara Speybroeck & Dieter Vanderelst. 2008. Syntactic priming persists while the lexical boost decays: Evidence from written and spoken dialogue. *Journal of Memory and Language* 58(2). 214–238. https://doi.org/10.1016/j.jml.2007.07.003

Hole, Daniel. 2014. *Dativ, Bindung und Diathese*. Berlin & Boston: De Gruyter. https://doi.org/10.1515/9783110347739.

Hwang, Heeju & Elsi Kaiser. 2014. The role of the verb in grammatical function assignment in English and Korean. *Journal of Experimental Psychology: Learning, Memory, and Cognition* 40(5). 1363–1376. http://doi.org/10.1037/a0036797.

Jaeger, T. Florian & Neal E. Snider. 2007. Implicit learning and syntactic persistence: Surprisal and cumulativity. In Lynsey Wolter & Jill Thoerson (eds.), *University of Rochester Working Papers in the Language Sciences* 3(1), 26–44.

Kempen, Gerard. 2014. Prolegomena to a neurocomputational architecture for human grammatical encoding and decoding. *Neuroinform* 12(1). 111–142. https://doi.org/10.1007/s12021-013-9191-4.

Kempen, Gerard & Edward Hoenkamp. 1987. An incremental procedural grammar for sentence formulation. *Cognitive Science* 11(2). 201–258. https://doi.org/10.1207/s15516709cog1102_5.

Kittilä, Seppo. 2005. Recipient-prominence vs. beneficiary-prominence. *Linguistic Typology* 9(2). https://doi.org/10.1515/lity.2005.9.2.269.

Köhne, Judith, Martin J. Pickering & Holly P. Branigan. 2014. The relationship between sentence meaning and word order: Evidence from structural priming in German. *Quarterly Journal of Experimental Psychology* 67(2). 304–318. https://doi.org/10.1080/17470218.2013.807855.

Konopka, Agnieszka E. & Antje S. Meyer. 2014. Priming sentence planning. *Cognitive Psychology 73*. 1–40. https://doi.org/10.1016/j.cogpsych.2014.04.001.

Kratzer, Angelika. 1996. Severing the external argument from its verb. In Johan Rooryck & Laurie Zaring (eds.), *Phrase structure and the lexicon*, 109–137. Dordrecht: Kluwer. https://doi.org/10.1007/978-94-015-8617-7_5.

Lehmann, Christian. 2005. Participant roles, thematic roles and syntactic functions. In Tasaku Tsunoda & Taro Kageyama (eds.), *Voice and grammatical relations: Festschrift for Masayoshi Shibatani*, 167–190. Amsterdam: Benjamins.

Lenerz, Jürgen. 1977. *Zur Abfolge nominaler Satzglieder im Deutschen*. Tübingen: Narr.

Levelt, Willem J. M. 1989. *Speaking: From intention to articulation*. Cambridge, MA: MIT Press.

Levelt, Willem J. M. & Stephanie Kelter. 1982. Surface form and memory in question answering. *Cognitive Psychology* 14. 78–106. https://doi.org/10.1016/0010-0285(82)90005-6.

Levelt, Willem J. M., Ardi Roelofs & Antje S. Meyer. 1999. A theory of lexical access in speech production. *Behavioral and Brain Sciences* 22(1). 1–38. https://doi.org/10.1017/S0140525X99001776.

Levin, Beth & Malka Rappaport Hovav. 2005. *Argument realization* (Research Surveys in Linguistics). Cambridge, UK: Cambridge University Press.

Mahowald, Kyle, Ariel James, Richard Futrell & Edward Gibson. 2016. A meta-analysis of syntactic priming in language production. *Journal of Memory and Language* 91. 5–27. http://doi.org/10.1016/j.jml.2016.03.009.

Malchukov, Andrej, Martin Haspelmath & Bernard Comrie. 2010. Ditransitive constructions: A typological overview. In Andrej Malchukov, Martin Haspelmath & Bernard Comrie (eds.), *Studies in ditransitive constructions: A comparative handbook*, 1–64. Berlin: DeGruyter.

Malhotra, Gaurav, Martin J. Pickering, Holly P. Branigan & James A. Bednar. 2008. On the persistence of structural priming: Mechanisms of decay and influence of word forms. In Bradley C. Love, Ken McRae & Vladimir M. Sloutsky (eds.), *Cognitive Science Society (CSS) 30*, 657–662. Austin, TX.

Marantz, Alec. 2013. Verbal argument structure: Events and participants. *Lingua* 130. 152–168. https://doi.org/10.1016/j.lingua.2012.10.012.

Matuschek, Hannes, Reinhold Kliegl, Shravan Vasishth, Harald Baayen & Douglas Bates. 2017. Balancing Type I error and power in linear mixed models. *Journal of Memory and Language* 94. 305–315. https://doi.org/10.1016/j.jml.2017.01.001.

McFadden, Thomas. 2006. German inherent datives and argument structure. In Daniel Hole, André Meinunger & Werner Abraham (eds.), *Datives and other cases: Between argument structure and event structure*, 49–77. Amsterdam: Benjamins. https://doi.org/10.1075/slcs.75.05mcf.

McIntyre, Andrew. 2006. The interpretation of German datives and English *have*. In Daniel Hole, André Meinunger & Werner Abraham (eds.), *Datives and other cases: Between argument structure and event structure*, 185–211. Amsterdam: Benjamins. https://doi.org/10.1075/slcs.75.09mci.

Melinger, Alissa, Thomas Pechmann & Sandra Pappert. 2009. Case in language production. In Andrej L. Malchukov & Andrew Spencer (eds.), *The Oxford handbook of case*, 384–401. Oxford: Oxford University Press. https://doi.org/10.1093/oxfordhb/9780199206476.013.0026.

Meyer, Antje S. 1996. Lexical access in phrase and sentence production: Results from picture-word interference experiments. *Journal of Memory and Language* 35. 477–496. https://doi.org/10.1006/jmla.1996.0026.

Momma, Shota, L. Robert Slevc & Colin Phillips. 2016. The timing of verb selection in Japanese sentence production. *Journal of Experimental Psychology: Learning, Memory, and Cognition* 42(5). 813–824. http://doi.org/10.1037/xlm0000195.

Müller, Gereon. 1999. Optimality, markedness, and word order in German. *Linguistics* 37(5). 777–818. https://doi.org/10.1515/ling.37.5.777.

Müller, Stefan. 2016. Flexible phrasal constructions, constituent structure and (cross-linguistic) generalizations: A discussion of template-based phrasal LFG approaches. In Doug Arnold, Miriam Butt, Berthold Crysmann, Tracy Holloway King & Stefan Müller (eds.), *Proceedings of the Joint 2016 Conference on Head-driven Phrase Structure Grammar and Lexical Functional Grammar*, 457–477. Stanford: CSLI Publications.

Osgood, Charles E. & J. Kathryn Bock. 1977. Salience and sentencing: some production principles. In Sheldon Rosenberg (ed.), *Sentence production: Developments in research and theory*, 89–140. Hillsdale, N.J.: Erlbaum.

Pappert, Sandra. 2016. Towards an account of prediction in a serial model of comprehension and production: Processing verb-second and verb-final sentences. Ms., Bielefeld.

Pappert, Sandra & Thomas Pechmann. 2013. Bidirectional structural priming across alternations: Evidence from the generation of dative and benefactive alternation structures in German. *Language and Cognitive Processes* 28(9). 1303–1322. https://doi.org/10.1080/01690965.2012.672752.

Pappert, Sandra & Thomas Pechmann. 2014. Priming word order by thematic roles: No evidence for an additional involvement of phrase structure. *Quarterly Journal of Experimental Psychology* 67(11). 2260–2278. https://doi.org/10.1080/17470218.2014.918632.

Pechmann, Thomas. 1989. Incremental speech production and referential overspecification. *Linguistics* 27. 89–110. https://doi.org/10.1515/ling.1989.27.1.89.

Pickering, Martin J. & Holly P. Branigan. 1998. The representation of verbs: Evidence from syntactic priming in language production. *Journal of Memory and Language* 39(4). 633–651. https://doi.org/10.1006/jmla.1998.2592.

Pickering, Martin J. & Holly P. Branigan. 1999. Syntactic priming in language production. *Trends in Cognitive Sciences* 3(4). 136–141. http://doi.org/10.1016/S1364-6613(99)01293-0.

Pickering, Martin J., Holly P. Branigan & Janet F. McLean. 2002. Constituent structure is formulated in one stage. *Journal of Memory and Language* 46(3). 586–605. https://doi.org/10.1006/jmla.2001.2824.

Pickering, Martin J. & Victor S. Ferreira. 2008. Structural priming: A critical review. *Psychological Bulletin* 134(3). 427–459. https://doi.org/10.1037/0033-2909.134.3.427.

Pickering, Martin & Roger P. G. van Gompel. 2006. Syntactic parsing. In Morton Ann Gernsbacher & Matthew J. Traxler (eds.), *Handbook of psycholinguistics*, 2nd edn., 455–503. San Diego, CA: Academic Press.

Prat-Sala, Mercè & Holly P. Branigan. 2000. Discourse constraints on syntactic processing in language production: A cross-linguistic study in English and Spanish. *Journal of Memory and Language* 42(2). 168–182. https://doi.org/10.1006/jmla.1999.2668.

Primus, Beatrice. 1999. *Cases and thematic roles: Ergative, Accusative and Active*. Tübingen: Niemeyer.

Prince, Ellen. 1981. Toward a taxonomy of given-new information. In Peter Cole (ed.), *Radical pragmatics*, 223–255. New York, NY: Academic Press.

Pylkkänen, Liina. 2008. *Introducing arguments*. Cambridge, MA: MIT Press.

R Core Team. 2014. R: A language and environment for statistical computing. Vienna, Austria: R Foundation for Statistical Computing. Retrieved from http://www.R-project.org. (2021-04-13).

Scheepers, Christoph, Claudine N. Raffray & Andriy Myachykov. 2017. The lexical boost effect is not diagnostic of lexically-specific syntactic representations. *Journal of Memory and Language* 95. 102–115. https://doi.org/10.1016/j.jml.2017.03.001.

Schriefers, Herbert 1993. Syntactic processes in the production of noun phrases. *Journal of Experimental Psychology: Learning, Memory, and Cognition* 19(4). 841–850. http://doi.org/10.1037/0278-7393.19.4.841.

Schriefers, Herbert, Encara Teruel & Raik-Michael Meinshausen. 1998. Producing simple sentences: Results from picture-word interference experiments. *Journal of Memory and Language* 39(4). 609–632. https://doi.org/10.1006/jmla.1998.2578.

Segaert, Katrien, Kirsten Weber, Mira Cladder-Micus & P. Hagoort. 2014. The influence of verb-bound syntactic preferences on the processing of syntactic structures. *Journal of Experimental Psychology: Learning, Memory, and Cognition* 40(5). 1448–1460. https://doi.org/10.1037/a0036796.

Shibatani, Masayoshi. 1996. Applicatives and benefactives: A cognitive account. In Masayoshi Shibatani & Sandra A. Thompson (eds.), *Grammatical constructions*, 157–196. Oxford: Clarendon Press.

Shin, Jeong-Ah & Kiel Christianson. 2009. Syntactic processing in Korean-English bilingual production: Evidence from cross-linguistic structural priming. *Cognition* 112(1). 175–180. https://doi.org/10.1016/j.cognition.2009.03.011.

Singmann, Henrik, Ben Bolker, Jake Westfall & Frederik Aust. 2016. afex: Analysis of Factorial Experiments. R package version 0.16-1. Retrieved from https://CRAN.R-project.org/package=afex. (2021-04-13).

Song, Jae Jung 2010. Korean benefactive particles and their meanings. In Fernando Zuñiga & Seppo Kittilä (eds.), *Benefactives and malefactives: Typological perspectives and case studies*, 393–418. Amsterdam: Benjamins. https://doi.org/10.1075/tsl.92.17son.

Tooley, Kristen M. & Kathryn Bock. 2014. On the parity of structural persistence in language production and comprehension. *Cognition* 132(2). 101–136. https://doi.org/10.1016/j.cognition.2014.04.002.

Van Valin, Robert D. & Randy J. LaPolla. 1997. *Syntax: Structure, meaning and function*. Cambridge, UK: Cambridge University Press.

Verhoeven, Elisabeth. 2014. Thematic prominence and animacy asymmetries: Evidence from a cross-linguistic production study. *Lingua* 143. 129–161. https://doi.org/10.1016/j.lingua.2014.02.002.

Vogel, Ralf & Markus Steinbach. 1998. The dative – an oblique case. *Linguistische Berichte* 173. 65–90.

Wagner, Valentin, Jörg D. Jescheniak & Herbert Schriefers. 2010. On the flexibility of grammatical advance planning during sentence production: Effects of cognitive load on multiple lexical access. *Journal of Experimental Psychology: Learning, Memory, and Cognition* 36(2). 423–440. https://doi.org/10.1037/a0018619.

Wegener, Heide. 1985. *Der Dativ im heutigen Deutsch*. Tübingen: Narr.

Wegener, Heide. 1991. Der Dativ: Ein struktureller Kasus? In Gisbert Fanselow & Sascha W. Felix (eds.), *Strukturen und Merkmale syntaktischer Kategorien*, 70–103. Tübingen: Narr.

Weiner, E. Judith & William Labov. 1983. Constraints on the agentless passive. *Journal of Linguistics* 19(01). 29–58. https://doi.org/10.1017/S0022226700007441.

Wunderlich, Dieter. 2006. Argument hierarchy and other factors of argument realization. In Ina Bornkessel, Matthias Schlesewsky, Bernard Comrie & Angela D. Friederici (eds.), *Semantic role universals: Perspectives from linguistic theory, language typology and psycho-/neurolinguistics*, 15–52. Berlin & New York: Mouton de Gruyter.

Zschernitz, Susann, Sandra Pappert & Thomas. Pechmann 2010. *The production of prosody in German PP-attachment ambiguities*. Poster, Prosody Frontiers, Leiden.

Anna Czypionka, Carsten Eulitz
Case marking affects the processing of animacy with simple verbs, but not particle verbs
An event-related potential study

Abstract: In sentence comprehension, animate-animate argument sequences are associated with higher processing costs than animate-inanimate argument sequences. This increase in processing costs is reflected in enhanced N400 components in ERP measurements. In German, a language that morphologically marks case on the arguments of verbs, this increase in processing cost is only found for standard nominative-accusative assigning verbs, but not for nominative-dative assigning verbs. So far, it is unclear whether this interplay between object animacy and case marking in sentence comprehension reflects the non-standard syntax or semantics of nominative-dative assigning verbs.

We present the results of two ERP experiments designed to tease apart syntactic and semantic contributions to lexical case marking effects in sentence comprehension. Our first experiment monitored the interaction of object animacy and case marking for non-separable simple verbs. This experiment revealed an enhanced N400 for animate objects with simple verbs assigning nominative-accusative, but not for those assigning nominative-dative. Our second experiment monitored the same interaction for separable particle verbs. This experiment revealed an enhanced N400 for animate relative to inanimate objects, both for particle verbs assigning nominative-accusative and nominative-dative. Our results suggest that the attenuation of the object animacy effect for simple nominative-dative verbs reflects the processing of syntactic, rather than semantic, differences between verb classes.

Keywords: sentence comprehension, argument processing, animacy, case, lexical case, particle verbs, German, ERP, N400

Note: An alternative analysis of the experiments presented here was published as Czypionka & Eulitz (2018).

Anna Czypionka, Department of Linguistics, Constance University, Universitätsstraße 10, 78457 Constance, Germany, e-mail: anna.czypionka@uni-konstanz.de
Carsten Eulitz, Department of Linguistics, Constance University, Universitätsstraße 10, 78457 Constance, Germany, e-mail: carsten.eulitz@uni-konstanz.de

1 Introduction

During the comprehension of transitive sentences, different cues are used for grammatical and thematic role assignment. These cues can be divided into different groups: Information like word order, person and number congruency of subject and verb, and case marking on the arguments, could be described as formal cues (Bader & Meng 1999; Carminati 2005; Frazier & Flores d'Arcais 1989; Frisch & Schlesewsky 2001; Hemforth et al. 1993; Pearlmutter et al. 1999; Schlesewsky et al. 2000; Schriefers et al. 1995). Semantic information like argument animacy also has an influence on grammatical and thematic role assignment (e.g. Czypionka 2014; Frisch & Schlesewsky 2001; McDonald et al. 1994; Paczynski & Kuperberg 2011; Trueswell et al. 1994). In German, one of the main cues for argument processing in transitive sentences is case marking. Subjects are nominative, and objects are usually accusative. A small group of two-place verbs, however, assign lexical dative instead of structural accusative to their objects. These verbs show lexical, semantic and syntactic differences from 'standard' nominative-accusative assigning verbs (e.g. Bayer et al. 2001; Blume 2000; Grimm 2010; Haider 2010; McFadden 2004), and the processing of both verb classes is measurably different (Bader et al. 2000; Bayer et al. 2001; Bornkessel et al. 2004; Czypionka 2014; Czypionka et al. 2017; Hopf et al. 1998; Hopf et al. 2003). It is still unclear whether these processing differences reflect syntactic, semantic or lexical differences between both verb classes.

Here, we present data from two ERP experiments aimed to disentangle the syntactic and semantic contributions to processing differences of nominative-accusative and nominative-dative assigning verbs. To this end, we used well-established effects from the processing of argument animacy contrasts in a variety of sentence backgrounds. In the remainder of the introduction, we will set out by introducing the role of argument animacy in sentence comprehension, followed by an overview of the existing literature on the processing of nominative-accusative and nominative-dative marking verbs in German. This will allow us to explain how argument animacy contrasts can be used to monitor the processing of lexical case marking. We will then introduce another distinction between German verb types, namely, the one between non-separable simple verbs and separable particle verbs. In combination with argument animacy contrasts, this distinction will allow us to disentangle the semantic and syntactic contributions to lexical case marking effects.

1.1 Animate and inanimate objects

The animacy of a noun's referent is a semantic property that has different linguistic reflections across the world's languages. Examples are different interrogative pronouns (English *who* or German *wer* for animates, but English *what* or German *was* for inanimates), number marking (Corbett 2000; Croft 1990; Haspelmath 2013) or case marking (in Differential Object Marking languages, see e.g. Bossong 1985, 1991; Næss 2004). Based on observations from corpus linguistics and typology (Aissen 2003; Bossong 1985; Comrie 1989; Dahl 2008; Dixon 1994; Jäger 2004; Malchukov 2008; Silverstein 1976), sentences with an animate subject and an inanimate object are often considered the "most natural" transitive constructions in psycholinguistics.

Argument animacy plays a central role in sentence production and comprehension. In production, argument animacy has an influence on word order and the assignment of syntactic function (Bock 1987; Bock & Loebell 1990; Bock & Warren 1985; Branigan et al. 2008; Branigan & Feleki 1999; Ferreira 1994; McDonald et al. 1993; Prat-Sala & Branigan 2000), and interacts with the assignment of thematic roles (Ferreira 1994; van Nice & Dietrich 2003), sometimes interacting with case marking (Verhoeven 2009, 2014). In comprehension, contrasts in argument animacy are used for assigning grammatical roles.[1] The general pattern is that sentences with animate objects have higher processing costs than sentences with inanimate objects (Czypionka 2014; Czypionka et al. 2017; Frisch & Schlesewsky 2001; Kuperberg et al. 2007; Paczynski & Kuperberg 2011; Trueswell et al. 1994; Weckerly & Kutas 1999).

The ERP component usually associated with animate-animate argument sequences relative to animate-inanimate argument sequences is an enhanced N400. Frisch and Schlesewsky (2001) monitored the comprehension of German embedded verb-final transitive sentences. Objects in these sentences were either inanimate or animate objects, and all arguments were marked nominative, which made the sentences ungrammatical. Animate-inanimate argument sequences elicited an enhanced P600 on the clause-final verb, but animate-animate argument sequences elicited an enhanced N400 in addition to the P600. For English, Paczynski and Kuperberg (2011) found an enhanced N400 for postverbal animate compared to

---

[1] For reasons of space, we cannot give a detailed outline of the earlier uses of argument animacy in the sentence comprehension literature, which was mainly concerned with assessing the time point at which semantic information influenced the buildup of syntactic structure (e.g. Clifton et al. 2003; Ferreira & Clifton 1986; Frazier & Rayner 1982; MacDonald et al. 1994; Trueswell et al. 1994).

inanimate objects in grammatically and semantically well-formed sentences. They did not find differences between animate objects that were patients or experiencers. This suggests that the enhanced N400 for animate objects is not caused by (mis)matches of the arguments' semantic properties with their assigned thematic roles.

The findings outlined above suggest that argument animacy is a central cue in sentence comprehension, and is used during the assignment of grammatical and thematic roles. It is processed differently from other aspects of a sentence's semantics (for example, the checking of plausibility, or whether the verb's semantic selectional restrictions are met). The processing of animate-animate argument sequences is more costly than that of animate-inanimate sequences. This enhanced processing load is reflected in an enhanced N400 component. The important role of argument animacy contrasts for the assignment of grammatical and thematic roles is reflected in different models of sentence comprehension (Bornkessel-Schlesewsky & Schlesewsky 2006, 2009, 2013; Kuperberg 2007).

In this chapter, we will call the increased processing cost for animate-animate argument sequences the *object animacy effect*. We will take advantage of the object animacy effect to investigate another issue in German sentence comprehension, namely, the processing of different verb types. To give a more detailed outline of our research question, we will introduce two possible distinctions between German verb types: By the case assigned to their direct objects, and by their separability.

1.2 Structural and lexical case marking verbs

In German, arguments are marked with morphological case (although case syncretism sometimes leads to grammatical, but case-ambiguous arguments).

Case marking is one of the most important cues for grammatical role assignment in German sentence comprehension. Subjects are nominative, direct objects are accusatives, and indirect objects of ditransitive verbs are dative. There is, however, a class of German transitive verbs that assign dative instead of accusative to their direct objects. Here, we will call these transitive verbs that assign noncanonical case NOM-DAT verbs or *lexical case marking verbs*. The verbs assigning canonical case will be called *structural case marking verbs* or NOM-ACC verbs. Lexical case marking verbs are not restricted to German, but occur in many different case marking languages. Interestingly, they seem to always refer to situations with a special type of argument semantics (Blume 2000). These are situations that deviate from prototypical (Dowty 1991) or maximal (Grimm 2010) transitivity, meaning that they do not describe situations with a prototypical (i.e. unaffected, volitional, sentient . . .) agent doing something to a prototypical (i.e. affected, moved) participant. Instead, they encode situations where the semantic features or properties associated with a specific semantic proto-role are distributed among both participants. A simplification would be to say that their objects tend to be more agentive relative to their subjects than those in prototypically transitive situations.[2] However, this diagnostic for non-prototypical argument semantics does not work both ways: NOM-DAT verbs always denote situations that deviate from prototypical transitivity. At the same time, non-prototypically transitive situations may be encoded by a NOM-ACC verb. In the literature, this is often illustrated with the verb pair *helfen* ('to help', NOM-DAT) and *unterstützen* ('to support', NOM-ACC). Different authors have claimed that this verb pair shows that case marking can be predicted from verbal semantics (Meinunger 2007) or that case marking is unpredictable and idiosyncratic (Haider 2010). For the purposes of our study, we will assume that NOM-DAT verbs are always non-prototypically transitive, while NOM-ACC verbs may encode all kinds of situations with respect to transitivity.

Dative on direct objects is an idiosyncratic or lexical case (Czepluch 1996; Haider 1993, 2010; Woolford 2006) (in contrast to dative for indirect objects, see Woolford 2006; but see also Meinunger 2007). Many syntactic analyses propose that the structure of NOM-DAT verbs is different from that of NOM-ACC verbs. Following Fanselow (2000) and Woolford (2006), lexical datives must be assigned by lexical heads like V^0 or P^0. McFadden (2004) suggests that there are different base positions for indirect objects, depending on the verb, and that lexical case marking verbs assign dative in one of the indirect object positions. Bayer suggests that lexical case is assigned in an additional syntactic layer of projection called KP for Kase Phrase (Bader et al. 2000; Bayer et al. 2001; since this analysis has already informed psycholinguistic experiments, we will return to this in more detail below).

In German sentence comprehension, NOM-DAT verbs are associated with higher processing costs than NOM-ACC verbs. It seems that this increase in processing cost only occurs when case marking on the arguments is ambiguous (Bader et al. 2000). In ERP studies, clause-final NOM-DAT verbs elicited an enhanced N400 relative to NOM-ACC verbs (Hopf et al. 1998, 2003) with case-ambiguous arguments. In contrast to NOM-ACC verbs, NOM-DAT verbs can have either subject-object or object-

---

[2] Importantly, neither Dowty (1991) nor Grimm (2010) include animacy in their list of proto-agent properties; in fact, both some of the proto-agent properties like *volitional involvement*, and some of the proto-patient properties, like *affectedness*, imply animacy. We can therefore not assume that the non-prototypically transitive argument semantics of NOM-DAT verbs always translate to a clear preference for animate objects.

subject as their pragmatically unmarked argument order. This fact is also reflected in sentence comprehension, and object-subject verb orders lead to reduced garden-path effects and different ERP patterns with NOM-DAT verbs relative to NOM-ACC verbs (Bader 1996; Bornkessel et al. 2004). Argument animacy is also processed differently for NOM-ACC and NOM-DAT verbs. Czypionka (2014) and Czypionka et al. (2017) showed that the contrast between grammatical sentences with animate and inanimate objects was reduced for NOM-DAT compared to NOM-ACC verbs, using behavioural and ERP measures. Processing differences between NOM-DAT and NOM-ACC verbs have been explained in different ways in the psycholinguistic literature. In the extended Argument Dependency Model (eADM; Bornkessel-Schlesewsky & Schlesewsky 2006, 2009, 2013), processing differences between both verb classes are predicted (Bornkessel-Schlesewsky & Schlesewsky 2006: 792), although currently, the specific processing differences are not formulated in greater detail. In the context of this model, it is assumed that this difference arises from the non-prototypically transitive semantics of NOM-DAT verbs (Bornkessel-Schlesewsky & Schlesewsky 2009: 43). In the KP-based account (Bader et al. 2000; Bayer et al. 2001), it is assumed that sentences with case-ambiguous arguments lead to two additional processing steps. The first is the insertion of an additional projection (KP for Kase Phrase), allowing the assignment of lexical case. The second step is lexical reaccess to the object to check if its morphology licenses lexical case (this step is assumed to cause the N400 reported by Hopf et al. 1998, 2003).

Taken together, NOM-DAT verbs are processed differently from NOM-ACC verbs in sentences without overt morphological case marking. These processing differences can surface as additional processing load for NOM-DAT verbs, but also in different effects of word order and attenuated object animacy effects.

For now, it remains unclear what exactly is reflected in the processing differences of NOM-DAT and NOM-ACC verbs – differences in lexical, syntactic or semantic processing, or a mix of these factors. Our aim in the current study is to disentangle the contributions of these different factors, focusing on one of the many differences, namely, the attenuation of the object animacy effect with NOM-DAT verbs. This attenuated object animacy effect could be explained in two different ways:

- The attenuated object animacy effect could reflect the non-prototypically transitive semantics of NOM-DAT verbs. As outlined above, these verbs have objects that bear semantic properties that do not correspond to the thematic role of proto-agent (Blume 2000; Dowty 1991; Grimm 2010). Under this assumption, the non-prototypically transitive semantics of these verbs interact with semantic argument information, i.e. animacy. This could enable them to license noncanonical animacy patterns like animate-animate argument sequences. This explanation fits the explanation given in the eADM for the

processing differences found with NOM-DAT and NOM-ACC verbs (Bornkessel-Schlesewsky & Schlesewsky 2006, 2009).
- The attenuated object animacy effect could reflect the syntactic differences between NOM-DAT and NOM-ACC verbs, leading to mild syntactic reanalysis and lexical reaccess to the object, as proposed by the KP-based account (see above). While some earlier studies reported results that could be interpreted as reflecting increased processing cost for NOM-DAT compared to NOM-ACC verbs (i.e. the N400 reported in Hopf et al. 1998, 2003), it is also possible that case-marking effects in some way interfere with the effects of argument animacy contrasts during the buildup of the sentence representation, leading to seemingly absent effects of argument animacy (we give an outline of a more detailed proposal in the discussion section). Although not explicitly predicted by the KP-based account (Bader et al. 2000; Bayer et al. 2001), this assumption fits the KP-based account.

To distinguish between these two possible explanations, we will introduce another distinction between different verb types. This distinction is the one between non-separable simple verbs and separable particle verbs. Both of these verb types include two-place verbs assigning NOM-ACC or NOM-DAT to their arguments. Below, we will give a short outline about the characteristics of particle verbs. This in turn will allow us to give a more detailed explanation of how particle verbs can contribute to solving the underlying reasons for attenuated object animacy effects with NOM-DAT verbs.

1.3 Simple and particle verbs

German verbs can either be non-separable or separable. Non-separable verbs can be simple, like *folgen*, 'to follow', or prefixed like *verfolgen*, 'to pursue'. (For the sake of readability, we will refer to both kinds of verbs together as *simple verbs* in this text). In main clauses, simple verbs are realized as the second constituent; in embedded clauses, they are realized as the clause-final constituent. In contrast, separable or particle verbs, like *nachlaufen* ('to run after'), are compounds that can be realized as multiple or single words in a sentence (see Olsen et al. 1996 for a definition; see also Dehé 2015 or McIntyre 2007 for overviews). They consist of a particle and base. The base may often function as a stand-alone verb (here: *laufen*, meaning 'to run' when not combined with a particle). The particle (here: *nach*) is often homologuous to a preposition. Just like simple verbs, particle verbs occur as one orthographical unit in clause-final positions. In main clauses, only the base verb is realized as the second constituent, while the particle is realized as the clause-final constituent. Although particle verbs are regularly realized as two separate words, they are assumed to have one single lexical entry (Cappelle et al. 2010; Jackendoff 2002).[3]

Different syntactic analyses for particle verbs have been proposed. Perhaps trivially, their structure must be morphosyntactically more complex that of simple NOM-ACC verbs, if only because of their unusual property of occurring as two words in main clauses (see e.g. Lüdeling & de Jong 2002 for an analysis of particle verbs as phrasal units). One type of analysis is based on the idea that the objects of particle verbs are not objects of the verb, but of the particle (e.g. Zeller 2001a). Another type of analysis is based on the idea that the objects of particle verbs are either objects of the verb or of a complex predicate including the particle and the verb (Neeleman & Weerman 1993; Neeleman 1994 for Dutch; Stiebels & Wunderlich 1994 for German). McIntyre (2007, 2015) provides a detailed comparison of many different types of theoretical descriptions.

Two-place particle verbs occur with canonical NOM-ACC and noncanonical NOM-DAT case marking patterns, just like simple verbs. The case assigned by particle verbs does not necessarily correspond to the case assigned by the prepositions that are homologuous to the particle (see Zeller 2001b), for prepositions, case marking encodes spatial semantics (Svenonius 2010). Neither is it possible to reliably link a specific particle with exclusively accusative or dative objects. NOM-DAT particle verbs are never prototypically transitive (Meinunger 2007); thus, the generalizations about special argument semantics of NOM-DAT verbs hold for both simple and particle verbs.

Syntactic accounts of particle verbs hardly ever mention different case assignment patterns, and to our knowledge, none offers a direct contrast of structures for NOM-ACC and NOM-DAT assigning particle verbs. Just as for simple verbs, dative seems to be a lexical case for direct objects of particle verbs, one important diagnostic being that unlike accusative, it is retained under passivization (*Dem Jungen wird zugeschaut*, 'The.DAT boy(.DAT) is being watched', but *Der Junge wird angeschaut* 'The.NOM boy(.NOM) is being looked at'). (This example also illustrates that accusative assigned by particle verbs is likely to function like a structural case syntactically, no matter which analysis of case assignment with particle verbs is ultimately chosen.)

For our current studies, we will not choose a specific syntactic analysis of particle verbs. However, we will base our hypotheses on some assumptions: We

---

[3] Importantly, this only refers to the storage of particle verbs in the mental lexicon, not to their semantic compositionality and neither to the semantic and syntactic relations between particle verbs and their bases.

assume that because of their morphosyntactic complexity and separability, the syntactic processing cost for particle verbs should be higher than that for simple NOM-ACC assigning verbs (see below for psycholinguistic studies aiming to investigate this issue). We further assume that for sentence comprehension, deviations from the "standard" structure of simple NOM-ACC verbs are the most relevant contrast. Therefore, potential contrasts between particle verbs assigning NOM-ACC and NOM-DAT should not influence processing to the same extent as contrasts between simple verbs assigning NOM-ACC and NOM-DAT. The underlying reasoning is that with particle verbs, the contrast of NOM-ACC and NOM-DAT is between two structures that are already more complex than the simple NOM-ACC verb "standard" structure. Finally, we assume that the differences in argument semantics and thematic role assignment for NOM-ACC and NOM-DAT verbs are the same for simple and particle verbs, and that NOM-DAT case assignment reliably signals non-prototypically transitive argument semantics (following Meinunger 2007, and, in our interpretation, implicitly in Grimm 2010).

Psycholinguistic research on particle verbs in sentence comprehension is mostly concerned with the processing of separate base-particle combinations in Dutch and German main clauses (Cappelle et al. 2010; Isel et al. 2005; Piai et al. 2013; Urban 2001, 2002; an exception is Roehm & Haider 2009, who report increased processing costs for particle verbs relative to non-separable prefix verbs). We do not know of any study testing the influence of case marking patterns on the processing of particle verbs. In a similar vein, models of sentence comprehension do not currently use the distinction between simple and particle verbs, and in many experiments, stimuli are not controlled for this factor.

In summary, simple verbs and particle verbs with two arguments come with canonical NOM-ACC and noncanonical NOM-DAT case marking patterns. In both verb types, NOM-DAT case marking pattern signals non-prototypically transitive argument semantics. We assume that simple NOM-ACC and NOM-DAT verbs differ in syntactic complexity. At the same time, we assume that NOM-ACC and NOM-DAT particle verbs both differ in morphosyntactic complexity from simple verbs, and that syntactic differences between them are in principle possible, but too subtle to affect psycholinguistic measures of sentence comprehension.

1.4 Research question

Having given an outline of particle verbs, we can return to our research question, namely, finding out what is reflected in lexical case marking processes, and more specifically, in the attenuated object animacy effect for NOM-DAT relative to NOM-ACC verbs. As outlined above, it is possible to assume that this attenuation of the object animacy effect reflects the non-prototypically transitive argument semantics of NOM-DAT verbs, or the differences in syntactic and lexical processing between NOM-ACC and NOM-DAT verbs. The previous literature cannot give an answer to this question: The studies on the processing of NOM-DAT verbs cited above (Bornkessel et al. 2004; Czypionka 2014; Czypionka et al. 2017; Hopf et al. 1998, 2003) used a mix of simple and particle verbs in their stimuli. Therefore, earlier findings on the processing of lexical case marking verbs could reflect semantic, lexical and syntactic processing differences between NOM-ACC and NOM-DAT verbs.

In the current study, we will use the different properties of simple and particle verbs to disentangle the semantic and syntactic contributions to lexical case marking effects. More specifically, we will monitor object animacy effects with simple and particle verbs assigning NOM-ACC or NOM-DAT.

We make the following predictions for simple verbs and particle verbs:
(1) The attenuation of the object animacy effect with NOM-DAT verbs could reflect their non-prototypically transitive semantics. This could in turn reflect a better match of animate objects with the thematic roles assigned by NOM-DAT verbs. Following this assumption, we predict an interaction of object animacy and case marking for both simple and particle verbs, i.e. an attenuated object animacy effect for both verb types assigning NOM-DAT.
(2) The attenuation of the object animacy effect with NOM-DAT verbs could reflect the increased syntactic and lexical workload associated with NOM-DAT verbs. However, only simple verbs should lead to measurably increased syntactic workload. Particle verbs should have an increased syntactic workload, irrespective of their case marking pattern, and differences between NOM-ACC and NOM-DAT particle verbs should be subtle compared to these bigger differences. Under this assumption, we expect an interaction of object animacy and case marking for simple verbs, but only object animacy effects for particle verbs.[4]

Here, we present the results of two EEG experiments, monitoring the interaction of object animacy and case marking. In the first experiment, we monitored this interaction in sentences with simple verbs. In the second experiment, we monitored this interaction in sentences with particle verbs. To allow for a better comparison,

---

[4] Prediction (1) would match the explanation given for verb class processing differences in the eADM (Bornkessel-Schlesewsky & Schlesewsky 2009). Prediction (2) would roughly match the explanation given for verb class processing differences in the KP based account proposed by Bayer et al. (2001). However, the exact predictions for particle verbs are difficult to extract from this latter account. For the sake of brevity, we will limit ourselves to a detailed discussion of this issue in the Discussion section.

2 Language material

2.1 Stimulus set 1: Simple verbs

The simple verb stimulus set (used in Experiment 1) consisted of 36 items in four different conditions, i.e. 144 sentences. All sentences were grammatical, verb-final sentences with SOV word order that were embedded in a matrix clause. In each sentence quartet, we paired either NOM-ACC or NOM-DAT simple verbs with either inanimate or animate objects. Arguments were bare plural NPs without overt morphological case marking in their plural forms (due to case syncretism). This made grammatical role assignment via subject-verb number agreement or case marking impossible. We chose NOM-DAT verbs with unmarked subject-object word order from a list of German dative-assigning verbs (Meinunger 2007). The semantic selectional restrictions of all NOM-ACC and NOM-DAT verbs allow animate subjects and inanimate and animate objects, so that all conditions are syntactically and semantically well-formed. An adverb was inserted between the object NP and the critical verb. We constructed 36 critical sentence quartets using 33 animate subject NPs, 33 inanimate and 29 animate object NPs, 22 NOM-ACC and 16 NOM-DAT verbs, repeating some verbs with different subject and object NPs. Animate and inanimate object NPs in a sentence quartet were controlled for length ($t(60) = 1.49$, $p > .1$) and frequency ($t(52.3) = -.35$, $p > .5$; frequencies unavailable for five objects) according to the dlexDB corpus (Heister et al. 2011). NOM-ACC and NOM-DAT verbs in a sentence quartet were also controlled for length ($t(74) = -.18$, $p > .8$) and frequency ($t(73) = 1.23$, $p > .2$, frequency unavailable for eight verbs) according to the dlexDB corpus. A typical sentence quartet is given in Example 1.

Example 1: Example of a stimulus quartet, stimulus set 1, simple verbs
(A) inanimate object, accusative-assigning verb:
 Arno beklagt, dass Studentinnen Vorlesungen selten loben, und Uli beklagt es auch.
 Arno deplores that student.FEM.PL(.NOM) lecture.PL(.ACC) rarely praise.3PL and Uli deplores it too
 'Arno deplores (the fact) that students rarely praise lectures, and Uli deplores this, too.'
(B) animate object, accusative-assigning verb:
 Arno beklagt, dass Studentinnen Professoren selten loben, und Uli beklagt es auch.
 Arno deplores that student.FEM.PL(.NOM) professor.PL(.ACC) rarely praise.3PL and Uli deplores it too
 'Arno deplores (the fact) that students rarely praise professors, and . . .'

(C) inanimate object, dative-assigning verb:
Arno beklagt, dass Studentinnen Vorlesungen selten applaudieren, und Uli beklagt es auch.
Arno deplores that student.FEM.PL(.NOM) lecture.PL(.DAT) rarely applaud.3PL and Uli deplores it too
'Arno deplores (the fact) that students rarely applaud lectures, and . . .'

(D) animate object, dative-assigning verb:
Arno beklagt, dass Studentinnen Professoren selten applaudieren, und Uli beklagt es auch.
Arno deplores that student.FEM.PL(.NOM) professor.PL(.DAT) rarely applaud.3PL and Uli deplores it too
'Arno deplores (the fact) that students rarely applaud professors, and . . .'

2.2 Stimulus set 2: Particle verbs

A parallel stimulus set was used in Experiment 2. This stimulus set also consisted of 144 sentences, with 36 items in four different conditions. The structure of the sentences was identical to the ones in the simple verb stimulus set, but the NOM-ACC and NOM-DAT verbs were separable particle verbs, presented as one orthographic unit at the end of the embedded clause. We constructed 36 critical sentence quartets using 34 animate subject NPs, 36 inanimate and 28 animate object NPs, 25 NOM-ACC and 21 NOM-DAT verbs, also repeating some particle verbs with different subject and object NPs. A typical sentence quartet is given in Example 2. Animate and inanimate object NPs in a sentence quartet were controlled for length (t (58.05) = −.86, p > .3) and frequency (t (51.3) = −1.19, p > .2; frequencies unavailable for ten objects) according to the dlexDB corpus (Heister et al. 2011). NOM-ACC and NOM-DAT verbs in a sentence quartet were controlled for frequency (t (42.75) = −.96, p > .3, frequency unavailable for one verb) according to the dlexDB corpus and for length(t (37.9) = −2.64, p < .05). The mean length of NOM-ACC assigning particle verbs was 9.1 letters, the mean length of NOM-DAT assigning particle verbs was 10.7 letters. We accepted this small but statistically significant difference in length, mostly because there is only a limited choice of NOM-DAT verbs in German, and stimulus construction is further restricted by the need to find argument-verb combinations that are meaningful and acceptable for accusative and dative conditions. A typical sentence quartet is given in Example 2.

Example 2: Example of a stimulus quartet, stimulus set 2, particle verbs
(A) inanimate object, NOM-ACC verb:
Peter berichtet, dass Banditen Postkutschen häufig ausrauben, und Ida berichtet das gleiche.
Peter relates that bandit.PL(.NOM) stagecoach.PL(.ACC) often out.rob.3PL and Ida relates the same
'Peter relates that bandits often rob stage coaches, and Ida relates the same.'

(B) animate object, NOM-ACC verb:
Peter berichtet, dass Banditen Postboten häufig ausrauben, und Ida berichtet das gleiche.
Peter relates that bandit.PL(.NOM) postman.PL(.ACC) often out.rob.3PL and Ida relates the same
'... that bandits often rob postmen, and Ida ...'
(C) inanimate object, NOM-DAT verb:
Peter berichtet, dass Banditen Postkutschen häufig auflauern, und Ida berichtet das gleiche.
Peter relates that bandit.PL(.NOM) stagecoach.PL(.DAT) often on.lurk.3PL and Ida relates the same
'... that bandits often waylay stage coaches, and Ida ...'
(D) animate object, NOM-DAT verb:
Peter berichtet, dass Banditen Postboten häufig auflauern, und Ida berichtet das gleiche.
Peter relates that bandit.PL(.NOM) postman.PL(.DAT) often on.lurk.3PL and Ida relates the same
'... that bandits often waylay postmen, and Ida ...'

2.3 Sentence completion task

In a pen-and-paper sentence completion task, we monitored the relative likelihood of finding animate and inanimate objects with NOM-ACC and NOM-DAT verbs.[5] Participants saw the critical sentence printed until the final verb of the subordinate clause (i.e. minus the spillover region). The space of the object was left blank, and participants were asked to fill in the blank and to complete the sentence in a meaningful way. For each sentence quartet, participants saw either the NOM-ACC or the NOM-DAT condition. Each participant saw 36 sentences from stimulus set 1, and 36 sentences from stimulus set 2. The task was completed as part of a course assignment at Constance University. Completions were coded as either "inanimate", "animate" or "not applicable" (when the completion was not an argument, or when the space had been left blank). 28 participants successfully completed the task. 3 participants were male. Mean age was 23.3 years (SD = 2.0). Before data analysis, the responses coded as "not applicable" were removed from the data set. The majority of the completions were inanimate or animate arguments (93 % for simple verb conditions, 89 % for particle verb conditions), suggesting that a second argument is natural in this position in our stimulus material. An overview of the completions per condition is given in Table 1.

---

[5] While Bader & Häussler (2010) report a general pattern of more animate than inanimate datives in their extensive corpus study, they still find 13 % to 21 % inanimate datives. In addition, they find that animate-animate argument sequences are not more frequent with dative than with accusative objects. However, the sentences they investigated are much more diverse than our own stimulus material. This made it necessary to monitor the likelihood of finding animate objects with our specific stimuli.

Table 1: Results of the sentence completion task performed as a pretest for our stimulus material. Mean proportions of completions are given in percent, standard deviations are given in parentheses.

verb type	case marking	percentage of completions	
		inanimate	animate
simple	NOM-ACC	37.1 (12.6)	58.1 (14.8)
	NOM-DAT	22.6 (13.4)	68.3 (15.5)
particle	NOM-ACC	45.4 (18.3)	46.2 (15.1)
	NOM-DAT	22.6 (12.6)	64.3 (16.0)

The results of the sentence completion task were analyzed in R (R Development Core Team 2005) with a binomial generalized linear mixed model, using the packages lme4 (Bates et al. 2015, glmer function for binomial data) and LMERConvenienceFunctions (Tremblay & Ransijn 2015, summary function). The choice of argument (inanimate or animate) was the dependent variable. For the first model, we specified the main effects and interactions of CASE and SEPARABILITY as fixed effects. Participants and items were specified as random intercepts. In addition, random slopes were defined for participants (main effects of CASE and SEPARABILITY) and items (main effects of CASE). There was a statistically significant main effect of CASE ($p < .05$), with more animate completions for dative verbs than for accusative verbs. There was no interaction of CASE and SEPARABILITY, suggesting that this effect of case marking did not differ systematically between simple and particle verbs. Since we planned to use the two stimulus sets in two separate experiments that were to be analyzed separately, we performed planned comparisons for simple and particle verbs. The planned comparisons were performed with a second model. For the second model, we specified the main effect of CASE as fixed effect. Participants and items were specified as random intercepts, and random slopes were defined for participants and items (main effects of CASE). For simple verbs, there was a statistically significant main effect of CASE on the likelihood of choosing an animate object ($p < .05$). Overall, participants chose more animate than inanimate objects. This tendency was more pronounced for dative than for accusative conditions. For particle verbs, there was a statistically significant main effect of CASE on the likelihood of choosing an animate object $p < .05$). Participants chose more animate than inanimate objects for dative conditions. For accusative conditions, there was no marked preference for animate or inanimate objects.

The sentence completion study reveals that there are more animate completions for NOM-DAT than for NOM-ACC verbs. On the other hand, animate accusative objects are provided more often for our stimuli than in larger corpora, and inanimate datives contribute over 20 % of the completions. We are therefore confident that both animate and inanimate objects are in principle possible for all of our stimulus conditions, and that preferences for animate and inanimate objects do not differ depending on case marking between the simple and separable verb stimulus set.

3 Experiment 1: Interaction of object animacy and case marking with simple verbs

In the first experiment, we measured the interaction of ANIMACY and CASE for simple NOM-ACC and NOM-DAT verbs. For NOM-ACC VERBS, we expected enhanced processing difficulties for the animate-accusative compared to the inanimate-accusative condition, reflected in an enhanced N400 on the clause-final verb (Frisch & Schlesewsky 2001; Paczynski & Kuperberg 2009; Paczynski & Kuperberg 2011). We cannot make specific predictions as to the time course and shape of the lexical case marking effects and their interactions with object animacy, since our stimuli are the first to measure these effects without a mix of simple and particle verbs. Our general prediction from earlier studies would be that the contrast between animate and inanimate conditions is reduced for NOM-DAT verbs (based on Czypionka 2014; Czypionka et al. 2017).

3.1 Material and methods

3.1.1 Participants

24 participants participated in the first ERP experiment. All participants spoke German as their only native language and reported no known reading or language-related problems. Participants had normal or corrected to normal vision, were not taking any psychoactive medication and reported no neurological or psychiatric disorders. All participants were right-handed, scoring 70 % or higher on the Edinburgh handedness test (Oldfield 1971). All participants gave written informed consent. The data of 3 participants were excluded from the data analysis because of poor data quality. The mean age of the remaining 21 participants (11 male) was 23 years (SD = 2.4). Participants received 16 Euros compensation.

3.1.2 Language material

The simple verb set (stimulus set 1) was used as the language material, described in detail above in the Language material section. For the experiment, critical sentences were mixed with filler sentences. The final stimulus list consisted of 222 sentences and contained 144 critical sentences (36 per condition) interspersed with 78 filler sentences. Filler sentences were short main clauses beginning with animate or inanimate grammatical subjects. Representative examples of filler sentences are: *Der Affe ist vom Baum gefallen.* ('The monkey fell off the tree.'); *Die Säge hat einen roten Plastikgriff.* ('The saw has a red plastic handle.'). Sentences were pseudorandomized before the presentations. After 24 of the critical and 12 of the filler sentences, a comprehension question was asked. Answers were given via presses on a button box. Questions like "Do students rarely praise lectures?" were to be answered with "yes", the other half were to be answered with "no".

3.1.3 Procedure

Participants were seated in a comfortable chair in front of a computer screen, with an average distance of about 180 cm, in an electrically shielded EEG recording chamber. The experiment consisted of an instruction phase and the experimental phase. Participants were first instructed orally and then again in written form on the screen during the instruction phase. Words were presented visually in the center of a computer screen using the Presentation software by Neurobehavioral Systems Inc. (version 16.1). Words were presented in white 40 pt Arial font on a black screen. The first two and last three words of the matrix sentence were presented together, while the remaining words were presented in a word-by-word fashion. This means that the embedded sentence and the first two postverbal words (*und* and a personal name) were presented as single words: *Tim glaubt,| dass | Tauben | Luftballons | gerne | mögen, | und | Tom | glaubt das auch.* Each word or string of words was presented for 700 ms, followed by a 200 ms blank screen. During the experiment, participants held a two-button response box in their hands. Participants answered the questions by pressing the left or right response button, respectively. The sides for answering "yes" and "no" were switched for half of the participants. Feedback was presented for 500 ms. After 72 sentences, participants were offered to take a short break, resulting in 2 breaks during the course of the experiment. Before the actual experiment, participants performed three practice trials.

3.1.4 EEG recording

The EEG was recorded with 61 Ag/AgCl sintered ring electrodes attached to an elastic cap (EasyCap, Herrsching) and connected to an Easy-Cap Electrode Input Box (EiB32). Electrodes were positioned in the equidistant 61-channel arrangement provided by EasyCap (see http://easycap.brainproducts.com/e/electrodes/13_M10.htm for electrode layout). The EEG signal was amplified with a BrainAmp DC amplifier with a bandpass of 0.016–250 Hz (Brain Products, Gilching) connected to a computer outside of the EEG chamber (via USB2 Adapter, Brain Products, Gilching). The signal was recorded with a digitization rate of 500 Hz (Brain Vision Recorder, Brain Products, Gilching). Eye movements were monitored by recording the electrooculogram (IO1, IO2, Nz). The ground electrode was located on the left cheek.

3.1.5 Data processing

Data were processed using the Brain Vision Analyzer 2 software (Brain Products, Gilching). Raw data were inspected visually. Time windows including strong, visible artifacts and breaks were manually removed. Next, an ICA blink correction was performed for the remaining data, using the Slope Algorithm for blink detection. After blink correction, data were again inspected visually to monitor successful blink correction. A spline interpolation was performed for channels that showed long stretches of noisy data. Interpolation was only performed for electrodes with at least 3 surrounding non-interpolated electrodes. After the interpolation, all electrodes were re-referenced to average reference. An Automatic Raw Data Inspection was performed for the re-referenced data (maximal allowed voltage step: 50 μV/ms; maximal allowed difference: 100 μV/200ms; minimal/maximal allowed amplitudes 200 μV/–200 μV; lowest allowed activity: 0.5 μV/100ms). Before segmentation, the remaining raw data were filtered with Butterworth zero phase bandpass filters. The low cutoff frequency was 0.05 Hz (12 dB/oct), the high cutoff frequency was 70 Hz (12 dB/oct). After filtering, data were segmented into time windows time-locked to the onset of the critical verb. Time windows began at –2000 ms before the onset of the critical verb, and ended at 2000 ms after the onset of the critical verb.[6] A baseline correction was performed for the

---

6 This unusually long baseline was chosen to avoid transmission of ERP effects from preceding words while avoiding filter effects (see Bornkessel-Schlesewsky et al. 2011; Hung & Schumacher 2012; Tanner et al. 2015; Maess et al. 2016).

2000 ms before the onset of the critical verb. Averages were calculated per participant for all four conditions. Participants with less than 23 trials in one of the four conditions were excluded from data analysis. For the remaining 21 participants, on average 15 % of the data were rejected (SD = 7.5 %), so that all condition means were calculated from 23 to 36 segments. For data presentation, Grand Averages were smoothed with an additional 10 Hz low-pass filter.

3.1.6 Parametrization and statistical testing

The time window chosen for analysis was 400–600 ms after the onset of the critical verb. This time window was chosen based on visual inspection of the data, and because it matched time windows for object animacy effects and case marking interactions reported in the literature (Paczynski & Kuperberg 2011; Czypionka et al. 2014; Czypionka et al. 2017). A subset of 25 electrodes was selected for the statistical data analysis. Electrode position was coded by assigning electrodes to five medial-lateral as well as five anterior-posterior positions. Medial-lateral positions were: lateral-left (front to back: AF7, FT7, T7, TP7, P7), lateral-medial-left (front-to-back: FP1, C3, P1, O1, F1), midline (front-to-back: FPz, Cz, Pz, Oz, Fz), lateral-medial-right (front-to-back: FP2, C4, P2, O2, F2) and lateral-right (front-to-back: AF8, FT8, T8, TP8, P8). Anterior-posterior positions were: anterior (left to right: AF7, FP1, FPz, FP2, AF8), medial-anterior (left to right: FT7, F1, Fz, F2, FT8); medial (left to right: T7, C3, Cz, C4, T8), posterior-medial (TP7, P1, Pz, P2, TP8), posterior (left to right: P7, O1, Oz, O2, P8).

For data analysis, we performed a repeated measures ANOVA of the mean voltages in the selected electrode sites, with within-subject factors MEDIAL-LATERAL position (with five levels going from LATERAL LEFT to LATERAL-RIGHT), ANTERIOR-POSTERIOR position (with five levels going from ANTERIOR to POSTERIOR), CASE (with levels NOM-ACC and NOM-DAT) and ANIMACY (with levels INANIMATE and ANIMATE). Based on our initial hypothesis, we compared the effects of object animacy on two different verb classes, beginning at the presentation of the verb. Statistical analyses were performed in a hierarchical fashion, i.e. only statistically significant interactions were pursued, if they included at least one of the factors ANIMACY and CASE. Based on our hypotheses, we pursued interactions by separating the data by CASE and investigating ANIMACY and its interactions separately for each subset. A Huynh-Feldt correction was performed when the degree of freedom in the numerator was higher than 1. We report original degrees of freedom and corrected probability levels. Analyses were performed in R (R Development Core Team 2005) using the ezANOVA function (ez package,

Lawrence 2011). Data were prepared for analysis using functions from the packages reshape (Wickham 2007) and plyr (Wickham 2011).

3.2 Results

Mean answer accuracy was 83 % (SD = 7 %). ERP results are reported for the time window from 400–600 ms after the onset of the critical verb. We only report results containing main effects or interactions of ANIMACY or CASE. Mapping views for this time window and curves for selected electrodes are given in Figure 2.

In the selected time window, waveforms for central electrodes were more negative-going for the animate-accusative than for the inanimate-accusative condition. In contrast, waveforms for the two dative conditions did not differ from each other, and ran close to the waveforms for the inanimate-accusative condition. Results are illustrated in Figure 1.

The statistical analysis revealed an interaction of ANIMACY, CASE and MEDIAL-LATERAL position ($F(4,80) = 3.3$, $\varepsilon = .66$, $p < .05$). To assess whether animacy effects were similar or different for accusative and dative conditions, we resolved the three-way interaction by calculating separate two-way ANOVAs with the factors ANIMACY and MEDIAL-LATERAL position for the two cases.

For the accusative conditions, there was an interaction of ANIMACY and MEDIAL-LATERAL position ($F(4,80) = 4.2$, $\varepsilon = .62$, $p > .05$). The simple main effect of animacy was statistically significant for MEDIAL-LATERAL positions lateral-medial-left ($t(20) = -2.5$, $p < .05$), midline ($t(20) = -2.7$, $p < .05$), and lateral-right ($t(20) = 2.3$, $p < .05$). For dative conditions, there were no main effects and no interactions of ANIMACY.

The original four-way ANOVA showed an interaction of ANIMACY and CASE. As illustrated in the difference maps of Figure 1, this was most clearly visible at central electrodes.

We will discuss the results of this experiment in the Discussion section, together with the results of Experiment 2.

4 Experiment 2: Particle verbs

In the first experiment, we found an interaction of ANIMACY and CASE, with an enhanced N400 for animate-accusative relative to inanimate-accusative conditions. For dative conditions, we did not find this effect of object animacy. Following our

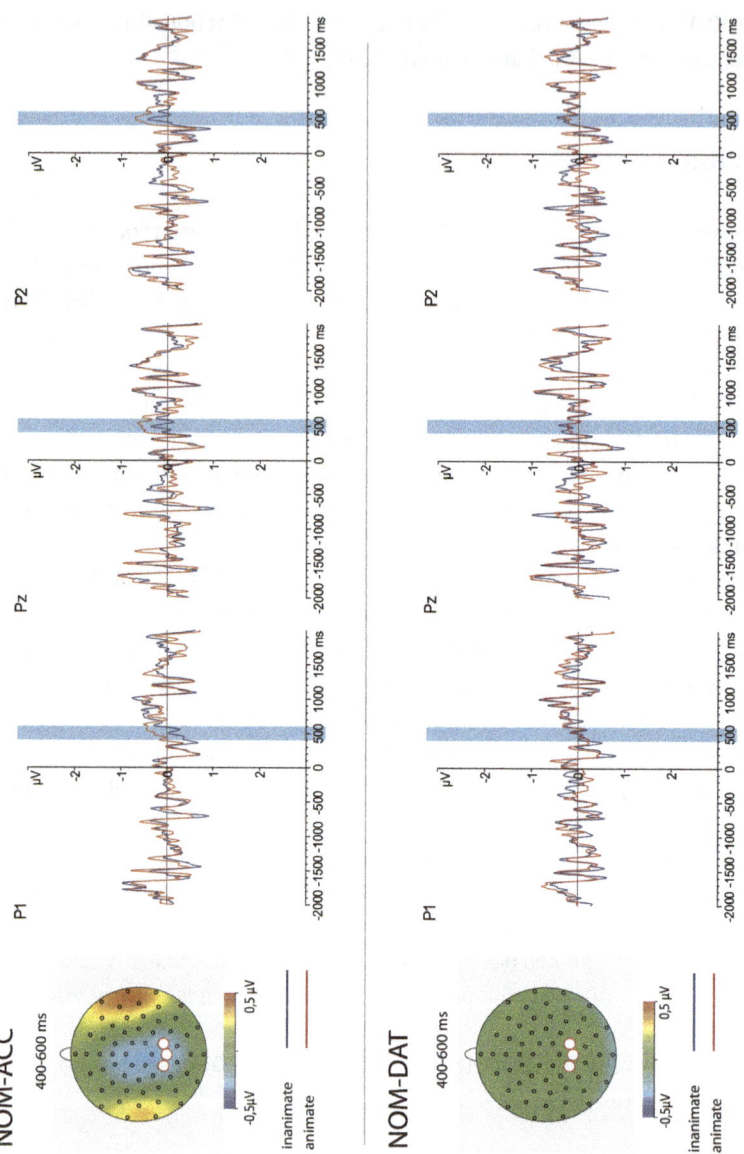

Figure 1: Experiment 1, simple verbs. Grand average ERPs for selected electrode sites and difference maps. Accusative conditions are depicted in the upper part, dative conditions are depicted in the lower part. Mean voltage difference maps (animate minus inanimate) for the marked time window from 400–600 ms are given on the left side. The electrodes selected for illustration are marked in the maps.

guiding hypothesis, this interaction of ANIMACY and CASE could reflect the special syntax, or else the noncanonical argument semantics of simple NOM-DAT verbs.

In the second experiment, we measured the interaction of ANIMACY and CASE for NOM-ACC and NOM-DAT verbs that were separable particle verbs. Following our initial hypotheses, we predict the following possible outcomes:
- If the interaction of ANIMACY and CASE visible in Experiment 1 reflects semantic differences between simple NOM-ACC and NOM-DAT verbs, then we expect an interaction of ANIMACY and CASE in Experiment 2, too. The object animacy effect should be small or absent with NOM-DAT assigning particle verbs.
- If the interaction of ANIMACY and CASE visible in Experiment 1 reflects syntactic differences between simple NOM-ACC and NOM-DAT verbs, then we expect no effects of Case marking and no interaction of ANIMACY and CASE in Experiment 2. Instead, we expect a main effect of ANIMACY for NOM-ACC and NOM-DAT assigning particle verbs.

4.1 Material and methods

4.1.1 Participants

25 participants participated in the Experiment 2. All participants were right-handed, scoring 70 % or higher on the Edinburgh handedness test. All participants spoke German as their only native language and reported no known reading or language-related problems. Participants had normal or corrected to normal vision, were not taking any psychoactive medication and reported no neurological or psychiatric disorders. All participants gave written informed consent. None of the participants had participated in Experiment 1. The data of 4 participants were excluded from the data analysis because of poor data quality. The mean age of the remaining 21 participants (10 male) was 24 years (SD = 3.7). Participants received 16 Euros compensation.

4.1.2 Language material

The stimulus material used in Experiment 2 was the particle verb stimulus set, described in more detail in the Language Material section. Filler sentences were the same as described for Experiment 1.

4.1.3 Procedure

The experimental procedure was the same as described for Experiment 1.

4.1.4 EEG recording

EEG recording was the same as described for Experiment 1.

4.1.5 Data processing, parametrization and statistical analysis

Data processing and analysis were the same as described for Experiment 1. On average 12 % of the data were removed during artifact removal, so that all condition means were calculated from a maximum of 36 and a minimum of 23 segments. The time window chosen for analysis was the same as in Experiment 1, namely, 400–600 ms after the onset of the critical verb. This time window was chosen based on visual inspection, expectations from the literature (see Experiment 1), and to allow a qualitative comparison of the results with those of Experiment 1.

4.2 Results

Mean answer accuracy was 86 % (SD = 8 %).

ERP results are reported for the time window from 400–600 ms after the onset of the critical verb. Mapping views for this time window and curves for selected electrodes are given in Figure 2.

In the selected time window, waveforms at central-anterior sites were more negative-going for the animate than for the inanimate conditions. There were no visible differences between waveforms for accusative and dative conditions during the presentation of the critical verb and the first postverbal word.

In the time window from 400 to 600 ms, there was an interaction of ANIMACY and ANTERIOR-POSTERIOR position ($F(16,320) = 3.6$, $\varepsilon = .50$, $p < .05$) and an interaction of ANIMACY, MEDIAL-LATERAL position and ANTERIOR-POSTERIOR position ($F(16,320) = 2.3$, $\varepsilon = .45$, $p < .05$). No main effects of CASE and no interactions of ANIMACY and CASE were found in this time window, and none were visible during the visual inspections of other time windows. The three-way interaction of ANIMACY, MEDIAL-LATERAL position and ANTERIOR-POSTERIOR position was pursued by pursuing the two-way interaction of ANIMACY with each

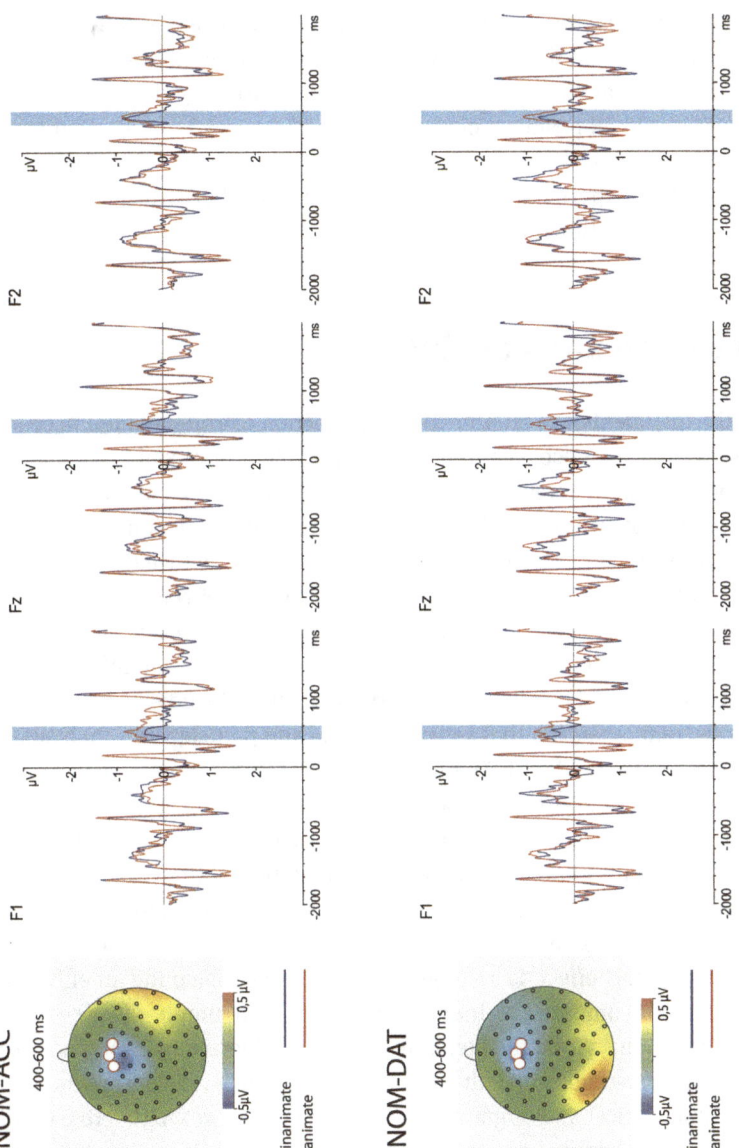

Figure 2: Experiment 2, particle verbs. Grand average ERPs for selected electrode sites and difference maps. Accusative conditions are depicted in the upper part, dative conditions are depicted in the lower part. Mean voltage difference maps (animate minus inanimate) for the marked time window from 400–600 ms are given on the left side. The electrodes selected for illustration are marked in the maps.

of the topographical factors separately. There was a statistically significant interaction of ANIMACY and ANTERIOR-POSTERIOR position ($F(4,80) = 3.6$, $\varepsilon = .50$, $p < .05$). The simple main effect of ANIMACY was statistically significant for the ANTERIOR-POSTERIOR positions medial-anterior ($t(20) = -3.5$, $p < .01$) and posterior ($t(20) = 2.1$, $p < .05$).

The results of Experiment 2 will be discussed together with the results of Experiment 1 in the following section.

5 Discussion and conclusion

In two EEG experiments, we monitored the interaction of argument animacy and object case during sentence comprehension. This interaction could be driven by semantic or syntactic differences between NOM-ACC and NOM-DAT verbs. To distinguish between these two possibilities, we monitored the interaction of object animacy and case marking in the processing of sentences with either simple or particle verbs assigning NOM-ACC or NOM-DAT. While dative effects in simple verbs could reflect syntactic, lexical or semantic differences from accusative verbs, dative effects in particle verbs should only reflect semantic or lexical differences. To our knowledge, the studies reported here are the first EEG studies on case marking effects in comprehension that separate simple and particle verbs. In a similar vein, Experiment 2 is the first EEG study on the processing of particle verbs that distinguishes between NOM-ACC and NOM-DAT assigning particle verbs.

For simple verbs, we found an interaction of object animacy and case marking on the verb. For 400–600 ms after the presentation of the verb, waveforms for the animate-accusative condition were more negative-going than waveforms for the inanimate-accusative condition. This effect was visible at central electrodes. We interpret this effect as an object animacy effect, meaning an enhanced N400 for animate compared to inanimate objects with simple NOM-ACC verbs. This fits earlier findings from the literature (Frisch & Schlesewsky 2001; Paczynski & Kuperberg 2011), reporting an enhanced N400 for animate-animate argument sequences in grammatical and ungrammatical sentences. For NOM-DAT verbs, we did not find a difference between animate and inanimate objects. Waveforms ran close to the inanimate-accusative conditions. We interpret this as an indication that the object animacy effect is attenuated for simple NOM-DAT verbs. This finding is in line with our initial assumption that the effect of object animacy is different for simple NOM-ACC and NOM-DAT verbs. As described above, there could be different possible explanations for this finding. Each of these in turn leads to different predictions for case marking effects with particle verbs (marked in bold):

- The attenuated object animacy effect for simple NOM-DAT verbs could reflect the non-prototypically transitive argument semantics of these verbs (Blume 2000; Dowty 1991; Grimm 2010). This would lead to the prediction that **the same attenuation of object animacy effects should be found for NOM-DAT assigning particle verbs relative to NOM-ACC assigning particle verbs,** since both simple and particle NOM-DAT verbs should reliably signal non-prototypically transitive argument semantics (Meinunger 2007).
- The attenuated object animacy effect for simple NOM-DAT verbs could reflect syntactic differences between both verb classes. Following the KP-based account (Bayer et al. 2001; psycholinguistically tested in Hopf et al. 1998, 2003), this would reflect the build-up of a more complex syntactic structure in the case of NOM-DAT verbs, followed by lexical reaccess to the object. While Hopf et al. do not assume that the insertion of the KP projection is associated with high processing costs, it is possible to assume that this processing step interferes with the use of object animacy in the buildup of the sentence representation, in turn attenuating the object animacy effect. One possible mechanism for this could be that the syntactic rearrangements necessary upon encountering a simple NOM-DAT verb elicit a P345, similar to findings for object compared to subject relative clauses in German (Mecklinger et al. 1995; Friederici et al. 1998; Frisch et al. 2004). A positivity that overlaps with the N400 time window might effectively attenuate an N400 elicited by animate-animate argument sequences.[7]

In contrast, upon encountering a particle verb, the parser would always have to deal with a verb that is morphosyntactically more complex than the 'standard' structure, no matter what the particle verb's case marking pattern is. This assumption would lead us to **predict no interaction of object animacy and case, i.e. the same behaviour for NOM-ACC and NOM-DAT particle verbs.**

---

[7] In general, the P345 has been associated with simple syntactic reanalysis processes (Friederici & Mecklinger 1998; Frisch et al. 2004), mainly reassignment of subject and object roles. However, Frisch et al. (2004) suggest that the short latency of the P345 in contrast to the P600 reflects comparatively easy syntactic rearrangement processes without adding new nodes to the tree – which would not match the KP-based account. Also, this explanation for the absent N400 with animate-animate-dative sequences could raise the expectation that datives with inanimate objects should elicit a P345 in contrast to the accusative baseline, since there is no N400 to attenuate the P345. This is not found in our data. In sum, it is possible to assume a more complex interplay of these two components for dative verbs, but further speculation should be based on new data.

For particle verbs, we found a clear main effect of object animacy from 400 to 600 ms after the onset of the critical verb; this effect was visible for both NOM-ACC and NOM-DAT particle verbs. Waveforms for animate conditions were more negative-going than for inanimate conditions. This effect was visible in central electrodes. We interpret this effect as an object animacy effect, meaning an enhanced N400 for animate compared to inanimate objects with particle verbs assigning NOM-ACC and NOM-DAT verbs. This general effect of object animacy is in line with the literature (Frisch & Schlesewsky 2001; Paczynski & Kuperberg 2011), reporting an enhanced N400 for animate-animate argument sequences in grammatical and ungrammatical sentences. They also match the object animacy effect found for simple NOM-ACC verbs in Experiment 1.[8]

Taken together, the object animacy effects found in our two experiments for all verb types but one (simple NOM-DAT verbs) support findings from the literature: Even in grammatical sentences without syntactic or semantic violations, object animacy effects occur. This matches the predictions made by different models of sentence comprehension that assume a central role for argument animacy during representation building (Bornkessel-Schlesewsky & Schlesewsky 2006, 2009, 2013; Kuperberg 2007; see Bornkessel-Schlesewsky & Schlesewsky 2009: 44 for a detailed outline).

With particle verbs, there were no effects of verbal case marking, and no interactions of verbal case marking with object animacy (Experiment 2). This suggests that the difference between NOM-ACC and NOM-DAT particle verbs does not affect the processing of object animacy to any extent that is detectable with our current methods.[9] Following our hypotheses outlined above, this implies that the attenuated object animacy effect found for simple NOM-DAT verbs is unlikely to reflect thematic or semantic differences between simple NOM-DAT and NOM-ACC verbs, since these should essentially be parallel for simple and particle verbs.

---

[8] The object animacy effect reported in Czypionka (2014) and Czypionka et al. (2017) was elicited using stimuli that are very similar to the ones in the current study. The effect in the earlier studies was reported for the same time window, but descriptively looked like a longer-lasting negativity than the one found in the current study. Our current results are more similar to the ones reported in the wider literature. We assume that this descriptive difference (that is, between the older studies on the interaction of animacy and case marking in German and our current one) reflects the fact that in the older studies, the stimuli included a mix of simple and particle verbs, whereas in the current study, simple and particle verbs were separated.

[9] A direct quantitative comparison between the results for simple and particle verbs would not be informative, mainly because there is currently no possibility to assess the frequencies of simple verbs and particle verbs in corpora; and because of the systematic difference in morphological complexity between both verb types. However, our design allows a meaningful qualitative comparison of the parallels and differences found for both experiments.

On the other hand, syntactic processing differences would lead us to expect effects of case marking (here, an attenuated object animacy effect) for simple, but not for particle NOM-DAT verbs. This prediction is motivated by the idea that the contrast between simple NOM-ACC and NOM-DAT verbs is one between the 'standard' structure and a more complex one, which should be reflected in processing workload. However, the contrast between particle verbs assigning NOM-ACC and NOM-DAT is not one between a "standard" structure and a more complex one. Instead, it is a contrast between either two morpho-syntactically complex structures, or there is no systematic contrast between both particle verb types (depending on the syntactic analysis; syntactic proposals for the analysis of particle verbs tend to not offer side-by-side structures for particle verbs assigning NOM-ACC and NOM-DAT, and particle verbs may in general be syntactically heterogenous, see below for further discussions). This prediction matches our findings. It therefore seems likely that the attenuated object animacy effect we find for simple NOM-DAT verbs reflects the processing of syntactic differences between simple NOM-ACC and NOM-DAT verbs, rather than semantic or thematic differences between both simple verb classes. Thus, our findings fit with any account that proposes a more complex syntactic structure for simple NOM-DAT verbs (Bayer et al. 2001; but also McFadden 2004).[10]

A closer look at the result pattern opens some new question about the role of lexical case marking in sentence comprehension. So far, the only syntactic account of NOM-DAT verb processing that has been psycholinguistically tested (the KP-based account proposed by Bayer et al. (2001); see Hopf et al. (1998, 2003) for EEG data) assumes that the increased processing cost for NOM-DAT verbs mainly reflects lexical reaccess to the object position. In these earlier studies, this becomes visible as an enhanced N400 for NOM-DAT relative to NOM-ACC verbs, whereas our own study does not find an enhanced N400 for inanimate-dative relative to inanimate-accusative conditions. This suggests that lexical reaccess to the object may not be the only contributing factor to processing differences between simple NOM-ACC and NOM-DAT verbs. However, it is important to keep in mind that most of the earlier psycholinguistic literature on case marking effects in German used a mix of simple and particle verbs in their stimuli, even though the underlying assumptions for the guiding

---

10 Our current findings are harder to reconcile with accounts proposing that lexical dative is assigned by V^0; however, we wish to refrain from suggesting that our findings provide an explicit argument against such accounts. We believe that our findings may provide groundwork for future experiments investigating the proposals of competing syntactic analyses of simple NOM-DAT verbs; these will be more fruitful now that the influence of argument animacy has been assessed.

hypotheses seem to be based on the syntactic analysis of simple verbs alone (see Hopf et al. 1998, 2003; Bornkessel et al. 2004; Czypionka 2014; Czypionka et al. 2017). Thus, we actually do not know what case-marking effects (apart from the attenuation of object animacy effects) would look like for syntactically homogenous stimulus sets.[11]

The question of lexical reaccess is further complicated by the fact that NOM-DAT particle verbs also assign lexical case. Although the syntactic status of their objects remains unclear, it seems safe to assume this, given that dative, but not accusative, assigned by particle verbs is retained under passivization.[12] If earlier case-marking effects were triggered mainly by lexical reaccess to the object (as proposed by Hopf et al. 1998, 2003), then we could have expected case-marking effects for particle verbs, too (although they could arguably be expected to be weaker than for simple verbs, given that any potential difference in syntactic complexity is unlikely to be systematic). The fact that we did not find any differences between NOM-ACC and NOM-DAT assigning particle verbs suggests that with the stimuli we used, lexical reaccess to the object does not seem to contribute to a measurable extent to our findings.

Future studies are needed to reassess the relative contributions of syntactic and lexical processing differences in the processing of lexical case marking verbs. Our current study shows that these studies will need to carefully control for syntactically homogenous stimulus material, and for potential confounds with the processing of argument semantics.

---

11 The mixing of simple verbs and particle verbs in the stimuli of the older studies may have affected the relative frequencies of accusative- and dative-assigning verbs, and also the syntactic variability of both groups. There are also some additional differences between older studies and our own that make a direct comparison difficult. These older studies used more complex sentences including relative clauses and variations of argument order. Furthermore, the studies by Hopf et al. (1998, 2003) potentially primed for accusative over dative; while the study by Bornkessel et al. (2004) did not compare accusative and dative verbs directly. Taken together, the literature suggests that assuming higher processing cost for dative compared to accusative in difficult sentence structures is reasonable. However, there is no reason to assume that datives should always elicit N400 when compared to accusatives.

12 Only some accounts explicitly mention individual examples of NOM-DAT assigning particle verbs. McIntyre (2007: 359) proposes that the object of *nachlaufen* gets case from the particle *nach*. Zeller (2001c) writes that NOM-ACC assigning particle verbs assign structural case, and that incorporated particles cannot assign case. In footnote 7, he writes "Some prepositions, (like *zu*, 'to', or *nach*, 'after') that assign dative case to their reference objects may transfer this property onto a structurally adjacent verb, such that the particle verb also assigns dative case to its object." (Importantly, these accounts assume that there may be different possible structures for particle verbs.)

The difference between the roles of case marking for simple and particle verbs also needs to be discussed in the context of current models of sentence comprehension. In the eADM (Bornkessel-Schlesewsky 2006, 2009, 2013), NOM-DAT verbs are expected to be processed differently from NOM-ACC verbs, and our findings match this general prediction. However, these processing differences are assumed to reflect the semantic differences of both verb classes; syntactic and lexical differences between both verb classes do not figure in current versions of the model, and neither does the difference between simple and particle verbs. This would lead us to expect an attenuated object animacy effect both for simple and particle verbs assigning NOM-DAT, as NOM-DAT particle verbs also encode non-prototypically transitive situations. Thus, our findings on case marking match the general predictions of the model, but they are difficult to reconcile with its underlying assumptions and its implicit predictions.[13]

In sum, our experiments illustrate that argument animacy is routinely used in sentence comprehension, and has an influence even for structures without grammatical or semantic violations. This influence is reflected in a slightly enhanced N400 component for animate compared to inanimate objects. For particle verbs, this holds for both NOM-ACC and NOM-DAT verbs. For simple verbs, only NOM-ACC verbs show this object animacy effect. Simple NOM-DAT verbs do not show an enhanced N400 for animate objects. This contrast suggests that this particular lexical case marking effect (i.e. the attenuation of the object animacy effect with simple NOM-DAT verbs) reflects syntactic, rather than semantic-thematic or lexical differences between simple NOM-DAT and NOM-ACC verbs. More generally, our findings illustrate that the theoretical distinction between different morphosyntactic classes of verbs assigning NOM-DAT and NOM-ACC is also informative for research in sentence comprehension, and needs to be taken into account during stimulus construction. Future work will need to address the relative contributions of lexical and syntactic processing differences between NOM-ACC and NOM-DAT verbs to lexical case marking effects in sentence comprehension. These studies would also benefit greatly by theoretical accounts offering explicit side-by-side illustrations of syntactic analyses for a wide variety of morphosyntactic verb types.

---

[13] We would like to stress that our findings do not suggest that semantic and thematic differences between NOM-ACC and NOM-DAT verbs do not play any role in sentence comprehension. Our findings merely suggest that some of the effects of lexical case marking are driven by syntactic differences between both verb classes, and that both semantic and syntactic differences should be reflected in models of sentence comprehension.

References

Aissen, Judith. 2003. Differential Object Marking: Iconicity vs. economy. *Natural Language & Linguistic Theory* 21(3). 435–483. https://doi.org/10.1023/A: 1024109008573.
Bader, Markus. 1996. *Sprachverstehen: Syntax und Prosodie beim Lesen*. Opladen: Westdeutscher Verlag.
Bader, Markus & Jana Häussler. 2010. Word order in German: A corpus study. *Lingua* 120(3). 717–762. https://doi.org/10.1016/j.lingua.2009.05.007.
Bader, Markus & Michael Meng. 1999. Subject-object ambiguities in German embedded clauses: An across-the-board comparison. *Journal of Psycholinguistic Research* 28(2). 121–143. https://doi.org/10.1023/A: 1023206208142.
Bader, Markus, Michael Meng & Josef Bayer. 2000. Case and reanalysis. *Journal of Psycholinguistic Research* 29(1). 37–52. https://doi.org/10.1023/A: 1005120422899
Bates, Douglas, Martin Mächler, Ben Bolker & Steve Walker. 2015. Fitting linear mixed-effects models using lme4. *Journal of Statistical Software* 67(1). 1–48. https://doi.org/10.18637/jss.v067.i01.
Bayer, Josef, Markus Bader & Michael Meng. 2001. Morphological underspecification meets oblique case: Syntactic and processing effects in German. *Lingua* 111(4–7). 465–514. https://doi.org/10.1016/S0024-3841(00)00041-3.
Blume, Kerstin. 2000. *Markierte Valenzen im Sprachvergleich*. Tübingen: Niemeyer.
Bock, J. Kathryn. 1987. Coordinating words and syntax in speech plans. In Andrew W. Ellis (ed.), *Progress in the psychology of language*, vol. 3, 337–389. London: Erlbaum.
Bock, Kathryn J. & Helga Loebell. 1990. Framing sentences. *Cognition* 35(1). 1–39. https://doi.org/10.1016/0010-0277(90)90035-I.
Bock, Kathryn J. & Richard K. Warren. 1985. Conceptual accessibility and syntactic structure in sentence formulation. *Cognition* 21. 47–67. https://doi.org/10.1016/0010-0277(85)90023-X.
Bornkessel, Ina, Brian McElree, Matthias Schlesewsky & Angela D. Friederici. 2004. Multidimensional contributions to garden path strength: Dissociating phrase structure from case marking. *Journal of Memory and Language* 51(4). 495–522. https://doi.org/10.1016/j.jml.2004.06.011.
Bornkessel-Schlesewsky, Ina & Matthias Schlesewsky. 2006. The Extended Argument Dependency Model: A neurocognitive approach to sentence comprehension across languages. *Psychological Review* 113(4). 787–821. https://doi.org/10.1037/0033-295X.113.4.787.
Bornkessel-Schlesewsky, Ina & Matthias Schlesewsky. 2009. The role of prominence information in the real-time comprehension of transitive constructions: A cross-linguistic approach. *Language and Linguistics Compass* 3(1). 19–58. https://doi.org/10.1111/j.1749-818X.2008.00099.x.
Bornkessel-Schlesewsky, Ina, Franziska Kretzschmar, Sarah Tune, Luming Wang, Safiye Genç, Markus Philipp, Dietmar Roehm & Matthias Schlesewsky. 2011. Think globally: Cross-linguistic variation in electrophysiological activity during sentence comprehension. *Brain and Language* 117(3). 133–152. DOI: https://doi.org/10.1016/j.bandl.2010.09.010.
Bornkessel-Schlesewsky, Ina & Matthias Schlesewsky. 2013. Reconciling time, space and function: A new dorsal-ventral stream model of sentence comprehension. *Brain and Language* 125(1). 60–76. https://doi.org/10.1016/j.bandl.2013.01.010.

Bossong, Georg. 1985. *Empirische Universalienforschung: Differentielle Objektmarkierung in den neuiranischen Sprachen*. Tübingen: Narr.

Bossong, Georg. 1991. Differential object marking in Romance and beyond. In Douglas A. Kibbee & Dieter Wanner (eds.), *New analyses in Romance linguistics*, 143–170. Amsterdam: Benjamins.

Branigan, Holly P. & Elina Feleki. 1999. Conceptual accessibility and serial order in Greek language production. In *Cognitive Science Society (CSS) 21*. 96–101.

Branigan, Holly P., Martin J. Pickering & Mikihiro Tanaka. 2008. Contributions of animacy to grammatical function assignment and word order during production. *Lingua* 118. 172–189. https://doi.org/10.1016/j.lingua.2007.02.003.

Cappelle, Bert, Yury Shtyrov & Friedemann Pulvermüller. 2010. Heating up or cooling up the brain? MEG evidence that phrasal verbs are lexical units. *Brain and Language* 115(3). 189–201. https://doi.org/10.1016/j.bandl.2010.09.004.

Carminati, Maria Nella. 2005. Processing reexes of the Feature Hierarchy (Person >Number >Gender) and implications for linguistic theory. *Lingua* 115(3). 259–285.

Clifton, Charles Jr., Matthew J. Traxler, Taha Mohamed, Rihana S. Williams, Robin K. Morris & Keith Rayner. 2003. The use of thematic role information in parsing: Syntactic processing autonomy revisited. *Journal of Memory and Language* 49(3). 317–334. https://doi.org/10.1016/S0749-596X(03)00070-6.

Comrie, Bernard. 1989. *Language universals and linguistic typology*. Chicago, IL: University of Chicago Press.

Corbett, Greville G. 2000. *Number*. Cambridge, UK: Cambridge University Press.

Croft, William. 1990. *Typology and universals*. Cambridge, UK: Cambridge University Press.

Czepluch, Hartmut. 1996. *Kasus im Deutschen und Englischen: Ein Beitrag zur Theorie des abstrakten Kasus*. Tübingen: Narr.

Czypionka, Anna. 2014. *The interplay of object animacy and verb class in representation building*. Berlin: Humboldt-Universität zu Berlin dissertation.

Czypionka, Anna, Katharina Spalek, Isabell Wartenburger & Manfred Krifka. 2017. On the interplay of object animacy and verb type during sentence comprehension in German: ERP evidence from the processing of transitive dative and accusative constructions. *Linguistics* 55 (6). 1383–1433. https://doi.org/10.1515/ling-2017-0031.

Czypionka, Anna & Carsten Eulitz. 2018. Lexical case marking affects the processing of animacy in simple verbs, but not particle verbs: Evidence from event-related potentials. *Glossa: a journal of general linguistics* 3(1): 126. 1–33. https://doi.org/10.5334/gjgl.313.

Dahl, Östen. 2008. Animacy and egophoricity: Grammar, ontology and phylogeny. *Lingua* 118. 141–150. https://doi.org/10.1016/j.lingua.2007.02.008.

Dehé, Nicole. 2015. Particle verbs in Germanic. In Peter O. Müller, Ingeborg Ohnheiser, Susan Olsen & Franz Rainer (eds.), *Word-Formation: An International Handbook of the Languages of Europe*, vol. 1, 611–626. Berlin & Boston: Mouton de Gruyter.

Dixon, Robert M. W. 1994. *Ergativity*. Cambridge, UK: Cambridge University Press.

Dowty, David. 1991. Thematic proto-roles and argument selection. *Language* 67(3). 547–619. https://doi.org/10.2307/415037.

Fanselow, Gisbert. 2000. Optimal exceptions. In Barbara Stiebels & Dieter Wunderlich (eds.), *Lexicon in Focus*. 173–209. Berlin: Akademie Verlag.

Ferreira, Fernanda. 1994. Choice of passive voice is affected by verb type and animacy. *Journal of Memory and Language* 33(6). 715–736. https://doi.org/10.1006/jmla.1994.1034.

Ferreira, Fernanda & Charles J. Clifton. 1986. The independence of syntactic processing. *Journal of Memory and Language* 25(3). 348–368. https://doi.org/10.1016/0749-596X(86)90006-9.

Frazier, Lyn & Giovanni B. Flores d'Arcais. 1989. Filler driven parsing: A study of gap filling in Dutch. *Journal of Memory and Language* 28(3). 331–344. https://doi.org/10.1016/0749-596X(89)90037-5.

Frazier, Lyn & Keith Rayner. 1982. Making and correcting errors during sentence comprehension: Eye movements in the analysis of structurally ambiguous sentences. *Cognitive Psychology* 14(2). 178–210. https://doi.org/10.1016/0010-0285(82)90008-1.

Friederici, Angela D., Karsten Steinhauer, Axel Mecklinger & Martin Meyer. 1998. Working memory constraints on syntactic ambiguity resolution as revealed by electrical brain responses. *Biological Psychology* 47(3). 193–221.

Frisch, Stefan & Matthias Schlesewsky. 2001. The N400 reflects problems of thematic hierarchizing. *NeuroReport* 12(15). 3391–3394. https://doi.org/10.1097/00001756-200110290-00048.

Frisch, Stefan, Peter Beim Graben & Matthias Schlesewsky. 2004. Parallelizing grammatical functions: P600 and P345 reflect different cost of reanalysis. *International Journal of Bifurcation and Chaos* 14(2). 531–549.

Grimm, Scott. 2010. Semantics of case. *Morphology* 21(3–4). 515–544. https://doi.org/10.1007/s11525-010-9176-z.

Haider, Hubert. 1993. *Deutsche Syntax – generativ: Vorstudien zur Theorie einer projektiven Grammatik*. Tübingen: Narr.

Haider, Hubert. 2010. *The Syntax of German*. Cambridge, UK: Cambridge University Press.

Haspelmath, Martin. 2013. Occurrence of nominal plurality. In Matthew Dryer & Martin Haspelmath (eds.), *The World Atlas of Language Structures Online*. Leipzig: Max Planck Institute for Evolutionary Anthropology.

Heister, Julian, Kay-Michael Würzner, Johannes Bubenzer, Edmund Pohl, Thomas Hanneforth & Alexander Geyken. 2011. dlexDB | eine lexikalische Datenbank für die psychologische und linguistische Forschung. *Psychologische Rundschau* 32(4). 10–20. https://doi.org/10.1026/0033-3042/a000029.

Hemforth, Barbara, Lars Konieczny & Gerhard Strube. 1993. Incremental syntax processing and parsing strategies. *Cognitive Science Society (CSS)* 15, 539–545.

Hopf, Jens-Max, Markus Bader, Michael Meng & Josef Bayer. 2003. Is human sentence parsing serial or parallel? Evidence from event-related brain potentials. *Cognitive Brain Research* 15(2). 165–177. https://doi.org/10.1016/s0926-6410(02)00149-0.

Hopf, Jens-Max, Josef Bayer, Markus Bader & Michael Meng. 1998. Event-related brain potentials and case information in syntactic ambiguities. *Journal of Cognitive Neuroscience* 10(2). 264–280. https://doi.org/10.1162/089892998562690.

Hung, Yu-Chen & Petra B. Schumacher. 2012. Topicality matters: Position specific demands on Chinese discourse processing. *Neuroscience Letters* 511(2). 59–64.

Isel, Frédéric, Kai Alter & Angela D. Friederici. 2005. Influence of prosodic information on the processing of split particles: ERP evidence from spoken German. *Journal of Cognitive Neuroscience* 17(1). 154–167. https://doi.org/10.1162/0898929052880075.

Jackendoff, Ray. 2002. English particle constructions, the lexicon, and the autonomy of syntax. In Nicole Dehé, Ray Jackendoff, Andrew McIntyre and Silke Urban (eds.), *Verb-particle explorations*. 67–94. Berlin & New York: De Gruyter.

Jäger, Gerhard. 2004. Learning constraint sub-hierarchies: The bidirectional gradual learning algorithm. In Reinhard Blutner & Henk Zeevat (eds.), *Optimality Theory and Pragmatics*, 442–501. Basingstoke: Palgrave McMillan.

Kuperberg, Gina R. 2007. Neural mechanisms of language comprehension: Challenges to syntax. *Brain Research* 1146. 23–49. 10.1016/j.brainres.2006.12.063.

Kuperberg, Gina R., Donna. A. Kreher, Tatiana Sitnikova, David N. Caplan & Phillip J. Holcomb. 2007. The role of animacy and thematic relationships in processing active English sentences: Evidence from event-related potentials. *Brain and Language* 100. 223–237. https://doi.org/ 10.1016/j.bandl.2005.12.006.

Lawrence, Michael A. 2011. ez: Easy analysis and visualization of factorial experiments. http://CRAN.R-project.org/package=ez. R package version 3.0-0. (2021-04-13).

Lüdeling, Anke, and Nivja H. de Jong. 2002. German particle verbs and word-formation. In Nicole Dehé, Ray Jackendoff, Andrew McIntyre and Silke Urban (eds.), *Verb-particle explorations*. 315–333. Berlin & New York: De Gruyter.

MacDonald, Maryellen C., Neal J. Pearlmutter & Mark S. Seidenberg. 1994. The lexical nature of syntactic ambiguity resolution. *Psychological Review* 101(4). https://doi.org/10.1037/0033-295X.101.4.676.

Maess, Burkhard, Erich Schröger & Andreas Widmann. 2016. High-pass filters and baseline correction in M/EEG analysis. Commentary on: "How inappropriate high-pass filters can produce artefacts and incorrect conclusions in ERP studies of language and cognition". *Journal of Neuroscience Methods* 266. 164–165. DOI: https://doi.org/10.1016/j.jneumeth.2015.12.003

Malchukov, Andrej L. 2008. Animacy and asymmetries in differential case marking. *Lingua* 118(2). https://doi.org/10.1016/j.lingua.2007.02.005.

McDonald, Janet L., Kathryn Bock & Michael H. Kelly. 1993. Word and world order: Semantic, phonological, and metrical determinants of serial position. *Cognitive Psychology* 25(2). 188–230. https://doi.org/10.1006/cogp.1993.1005.

McFadden, Thomas. 2004. *The position of morphological case in the derivation: A study on the syntax-morphology interface*. Philadelphia, PA: University of Pennsylvania dissertation.

McIntyre, Andrew. 2007. Particle verbs and argument structure. *Language and Linguistics Compass* 1(4). 350–367. https://doi.org/10.1111/j.1749-818X.2007.00013.x.

McIntyre, Andrew. 2015. Particle verb formation. In Peter O. Müller, Ingeborg Ohnheiser, Susan Olsen & Franz Rainer (eds.), *Word-Formation: An International Handbook of the Languages of Europe*, vol. 1, 435–449. Berlin & Boston: Mouton de Gruyter.

Mecklinger, Axel, Herbert Schriefers, Karsten Steinhauer & Angela D. Friederici. 1995. Processing relative clauses varying on syntactic and semantic dimensions: An analysis with event-related potentials. *Memory & Cognition* 23 (4). 477–494.

Meinunger, André. 2007. Der Dativ im Deutschen – Eine Verständnishilfe für das Phänomen der gespaltenen Ergativität. *Linguistische Berichte* 209. 3–33.

Næss, Åshild. 2004. What markedness marks: The markedness problem with direct objects. *Lingua* 114(9–10). 1186–1212. https://doi.org/10.1016/j.lingua.2003.07.005.

Neeleman, Adriaan Dirk & Fred Weerman. 1993. The balance between syntax and morphology: Dutch particles and resultatives. *Natural Language & Linguistic Theory* 11(3). 433–475. https://doi.org/10.1007/BF00993166.

Neeleman, Adriaan Dirk. 1994. *Complex predicates*. Utrecht: Universiteit Utrecht dissertation.

Oldfield, Richard C. 1971. The assessment and analysis of handedness: The Edinburgh Inventory. *Neuropsychologia* 9(1). 97–113. https://doi.org/10.1016/0028-3932(71)90067-4.

Olsen, Susan. 1996. Partikelverben im deutsch-englischen Vergleich [Particle verbs in a comparison of German and English]. In Ewald Lang & Gisela Zifonun (eds.), *Deutsch – typologisch*. 261–288. Berlin & New York: De Gruyter.

Paczynski, Martin & Gina R. Kuperberg. 2009. Impact of grammatical voice and animacy on verb processing. In *Annual Meeting of the Psychonomic Society*. Boston, MA.

Paczynski, Martin & Gina R. Kuperberg. 2011. Electrophysiological evidence for use of the animacy hierarchy, but not thematic role assignment, during verb argument processing. *Language and Cognitive Processes* 26(9). 1402–1456. https://doi.org/ 10.1080/ 01690965.2011.580143.

Pearlmutter, Neal J., Susan M. Garnsey & Kathryn Bock. 1999. Agreement processes in sentence comprehension. *Journal of Memory and Language* 41(3). 427–456. https://doi.org/10.1006/jmla.1999.2653.

Piai, Vitória, Lars Meyer, Robert Schreuder & Marcel C. M. Bastiaansen. 2013. Sit down and read on: Working memory and long-term memory in particle verb processing. *Brain and Language* 127(2). 296–306. https://doi.org/10.1016/j.bandl.2013.09.015.

Prat-Sala, Mercé & Holly P. Branigan. 2000. Discourse constraints on syntactic processing in language production: A cross-linguistic study in English and Spanish. *Journal of Memory and Language* 42(2). 168–182. https://doi.org/10.1006/jmla.1999.2668.

R Development Core Team. 2005. R: A Language and Environment for Statistical Computing. R Foundation for Statistical Computing Vienna, Austria. http://www.R-project.org. ISBN 3-900051-07-0. (2021-04-13).

Roehm, Dietmar & Hubert Haider. 2009. Small is beautiful: The processing of the left periphery in German. *Lingua* 119(10). 1501–1522. https://doi.org/10.1016/j.lingua.2008.04.007.

Schlesewsky, Matthias, Gisbert Fanselow, Reinhold Kliegl & Josef Krems. 2000. The subject-preference in the processing of locally ambiguous wh-questions in German. In Barbara Hemforth & Lars Konieczny (eds.), *German Sentence Processing*, 65–93. Dordrecht: Kluwer.

Schriefers, Herbert, Angela D. Friederici & Katja Kühn. 1995. The processing of locally ambiguous relative clauses in German. *Journal of Memory and Language* 34(4). 499–520.

Silverstein, Michael. 1976. Hierarchy of features and ergativity. In Richard M. W. Dixon (ed.), *Grammatical categories in Australian languages*, 112–171. Canberra: Australian Institute of Aboriginal Studies.

Stiebels, Barbara & Dieter Wunderlich. 1994. Morphology feeds syntax: The case of particle verbs. *Linguistics* 32(6). 913–968. https://doi.org/10.1515/ling.1994.32.6.913.

Svenonius, Peter. 2010. Spatial P in English. In Guglielmo Cinque & Luigi Rizzi (eds.), *Mapping spatial PPs: The cartography of syntactic structures*, vol. 6, 127–160. New York: Oxford University Press.

Tanner, Darren, James J. S. Norton, Kara Morgan-Short & Steven J. Luck. 2016. On high-pass filter artifacts (they're real) and baseline correction (it's a good idea) in ERP/ERMF analysis. *Journal of Neuroscience Methods* 266. 166–170.

Tremblay, Antoine & Johannes Ransijn. 2015. Lmerconveniencefunctions: Model selection and post-hoc analysis for (g)lmer models. https://CRAN.R-project.org/package=LMERConvenienceFunctions. R package version 2.10.

Trueswell, John C., Michael K. Tanenhaus & Susan M. Garnsey. 1994. Semantic influences on parsing: Use of thematic role information in syntactic ambiguity resolution. *Journal of Memory and Language* 33(3). 285–318. https://doi.org/10.1006/jmla.1994.1014

Urban, Silke. 2001. *Verbinformationen im Satzverstehen*. Leipzig: MPI of Cognitive Neuroscience dissertation.

Urban, Silke. 2002. Parsing verb particle constructions: An approach based on event-related potentials. In Nicole Dehé, Ray Jackendoff, Andrew McIntyre & Silke Urban (eds.), *Verb-particle explorations*. 335–353. Berlin & New York: De Gruyter.

van Nice, Kathy Y. & Rainer Dietrich. 2003. Task sensitivity of animacy effects: Evidence from German picture descriptions. *Linguistics* 41(5). 825–849. https://doi.org/10.1515/ling.2003.027.

Verhoeven, Elisabeth. 2009. Experiencer object and object clitics in Modern Greek: Evidence from a corpus study. In Mary Baltazani, George K. Giannakis, Tasos Tsangalidis, George J. Xydopoulos (eds.), *8th International Conference on Greek Linguistics (ICGL)*, vol. 30, 574–588. Ioannina: University of Ioannina.

Verhoeven, Elisabeth. 2014. Thematic prominence and animacy asymmetries: Evidence from a cross-linguistic production study. *Lingua* 143. 129–161. https://doi.org/10.1016/j.lingua.2014.02.002.

Weckerly, Jill & Marta Kutas. 1999. An electrophysiological analysis of animacy effects in the processing of object relative sentences. *Psychophysiology* 36(5). 559–70. https://doi.org/10.1111/1469-8986.3650559.

Wickham, Hadley. 2007. Reshaping data with the reshape package. *Journal of Statistical Software* 21(12). http://www.jstatsoft.org/v21/i12/paper.

Wickham, Hadley. 2011. The split-apply-combine strategy for data analysis. *Journal of Statistical Software* 40(1). https://doi.org/10.18637/jss.v040.i01.

Woolford, Ellen. 2006. Lexical Case, Inherent Case, and Argument Structure. *Linguistic Inquiry* 37(1). 111–130. https://www.jstor.org/stable/4179352.

Zeller, Jochen. 2001a. How syntax restricts the lexicon: Particle verbs and internal arguments. *Linguistische Berichte* 188. 459–492.

Zeller, Jochen. 2001b. *Particle verbs and local domains*. Amsterdam: Benjamins.

Zeller, Jochen. 2001c. Lexical particles, semi-lexical postpositions. In Norbert Corver & Henk van Riemsdijk (eds.), *Semi-lexical categories: The function of content words and the content of function words*, vol. 59, Berlin & New York: De Gruyter.

Helen de Hoop, Peter de Swart
Unexpected (in)animate argument marking

Abstract: The present chapter discusses the phenomena of object-fronting and passivization in relation to animacy. Both phenomena can be the outcome of a competition between a general subject-first preference and a topic-first preference in language. We explore how different patterns of unexpected (in)animate marking in object-initial and passive sentences might be expressed in a formal bidirectional OT account of grammar. Patterns in Dutch, Kinyarwanda, and Biak can be explained using the same model, which integrates the speaker's taking into account the hearer's perspective in production and the hearer's taking into account the speaker's perspective in interpretation. We show that both the speaker's choice between competing forms and the hearer's choice between competing interpretations constrain the use of object-fronting and passivization in language.

Keywords: Object-fronting, passivization, animacy, bidirectional OT, Dutch, Kinyarwanda, Biak

1 Introduction

Languages use case, word order, and agreement to overtly encode the arguments of a predicate. Animacy is a crucial feature of arguments that provides information about their potential roles in the event described by the predicate. For instance, it has been noticed that there is a tight relation between animacy and the semantic role of Agent (Primus 2012). Some languages even exclude the possibility of inanimate Agents (cf. Fauconnier 2011). Also, Experiencers are by definition animate, since only sentient arguments can undergo "an event of emotion, cognition, volition, perception, or bodily sensation" (Verhoeven 2014: 130). Animacy is

---

Acknowledgements: We are most grateful to two anonymous reviewers, the editors, and our colleagues Cas Coopmans, Maria van de Groep, Joske Piepers, Saskia van Putten, Theresa Redl, Gert-Jan Schoenmakers, Lila San Roque, and Thijs Trompenaars for their constructive comments on an earlier version of this paper.

Helen de Hoop, Centre for Language Studies, Radboud University Nijmegen, P.O. Box 9103, 6500 HD Nijmegen, The Netherlands, e-mail: helen.dehoop@ru.nl
Peter de Swart, Centre for Language Studies, Radboud University Nijmegen, P.O. Box 9103, 6500 HD Nijmegen, The Netherlands, e-mail: peter.deswart@ru.nl

https://doi.org/10.1515/9783110757255-005

often thought of as an inherent property of arguments, whereas other prominence features such as specificity are not (cf. de Swart & de Hoop 2007, 2018). With animate referents being conceptually more prominent than inanimate ones, subjects being more prominent than objects, and Agents being more prominent than Patients, the question arises how speakers choose to encode messages in which the Patient rather than the Agent is the topic or high-prominent argument of the sentence (cf. Aissen 1999). Note that the topic can loosely be characterized as "the entity that is talked about", but their properties have been shown to vary. For example, topics are often subjects but not always, they usually occur sentence-initially but not necessarily, and they are generally definite, but they can be indefinite too (van Bergen & de Hoop 2009). Also, while they are often animate, they can also be inanimate.

This chapter discusses two syntactic structures, as well as the relation between them, in which the Patient is high-prominent, i.e. the topic, namely object-fronting and passivization. Object-fronting involves a change in word order, whereas passives are generally characterized by a grammatical demotion of the Agent with a concomitant promotion of the Patient. We examine the role of animacy in the realization of these structures.

The interplay between the possible structures in a language and prominence features of arguments is couched in the general framework of Optimality Theory, in which grammar is viewed as a set of violable and potentially conflicting constraints that interact with each other (Smolensky & Legendre 2006). Because there is no fixed meaning associated with any particular type of structure, we assume that the relation between structure and interpretation cannot be modelled as a one-to-one mapping from form to meaning or vice versa. In other words, it does not suffice to optimize from structure to (obtained) interpretation or from (intended) interpretation to structure only. Therefore, we study the interplay between structure and interpretation from a bidirectional perspective, taking into account both the constraints imposed by the speaker on the optimal structure and those by the hearer on the optimal interpretation, resulting in optimal *pairs* of form and meaning (Blutner et al. 2006).

We will argue that taking into account both the hearer's and speaker's perspectives in a bidirectional Optimality-Theoretic analysis can explain patterns of object-fronting and passivization in relation to animacy features of arguments across languages.

2 The hearer's perspective on object-fronting: Competing interpretations

A cross-linguistic generalization is that most transitive sentences have a human subject and an inanimate object (cf. Comrie 1989). Corpus studies in Swedish, Norwegian and Dutch have shown that in transitive sentences objects hardly ever outrank subjects in the animacy hierarchy, where humans outrank animate entities which in turn outrank inanimate ones (cf. Dahl and Fraurud 1996; Øvrelid 2004; Bouma 2008).

Another well-attested phenomenon across the languages of the world is the preference for subject-initial sentences. In more than 75 % of the languages the basic word order is subject-initial (Dryer 2013). Since object-fronting can be a type of topicalization (although not necessarily, because it can also be focus-preposing), we may expect object-fronting to occur when the object is the topic of the sentence. Since animate arguments are better topics than inanimate ones (Givón 1984; Brunetti 2009), we may expect object-fronting to happen more often when the object is animate (see also Bouma 2008; van Bergen 2011; Lamers & de Hoop 2014).

However, from the hearer's point of view, it is important to identify the subject and object of a transitive sentence (de Swart 2007). If the speaker simply fronts an animate object without taking into account the hearer's perspective, the hearer may arrive at the (non-intended) subject-initial interpretation. In fact, even inanimate sentence-initial arguments tend to be interpreted as the subject (Bickel et al. 2015). From the hearer's perspective, the subject and the object in a transitive clause should be distinguishable. Since usually the object of a transitive clause is not higher in animacy than the subject, hearers are likely to interpret a fronted (or first) argument as the subject, especially when it is animate. In other words, from the hearer's perspective, object-fronting should only be allowed when the fronted argument can be identified as the object of a transitive verb, which is more likely the case if it is inanimate.

Notoriously, sometimes the animacy of a subject is not just preferred, but actually required by the verb. This holds for example for the transitive verb *bijten* 'bite' in Dutch:

(1) De gorilla heeft de vrouw gebeten.
    the gorilla has the woman bitten
    'The gorilla bit the woman.'

The verb *bijten* 'bite' requires an animate subject. In (1) the two arguments are both animate, so each could function as the subject of the verb *bijten* 'bite'. Here, animacy cannot help us in determining what is the subject and what is the object. Since the object of a transitive clause can be fronted in Dutch, (1) would in principle be ambiguous between a subject-initial and an object-initial reading. However, unless a context is provided that would suggest otherwise, sentence (1) is not ambiguous. It is interpreted as subject-initial by default. Only an enriched context would allow for an object-initial interpretation of (1). The phenomenon that in the absence of other clues (such as case, agreement, or context/intonation), it is the word order preference which straightforwardly determines the interpretation of an ambiguous sentence, is called *word order freezing* (Lee 2003; Zeevat 2006; de Hoop & Lamers 2006; Bouma 2008). The following Finnish sentence (Seppo Kittilä, p.c.) illustrates word order freezing:

(2) Poja-t   näk-i-vät   tytö-t.
     boy-PL.NOM/ACC   see-PAST-3PL   girl-PL.NOM/ACC
     'The boys saw the girls.' **Not:** 'The girls saw the boys.'

In (2) case morphology does not distinguish between nominative and accusative, since the case-suffixes are the same for the plural nominative and accusative arguments in Finnish. Clearly, the agreement suffix cannot unambiguously determine the subject either: both arguments are plural and there is plural inflection on the verb, hence both could be the subject. Therefore, word order, which is otherwise relatively free in Finnish, determines that the sentence-initial argument is the subject. In spite of the morphological ambiguity with respect to case and agreement, the sentence cannot be interpreted as an object-initial sentence without additional context.

In Dutch, object-fronting is rare, and occurs only if the speaker believes there can be no misunderstanding on the hearer's side as to what is the subject and what is the object (Bouma 2008). If we replace the first constituent in (1) by a pronoun in its object (accusative) form, we get an instance of object-fronting, since the case of the pronoun ultimately determines its grammatical function in the sentence:

(3) Haar heeft de   gorilla gebeten.
     her   has   the gorilla bitten
     'The gorilla bit her.'

There could be a good reason to topicalize the pronominal Patient in (3), since the woman referred to is the victim in a newsworthy biting event. However, even though case marking excludes the possibility of misunderstanding in (3), Bouma's (2008) investigation of object-initial sentences in the Spoken Dutch Corpus shows that personal pronominal objects as in (3) hardly occur in sentence-initial position. Note that a passive sentence would be an alternative and perhaps better option to promote the Patient in this case (see section 5).

De Hoop & Lamers (2006) propose five violable and potentially conflicting constraints that help the hearer to determine what is the subject and what the object in a transitive clause. The constraints and their ranking (for Dutch and German) are given below (de Hoop & Lamers 2006):

DISTINGUISHABILITY constraints:
a. CASE: the subject is in the nominative case, the object is in the accusative case
b. AGREEMENT: the verb agrees with the subject
c. SELECTION: fit the selectional restrictions of the verb (animacy)
d. PRECEDENCE: the subject (linearly) precedes the object
e. PROMINENCE: the subject outranks the object in prominence (animacy)

Proposed Dutch/German ranking of the DISTINGUISHABILITY constraints:
{CASE, AGREEMENT} >> SELECTION >> PRECEDENCE >> PROMINENCE

Different sources of information can thus be viewed as violable and potentially conflicting constraints that play a role in the optimization process of interpretation. In order to see how these constraints work, we provide an OT-semantic tableau for the Dutch sentences (3) and (1), respectively. We only distinguish between the two relevant candidate *interpretations*, SO (subject before object) and OS (object before subject), respectively. Consider first the optimization process of the interpretation of sentence (3), repeated in the upper left cell of Tableau 1, which gives the input for the optimization.

Tableau 1: Deriving the optimal interpretation of sentence (3).

Haar heeft de gorilla gebeten her has the gorilla bitten	CASE	AGR	SEL	PREC	PROM
SO			*		*
☞ OS				*	*

Both candidate readings (SO and OS) satisfy the constraints AGREEMENT and SELECTION, and both violate the constraint PROMINENCE. These three constraints can therefore not determine which reading comes out as optimal. The constraints CASE and PRECEDENCE do distinguish between the two readings, but in opposite directions. Since CASE outranks PRECEDENCE, the OS reading, which violates PRECEDENCE but satisfies CASE, wins the competition. That is, the second candidate interpretation is the optimal (and therefore only) interpretation. For sentence (1) we obtain a different result, as illustrated in Tableau 2.

Tableau 2: Deriving the optimal interpretation of sentence (1).

De gorilla heeft de vrouw gebeten the gorilla has the woman bitten	CASE	AGR	SEL	PREC	PROM
☞ SO					*
OS				*	*

In Tableau 2, the constraint CASE does no longer distinguish the two interpretations and only PRECEDENCE makes a difference. As pointed out above, this is called *word order freezing*: in the absence of any other clues (activated constraints), only word order (PRECEDENCE) distinguishes the subject from the object. Hence, the subject-initial reading comes out as the winning interpretation. A similar analysis would hold for the Finnish example (2) above.

De Swart (2007) proposes that a speaker takes into account the hearer's perspective when calculating the optimal form. More specifically, object-fronting is only possible if the grammatical functions remain recoverable. But even if the grammatical functions are recoverable, object-fronting is not always allowed. In her discussion of object-fronting (also called *subject object reversal*) in Bantu languages, Morimoto (2008) notes that in Kinyarwanda, object-fronting is permitted if the subject outranks the object in animacy, as shown in (4) and (5) below, but not if it is the other way around (examples (8) and (9), to be discussed below).

(4) Umuhuûngu a-ra-som-a igitabo.
 1.boy 1-PRES-read-ASP 7.book
 'The boy is reading the book.'

(5) Igitabo ki-som-a umuhuûngu.
 7.book 7-read-ASP 1.boy
 'The boy is reading the book.' **Not:** 'The book is reading the boy.'

In (4) the verb agrees with the subject, whereas in (5) it agrees with the fronted object, i.e. the topic (Morimoto 2008: 201). In other words, agreement cannot distinguish between the subject and the object in Kinyarwanda, since the verb agrees with the sentence-initial topic, which can be either the subject or the object. Case cannot help us either in determining the subject and the object in (4)–(5), since Kinyarwanda has no morphological case marking. However, based on SELECTION, the grammatical roles are recoverable since only a boy can read a book and not the other way around. Also, the boy outranks the book in animacy, which is an important prerequisite for object-fronting in Kinyarwanda (Morimoto 2008). If either PROMINENCE or SELECTION overrules the word order constraint PRECEDENCE, this will give rise to the object-initial reading in (5). Morimoto's (2008: 218) descriptive generalization is that marked animacy relations (i.e. when the object outranks the subject in animacy) cannot be expressed in the marked syntactic construction (i.e. object-fronting).

Therefore, while AGREEMENT and CASE do not apply, we will demonstrate that PROMINENCE in Kinyarwanda is the most important constraint (see example (7) below). Unlike in Dutch and German, it is more important than SELECTION. The derivation of the object-initial interpretation is illustrated in Tableau 3:

Tableau 3: Deriving the optimal interpretation of sentence (5).

Igitabo kisoma umuhuûngu book read boy	PROM	SEL	PREC
SO	*	*	
☞ OS			*

When the subject and the object are equal in animacy and the selectional restrictions of the verb cannot distinguish the two either, we get word order freezing, and only the subject-initial reading is available (Morimoto 2008: 217). In this case the constraint PRECEDENCE disambiguates the sentence. Thus, sentence (6) below from Kinyarwanda only allows for a subject-initial reading, which is also predicted on the basis of the three relevant constraints and their ranking (as illustrated in Tableau 4):

(6) Umuhuûngu y-a-som-ye umukoôwa.
    1.boy   1-PAST-kiss-ASP 1.girl
    'The boy kissed the girl.' **Not:** 'The girl kissed the boy.'

Tableau 4: Deriving the optimal interpretation of sentence (6).

Umuhuûngu yasomye umukoôwa boy kissed girl	PROM	SEL	PREC
☞ SO	*		
OS	*		*

Morimoto (2008: 217) notes that in some cases, however, even when there is equal animacy, the object-initial interpretation *is* available, as long as no ambiguity can arise. This can be explained by the given ranking in which SELECTION outranks PRECEDENCE. In (7) the object-initial reading wins the competition, since a knife can cut bread but not the other way around (cf. Rissman & Rawlins 2017 for a recent semantic approach to instrumental subjects). This is illustrated in Tableau 5.

(7) Umugati w-a-kas-e icyuma.
    bread it-PAST-cut-ASP knife
    'The knife cut the bread.' **Not:** 'The bread cut the knife.'

Tableau 5: Deriving the optimal interpretation of sentence (7).

Umugati wakase icyuma bread cut knife	PROM	SEL	PREC
SO	*	*	
☞ OS	*		*

So far, we have seen that in Kinyarwanda, object-fronting is only possible when the grammatical roles are still recoverable via the constraint SELECTION. Strikingly, however, the selectional restrictions of the verb *pierce* are not sufficient to allow for object-fronting, as can be seen in (9). Object-fronting is not allowed in this case, because the object outranks the subject in animacy (Morimoto 2008: 217). Therefore, (9) must be interpreted as a subject-initial sentence, even though this leads to a pragmatically odd interpretation.

(8) Urushiinge ru-ra-joomb-a umwaana.
    needle it-AF-pierce-ASP child
    'The needle will pierce the child.'

(9) Umwaana a-joomb-a urushiinge.
　　 child　　　 he-pierce-ASP　needle
　　 # 'The child will pierce the needle.' **Not:** 'The needle will pierce the child.'

Thus, object-fronting is permitted when the subject outranks the object in animacy, but not when the object outranks the subject in animacy. This is accounted for by the high ranking of PROMINENCE, as illustrated in Tableau 6:

Tableau 6: Deriving the optimal interpretation of sentence (9).

Umwaana ajoomba urushiinge child pierce needle	PROM	SEL	PREC
☞ SO		*	
OS	*		*

As pointed out by Morimoto (2008: 218), only predicates that have an unmarked animacy relation between the subject and the object allow for object-fronting, in which case "DISTINGUISHABILITY is already guaranteed by their relative ranking on the animacy scale. (. . .) Therefore, even though argument linking in Bantu languages suggests that it is more important to identify the prominent (topical) argument than to distinguish between the subject and the object, this is only apparently so, since the preverbal object can only be marked as the topic if it is clear from its relative animacy that it is indeed the grammatical object." In other words, PROMINENCE is ranked higher than SELECTION in Kinyarwanda, which makes the subject-initial interpretation the winning candidate. Although the proposed ranking correctly yields the right optimal interpretations (the ones that hearers indeed arrive at in sentences (4)–(9)), it only takes into account the hearer's perspective, that is to say, the optimization from form to interpretation. However, the question arises why a speaker cannot use object-fronting when *the child* is the object and the topic of the clause, even though selectional restrictions of the verb *pierce* clearly distinguish between the subject and the object. We propose that the answer to this puzzle lies in markedness, which can be analyzed within bidirectional Optimality Theory (Blutner et al. 2006; Smolensky & Legendre 2006; de Swart 2007; Legendre et al. 2016).

3 Adding the speaker's perspective: Competing word orders in Kinyarwanda

Bidirectional Optimality Theory has been suggested as a framework that models how the speaker and the hearer co-ordinate their choices of (related) forms (alternative structures) and (related) interpretations (Blutner et al. 2006; de Swart 2007). As Legendre et al. (2016: 18) note, "[t]he fact that forms and meanings cannot be identical makes the directionality in OT syntax/semantics even more important [than in phonology] and raises the question whether speakers take the hearer's perspective into account in production, and whether hearers take the speaker's perspective into account in comprehension. The answer to this question requires a change in perspective from *unidirectional* to *bidirectional* optimization." To illustrate, Blutner et al. (2006: 27–28) discuss the following two related forms, an active and a passive sentence:

(10) Volkert killed Pim.

(11) Pim was killed (by Volkert).

The two forms describe the same event, but from a different perspective. As Blutner et al. (2006: 27) argue, (10) will be used when Volkert is the most salient discourse entity, whereas (11) will be used in a context where Pim is the most salient one. However, as Blutner et al. (2006: 28) point out, "even if Volkert were the most salient discourse entity in the context, we could use sentence [(11)], with the effect that now Pim becomes the most salient discourse entity." In other words, the choice of a certain form (active or passive) is not just constrained by the given context (either Pim or Volkert being discourse-prominent already), but also by the intention of the speaker, who wants to mark the fact that either Pim or Volkert should be interpreted as discourse-prominent (the topic) by the hearer. Sentence (10) would then be the best form in a context in which Volkert is to be interpreted as the topic, whereas (11) would be the best form in a context in which Pim must be interpreted as the topic.

This is illustrated by means of a simple bidirectional OT tableau with four competing form-meaning pairs that are subject to two relevant constraints, an ECONOMY constraint that penalizes the use of a marked (i.e. passive) structure, and a constraint MARK TOPIC, which requires the speaker to mark topicality, in this case by the use of a passive sentence to mark the Patient as topic.

Tableau 7: Bidirectional optimization of Pim being killed by Volkert.

English, examples (10) and (11)	MARK TOPIC	ECONOMY
☞ 1. Volkert killed Pim, kill' (Volkert, Pim); Volkert is topic		
2. Volkert killed Pim, kill' (Volkert, Pim); Pim is topic	*	
3. Pim was killed (by Volkert), kill' (Volkert, Pim); Volkert is topic	*	*
☞ 4. Pim was killed (by Volkert), kill' (Volkert, Pim); Pim is topic		*

Tableau 7 shows two related forms (an active and a passive structure) that each combine with two related interpretations (one in which the Agent is the topic, and one in which the Patient is the topic). The combinations of two forms and two interpretations constitute four form-meaning pairs. These are the four relevant candidates that enter the competition. Two of these pairs come out as winners. The first winning pair satisfies both constraints, and combines the unmarked structure (active sentence) with the unmarked interpretation (the Agent being the topic). The other winning pair (candidate 4 in Tableau 7) combines a marked structure (a passive sentence), which links ECONOMY, with a marked interpretation (the Patient being the topic). Both these winning pairs are indicated by the sign ☞; they are called *superoptimal* (Blutner et al. 2006). A form-meaning pair is called *superoptimal* if there is no other pair with the same form but a different meaning that is more harmonic, and no other pair with the same meaning but a different form that is more harmonic. Thus, there are two types of superoptimal form-meaning pairs: the ones that link an unmarked form to an unmarked interpretation, and the ones that link a marked form to a marked interpretation (Blutner et al. 2006: 23).

As illustrated below, bidirectional OT can account for the fact that object-fronting in Kinyarwanda is only possible when the hearer will arrive at the correct interpretation, that is, the meaning intended by the speaker. Consider the bidirectional optimization of the two competing forms presented in sentences (4) and (5) above, i.e. *boy reads book* and *book reads boy*. The verb *read* takes two arguments. In principle, unlike in English, word order does not necessarily identify the subject of the sentence.

The constraints that were used in the OT-semantics analyses in section 2 can be maintained. Lestrade et al. (2016) show that unidirectional constraints can be derived from a generalization over bidirectional optimization processes.

The speaker's (OT-syntactic) constraint MARK TOPIC is added to the constraint ranking, which requires the speaker to mark topicality. One way to satisfy this constraint is by topicalization or topic-fronting. In Kinyarwanda the topic can be marked by topicalization, i.e. starting the sentence with the topic. That means that we have four possible interpretations for each form. That is, the boy can be the subject and the topic, the boy can be the topic but not the subject, the boy can be the subject but not the topic, or the boy can be neither the subject nor the topic. However, only two different forms are available for these four potential interpretations. The first four candidates in the tableau combine the first form (*boy reads book*) with the four possible interpretations, and the last four candidates the other form (*book reads boy*) with the same four possible interpretations. Hence, we end up with eight candidate form-meaning pairs.

As can be seen from the violation pattern in Tableau 8, the first candidate is a winning pair of form and interpretation (indicated by the sign ☞) as it does not violate any of the constraints. This superoptimal form-meaning pair links the form *boy reads book* to the meaning 'boy reads book' with the boy being the topic. As a consequence, candidate pairs with either the same form (candidates 2, 3, and 4) or the same interpretation (candidate 5) are blocked, but candidates 6, 7, and 8 (with a different form and a different interpretation) are still in competition. The seventh candidate is the winner of this competition, and therefore the pair of the form *book reads boy* and the meaning 'boy reads book' in which the book is the topic, is the second superoptimal pair (again indicated by the sign ☞).

Tableau 8: Bidirectional optimization of *boy reads book* and *book reads boy*.

Kinyarwanda, examples (4) and (5)	MARK TOPIC	PROM	SEL	PREC
☞ 1. *boy reads book*, read' (boy, book); boy is topic				
2. *boy reads book*, read' (book, boy); boy is topic		*	*	*
3. *boy reads book*, read' (boy, book); book is topic	*			
4. *boy reads book*, read' (book, boy); book is topic	*	*	*	*
5. *book reads boy*, read' (boy, book); boy is topic	*			*
6. *book reads boy*, read' (book, boy); boy is topic	*	*	*	

Tableau 8 (continued)

Kinyarwanda, examples (4) and (5)	MARK TOPIC	PROM	SEL	PREC
☞ 7. *book reads boy*, read' (boy, book); book is topic				*
8. *book reads boy*, read' (book, boy); book is topic		*	*	

Tableau 9 provides a similar analysis of the possible form-meaning pairs of *boy kisses girl* and *girl kisses boy* in Kinyarwanda (see example (6) above). Since boy and girl are equal in animacy, all candidate interpretations violate prominence (the subject does not outrank the object in animacy) while no candidate interpretations violate selection (the verb kiss requires an animate subject, and both arguments satisfy this restriction). Therefore, the first and eighth pairs of form and interpretation win the competition and become superoptimal. This means that there are no forms left to be linked to the other potential interpretations. The form *girl kisses boy* cannot mean that the boy kisses the girl, not even when the girl is the topic (as in the seventh candidate). As pointed out above, this is a clear case of word order freezing: when no other constraints distinguish between the subject-initial or the object-initial interpretation, precedence does the job.

Tableau 9: Bidirectional optimization of *boy kisses girl* and *girl kisses boy*.

Kinyarwanda, example (6)	MARK TOPIC	PROM	SEL	PREC
☞ 1. *boy kisses girl*, kiss' (boy, girl); boy is topic		*		
2. *boy kisses girl*, kiss' (girl, boy); boy is topic		*		*
3. *boy kisses girl*, kiss' (boy, girl); girl is topic	*	*		
4. *boy kisses girl*, kiss' (girl, boy); girl is topic	*	*		*
5. *girl kisses boy*, kiss' (boy, girl); boy is topic	*	*		*
6. *girl kisses boy*, kiss' (girl, boy); boy is topic	*	*		

Tableau 9 (continued)

Kinyarwanda, example (6)	MARK TOPIC	PROM	SEL	PREC
7. *girl kisses boy*, kiss' (boy, girl); girl is topic		*		*
☛ 8. *girl kisses boy*, kiss' (girl, boy); girl is topic		*		

In sentence (7) above, we have seen that prominence is violated (the subject does not outrank the object in animacy) but in this case selection again helps to distinguish the subject from the object (the verb cut requires a subject that can cut, such as knife, but not bread). Tableau 10 shows the correct derivation of the two superoptimal form-meaning pairs.

Not surprisingly, the first candidate pair wins the competition, since it only violates PROMINENCE, which all candidates do. Hence, the form *knife cuts bread* gets associated with the interpretation that the knife is the subject as well as the topic. For the other form, *bread cuts knife*, the best remaining interpretation is that again, the knife is the subject (because of SELECTION), but now the bread is the topic (which is why PRECEDENCE is violated in order to satisfy MARK TOPIC). Hence, the seventh candidate becomes the second superoptimal form-meaning pair.

Tableau 10: Bidirectional optimization of *knife cuts bread* and *bread cuts knife*.

Kinyarwanda, example (7)	MARK TOPIC	PROM	SEL	PREC
☛ 1. *knife cuts bread*, cut' (knife, bread); knife is topic		*		
2. *knife cuts bread*, cut' (bread, knife); knife is topic		*	*	*
3. *knife cuts bread*, cut' (knife, bread); bread is topic	*	*		
4. *knife cuts bread*, cut' (bread, knife); bread is topic	*	*	*	*
5. *bread cuts knife*, cut' (knife, bread); knife is topic	*	*		*
6. *bread cuts knife*, cut' (bread, knife); knife is topic	*	*	*	

Tableau 10 (continued)

Kinyarwanda, example (7)	MARK TOPIC	PROM	SEL	PREC
☞ 7. *bread cuts knife*, cut' (knife, bread); bread is topic		*		*
8. *bread cuts knife*, cut' (bread, knife); bread is topic		*	*	

Let us now turn to the most problematic case, the bidirectional OT analysis of sentences (8) and (9). We have seen that object-fronting is not possible in this case. This can be explained by the interaction of PROMINENCE and SELECTION. In this particular case, satisfaction of the high-ranked constraint PROMINENCE goes hand in hand with a violation of SELECTION. This means that, quite counterintuitively, the pragmatically odd interpretation in combination with the form *child pierces needle* (as in (9) above) is in fact the first superoptimal pair, as it only violates SELECTION. The second superoptimal pair is the form *needle pierces child* (as in (8)) with the interpretation that satisfies SELECTION. This is shown in Tableau 11.

Tableau 11: Bidirectional optimization of *needle pierces child* and *child pierces needle*.

Kinyarwanda, examples (8) and (9)	MARK TOPIC	PROM	SEL	PREC
☞ 1. *needle pierces child*, pierce' (needle, child); needle is topic		*		
2. *needle pierces child*, pierce' (child, needle); needle is topic			*	*
3. *needle pierces child*, pierce' (needle, child); child is topic	*	*		
4. *needle pierces child*, pierce' (child, needle); child is topic	*		*	*
5. *child pierces needle*, pierce' (needle, child); needle is topic	*	*		*
6. *child pierces needle*, pierce' (child, needle); needle is topic	*		*	
7. *child pierces needle*, pierce' (needle, child); child is topic		*		*
☞ 8. *child pierces needle*, pierce' (child, needle); child is topic			*	

This section has illustrated the general concept of speaker-hearer interaction for the phenomenon of object-fronting in Kinyarwanda. Speakers take into account the hearers' perspective in that they only front an object if they can be sure that the hearer will be able to determine the correct (intended) interpretation. As a consequence, a speaker who wants to say about a child, who is the topic, that a needle pierces the child, cannot use object-fronting. Similarly, a speaker who wants to tell about a topic, the girl, that the boy kisses her, cannot use object-fronting either. In these cases, only subject-initial sentences are possible, whether the object is a topic or not. The question arises whether speakers can mark topicality at all in these cases. Besides object-fronting, languages often have alternative strategies to mark topicality, for example dislocation, pronominalization, or passivization. The next section investigates the role of animacy in the choice between active and passive structures.

4 Animacy and the competition between active and passive in Biak

Passives are sometimes argued to be a better construction choice than actives when the Patient is more prominent than the Agent (or alternatively, when the Agent is less prominent than the Patient), that is to say, when the Agent is demoted and the Patient is the most prominent argument, or the topic (Legendre et al. 1993; Aissen 1999). Malchukov (2006: 349) also argues that shifting to a passive structure can sometimes be the optimal solution, even though a passive structure is more marked than an active structure.

Animacy is one of the features that contributes to an argument's prominence, with animates being more prominent than inanimates. Cornelis (1997: 121) finds that while 66 % of the Agents in active transitive sentences are animate in written Dutch, only 35 % of the Agents in *by*-phrases (which she calls *causers*) in passive sentences are. This means that the majority of (overt) Agents in passive sentences is inanimate. Further investigation of the *animate* Agents in passives reveals that they have two main characteristics. First, animate Agents within Dutch passive constructions can be Agents with whom the speaker (and the hearer) should not want to identify, because of negative evaluation of the event or the Agent. For example, sentences with transitive verbs of violence such as *rape*, *stab*, and *kill* appear to be often passivized in Dutch newspapers (Cornelis 1997: 124). Second, animate Agents may be demoted to passive *by*-phrases when they are newly introduced to the discourse, hence non-topical (Cornelis 1997: 123).

Whether a verb allows passivization, may be dependent on what counts as an Agent in a given language (cf. de Hoop and Narasimhan 2005). For example, Dutch allows for (subject-less) impersonal passive constructions of intransitive verbs (cf. Perlmutter 1978), whereas other languages such as English do not allow passivization of intransitive verbs. In Dutch, stative transitive verbs like *bevatten* 'contain', *weten* 'know', *hebben* 'have' do not allow for passivization. One could argue that the subjects of these verbs are not Agents, which could explain why these verbs cannot passivize, since demotion of the Agent is the main reason for passivization across languages. Indeed, a verb such as *krijgen* 'receive', of which the subject is a Recipient and not an Agent, does not passivize either (see also section 5).

What counts as an Agent can apparently also vary per construction within one language. For example, the Mayan language Kaqchikel has two types of passives, one of which, the so-called *ki*-passive, requires the Agent to be animate and the Patient to be specific. If the Agent is inanimate, the *ki*-passive is not an option (see (14)), whereas the other passive is (see (13)) (Broadwell 2006: 386).

(12) Ri che' x-u-tzäq ri ja'y
 the tree PERF-3SG.ERG-knock.down the house
 'The tree knocked down the house.'

(13) Ri ja'y x-tzaq r-oma ri che'
 the house PERF-knock.down.PASS 3SG.ERG-by the tree
 'The house was knocked down by the tree.'

(14) *Ri ja'y x-ki-tzaq r-oma ri che'
 the house PERF-PASS-knock.down 3SG.ERG-by the tree
 'The house was knocked down by the tree.'

Inanimate Agents are low-prominent and may therefore lead to passivization. This is in accordance with Aissen's (1999) cross-linguistic analysis of passivization, although she focusses on person as a prominence feature and not on animacy. We will use two of Aissen's (1999) constraints in the analyses below:
1. *Su/Pat: Avoid subject Patient;
2. *Obj/X: Avoid high-prominent objects.

Aissen uses the constraint *Su/Pat to penalize passive clauses in general. *Su/Pat is violated if the argument with the greater number of Proto-Patient properties is realized as the subject (Aissen 1999: 684). Other constraints dealing with (relative) prominence of the arguments may be in conflict with a general ban on Patient subjects (or oblique Agents), leading to the realization of a passive. Most of these constraints do not pertain to all passives in a certain language, but depend on the prominence features of the arguments in the discourse. For example, *OBJ/X penalizes active clauses with high-prominent objects (Aissen 1999: 684). The approaches of Legendre et al. (1993) and Aissen (1999) suggest that some independent mechanism of determining discourse prominence will in fact trigger the use of passive constructions. However, even in languages that allow passivization, this process is not obligatory in case of a low-prominent Agent and a high-prominent Patient, as (15) illustrates (de Hoop 1999: 101).

(15) Then someone hit Robert/him with a stick.

A bidirectional optimization approach does not need Aissen's (1999) mechanism of local conjunction with a constraint that requires structural marking of semantically marked configurations, to derive the fact that passives are used in unexpected contexts (namely when the Agent is low-prominent and/or the Patient is high-prominent). Marking should follow from the bidirectional optimization procedure itself.

In Biak, an Austronesian language of Papua, passivization is extremely rare (van den Heuvel 2006: 296). Example (16) is an elicited example of a passive construction that is considered grammatical (van den Heuvel 2006: 297)

(16) Sansun naine neve-sawek.
    clothes these 3PL.PASS-tear
    'These clothes are torn.'

Van den Heuvel (2006: 297) points out that not all transitive verbs allow for passivization in Biak. He mentions the verb *marisn* 'enjoy' as an example of a formally transitive verb that cannot passivize. This is illustrated in (17).

(17) *Sup ine vyeve-marisn.
    land this 3SG.PASS-enjoy
    'This land is enjoyed.'

As van den Heuvel (2006: 297) notes, "[t]he limited distribution of the passive probably has to do with the fact that the language also has alternative strategies to demote the Agent, like the use of impersonal 3rd plural", as exemplified in (18) below. Van den Heuvel's informant judges the passive construction in (17) ungrammatical and provides him with the object-fronted (18) instead.

(18) Sup   ine   si-marisn   i.
     land   this 3PL.ANIM-enjoy   3SG
     'This land they like.'

Other transitive verbs that cannot passivize in Biak are *nan* 'eat', *inm* 'drink', *rowr* 'hear, listen', *mam* 'see, look', *swar* 'love', *sewar* 'look for', *ros* 'kick' (Hengki, p.c.). Transitive verbs that do passivize in Biak quite unexpectedly require the promoted object to be third person inanimate. A human subject in a passive construction is excluded (Hengki, p.c.). This runs counter to the common insight that high-prominent Patients (such as local pronouns or animate or specific noun phrases) trigger passivization (cf. Aissen 1999).

(19) Ankrai-bon   anya   vyeve-pów.
     orange-fruit   the   3SG.PASS-peel
     'The orange is being peeled.'

Example (19) is a description of film scene at which the researcher held his hand over the Agent, asking what was happening in the picture (van den Heuvel 2006: 296). Yet, whereas the passive sentence (19) is grammatical, the passive counterpart of the active sentence (20a) in (20b) is ungrammatical (Hengki, p.c.).

(20) a. S-pam   roma   ya.
        3PL.ANIM-shoot   boy   that
        'They shoot that boy.'
     b. *Roma ya   vyeve-pam.
        boy   that   3SG.PASS-shoot
        'That boy is being shot.'

This pattern is clearly unexpected and cannot be accounted for in Aissen's (1999) unidirectional OT-syntactic analysis. However, we will show that the pattern can be accounted for in bidirectional OT. In Biak passives occur predominantly with inanimate Patients (van den Heuvel 2006). Strikingly, the use of a formally marked passive construction is allowed in the unmarked context (i.e. when the Agent outranks the Patient in animacy) instead of in the marked case. Aissen's (1999: 684) basic insight is "that the unmarked situation is for a more prominent argument to be subject and for a less prominent one to be non-subject". Therefore, we predict the use of a marked passive construction if the Patient is animate rather than if it is inanimate. However, what is conceptually marked in (19) is the mere fact that the inanimate Patient is the topic. An inanimate Patient is exactly the type of argument that we normally do not expect to be the topic.

The pattern in Biak can be explained as follows: because passivization is extremely costly (and therefore extremely rare) in Biak, it only applies if the Patient is not sufficiently prominent by itself to be able to be interpreted as the topic. Therefore, the speaker has to mark the fact that an inanimate Patient is the topic explicitly. Human Patients count as inherently prominent because of their rank in the animacy hierarchy, and therefore they can independently be interpreted as the topic. As a consequence, passivization is not allowed. If the Patient is inanimate and therefore typically low-prominent, the speaker can use a passive construction to mark its high-prominence (topicality).

Tableau 12 sketches the bidirectional OT derivation of sentence (19). Because subject-verb agreement in Biak distinguishes between animate and inanimate subjects, AGREEMENT is a relevant constraint to consider, and because it goes hand in hand with SELECTION, we have collapsed the two as the highest ranked constraint in Tableau 12. Crucially, the constraint *SU/PAT that penalizes passives outranks *OBJ/X that penalizes a high-prominent object in Biak. Following van den Heuvel (2006: 297), we assume that passivization is not the only way to mark a topic in Biak. Satisfaction of this constraint is also possible by the use of lexical means such as specificity markers or pronouns, or by object-fronting (see (18) above). Therefore, MARK TOPIC would not be satisfied in the active counterpart of (19) if *the orange* is the topic, but it would be if the third person animate marker is the topic. In (19), the third person animate marker is implied, but not overt, which is why MARK TOPIC is not satisfied if 3PL is to be understood as the topic.

Tableau 12: Bidirectional optimization of active and passive in Biak.

Biak, example (19)	AGR/SEL	MARK TOPIC	*SU/PAT	*OBJ/X
☞ 1. 3PL *peel orange*, peel' (3PL, orange); 3PL is topic				
2. 3PL *peel orange*, peel' (orange, 3PL); 3PL is topic	*		*	*
3. 3PL *peel orange*, peel' (3PL, orange); orange is topic		*		*

Tableau 12 (continued)

Biak, example (19)	AGR/SEL	MARK TOPIC	*SU/PAT	*OBJ/X
4. 3PL peel orange, peel' (orange, 3PL); orange is topic	*	*	*	
5. orange is peeled, peel' (3PL, orange); 3PL is topic		*	*	
☞ 6. orange is peeled, peel' (3PL, orange); orange is topic			*	

Because passive constructions are necessarily constructions in which the Agent is demoted to an oblique phrase or omitted altogether, while the Patient is the grammatical subject, we do not need to take into account interpretations in which the Agent is the grammatical subject and the Patient is demoted (as these would be antipassive constructions, cf. Legendre et al. 1993). Hence, the passive structure only combines with two candidate interpretations, one in which the Agent is the topic and one in which the Patient is the topic.

Tableau 12 shows that for the inanimate Patient that is the topic, the passive form becomes superoptimal. By contrast, we have seen that in (20) passivization was prohibited because the Patient is human. This can be analyzed as in Tableau 13:

Tableau 13: Bidirectional optimization of active and passive in Biak.

Biak, example (20)	AGR/SEL	MARK TOPIC	*SU/PAT	*OBJ/X
☞ 1. 3PL shoot boy, shoot' (3PL, boy); 3PL is topic				*
2. 3PL shoot boy, shoot' (boy, 3PL); 3PL is topic	*		*	*
☞ 3. 3PL shoot boy, shoot' (3PL, boy); boy is topic				*

Tableau 13 (continued)

Biak, example (20)	AGR/SEL	MARK TOPIC	*Su/Pat	*Obj/X
4. 3PL *shoot boy*, shoot' (boy, (3PL); boy is topic	*		*	*
5. *boy is shot*, shoot' (3PL, boy); 3PL is topic		*	*	
6. *boy is shot*, shoot' (3PL, boy); boy is topic			*	

The difference between (19) and (20) is that the constraint mark topic is already satisfied by the overt expression of the human object in the active sentence (20a). A human object is necessarily high-prominent, which explains why the low-ranked constraint *Obj/X gets violated by both optimal readings of the active sentence, independently of whether 3pl or the boy is the topic. Thus, the active sentence is not only the optimal form when 3PL is the topic, but also when the boy is the topic. It is impossible to distinguish between the two interpretations on the basis of the structure alone. We assume the question which argument will be interpreted as the topic may be answered in a broader discourse context, or is left undecided. Hence, the pair that links the passive form to the interpretation in which the boy is the topic does not become superoptimal at all. This explains why the use of a passive in this case would lead to ungrammaticality (van den Heuvel 2006: 297; Hengki, p.c.). The next section will deal with another example of the competition between passivization and object-fronting as two possible topic-marking strategies in language.

5 Object-fronting versus passivization in Dutch psych verbs

Reconsider the subject-initial sentence in (1), repeated below as (21).

(21) De gorilla heeft de vrouw gebeten.
 the gorilla has the woman bitten
 'The gorilla bit the woman.'

We have seen that in the absence of further contextual clues, object-fronting is not possible in (21), because the sentence would be interpreted as subject-initial. However, if one would like to topicalize *the woman*, being the most prominent participant in the event, there is an alternative strategy to do so in Dutch, namely to passivize the sentence. This strategy is much more common than object-fronting. Thus, the object of the active sentence gets promoted to the grammatical function of subject and becomes the topic of the sentence, as in (22) or (23):

(22) De vrouw werd gebeten door de gorilla.
 the woman became bitten by the gorilla
 'The woman was bitten by the gorilla.'

(23) Zij werd gebeten door de gorilla.
 she became bitten by the gorilla
 'She was bitten by the gorilla.'

So, if the object of a transitive verb gets the status of topic, there is a good strategy available to topicalize it to the sentence-initial position without violating the constraint PRECEDENCE, which indeed appears to be a high-ranked constraint in Dutch (Bouma 2008 in a corpus study of spoken Dutch finds that around 70 % of all sentences start with the subject in Dutch).

Tableau 14: Bidirectional optimization of active and passive in Dutch.

Dutch, examples (21)–(22)	SEL	PREC	*SU/PAT	PROM	MARK TOPIC
☞ 1. *gorilla bites woman*, bite' (gorilla, woman); gorilla is topic				*	
2. *gorilla bites woman*, bite' (woman, gorilla); gorilla is topic		*	*	*	
3. *gorilla bites woman*, bite' (gorilla, woman); woman is topic			*	*	*
4. *gorilla bites woman*, bite' (woman, gorilla); woman is topic		*		*	*

Tableau 14 (continued)

Dutch, examples (21)–(22)	SEL	PREC	*SU/PAT	PROM	MARK TOPIC
5. *woman bites gorilla*, bite' (gorilla, woman); gorilla is topic		*		*	
6. *woman bites gorilla*, bite' (woman, gorilla); gorilla is topic			*	*	
7. *woman bites gorilla*, bite' (gorilla, woman); woman is topic		*	*	*	*
☞ 8. *woman bites gorilla*, bite' (woman, gorilla); woman is topic				*	*
9. *woman bitten by gorilla*, bite' (gorilla, woman); gorilla is topic			*		*
☞ 10. *woman bitten by gorilla*, bite' (gorilla, woman); woman is topic			*		

Tableau 14 shows the optimal form-meaning pairs of the Dutch sentences (21) and (22). The two competing forms are the active and the passive sentences, as in (21) and (22). In principle, object-fronting is a possible (grammatical) form in Dutch, but as illustrated in Tableau 14, this leads to word order freezing (i.e. a subject-initial interpretation). In order to account for the marked status of a passive form, we again adopt Aissen's alignment constraint *SU/PAT ("Avoid subjects with the grammatical role of Patient"). Note, however, that we do not necessarily consider this constraint to be the one and only reason for passives to be throughout languages (see e.g. de Hoop and Malchukov 2008 for a different account). In Aissen's (1999: 689) analysis this constraint is overruled by a constraint that penalizes low-prominent subjects in English, in order to derive the use of a passive in English when the Patient is high-prominent. High-prominence is taken to be equivalent to being the topic in our analysis. Note that high-prominence of the Patient goes hand in hand with low-prominence of the Agent. In the canonical (active, transitive) case, the Agent outranks the Patient in animacy, in topicality, and in grammatical function.

The first two winning form-meaning pairs, i.e. the first and the eighth pair in Tableau 14, are the active sentences in which the sentence-initial argument is the topic as well as the subject, one meaning 'The gorilla bit the woman' and the other one 'The woman bit the gorilla'. Both candidates satisfy the constraints PRECEDENCE (hence, the sentences are subject-initial) and *SU/PAT (which means that a passive construction is avoided, and the Agent ends up as the subject of the sentence). The third superoptimal form-meaning pair (candidate 10) violates this latter constraint. The result is a passive construction in which the Patient becomes the grammatical subject and is identified as the topic. The constraint PROMINENCE cannot be violated in a passive sentence, because it deals with the relation between subject and object in a transitive clause.

Whereas causative psych verbs that take an Experiencer object, such as *overtuigen* 'convince', can passivize in Dutch, unaccusative psych verbs such as *bevallen* 'please', which also take an Experiencer object, cannot (Lamers & de Hoop 2014). This relates to the different thematic roles of the subject of these two types of verbs. We have seen that passive formation is cross-linguistically characterized as demotion of the Agent. The subject of a causative psych verb is a Stimulus, which has more proto-Agent properties than the subject of an unaccusative psych verb, which is a Theme (cf. Primus 1999, 2012). As a consequence, the Stimulus subject of a causative psych verbs gets demoted in a passive construction, while the Theme subject of an unaccusative psych verb does not. The difference between causative and unaccusative psych verbs is reminiscent of the well-known distinction between unergative and unaccusative intransitive verbs. In Dutch, in general only unergative intransitives such as *werken* 'work' which have an Agent subject can passivize, while unaccusative intransitives such as *zakken* 'fail' can only incidentally (Hoekstra 1984; Zaenen 1993; Beliën 2016). The subject of unaccusative intransitives is not an Agent, but rather a Theme or a Patient. In other words, both unaccusative intransitive verbs and unaccusative psych verbs resist passivization, because there is no argument with sufficient proto-Agent properties to be demoted.

Lamers & de Hoop (2014) conducted a production experiment and found that object-fronting is relatively frequent in case of unaccusative psych verbs, while causative psych verbs give rise to the use of more passive sentences. Because a speaker cannot use a passive construction in the case of an unaccusative psych verb (as these verbs do not allow passivization), object-fronting is produced more easily and therefore also understood more easily. They claim that this can also account for the higher acceptability of object-fronting in the case of unaccusative psych verbs compared to causative psych verbs, that was found in Lamers (2001, 2007).

Lamers (2001) investigated how speakers of Dutch judge object-fronting in sentences with three different types of verbs, agentive verbs that select an animate subject, and the two types of psych verbs, which both require an animate object. She found an overall preference for subject-initial sentences (satisfaction of PRECEDENCE), but also that for the unaccusative psych verbs, the difference in rating between the subject-initial and object-initial sentences was smallest. Recall that there is no difference in animacy requirements between the two types of psych verbs. There is, however, another difference between the two: while causative psych verbs can passivize, unaccusative psych verbs cannot. The difference between the two types of psych verbs is shown in (24) and (25).

(24) a. De foto overtuigde de man.
 the photo convinced the man
 'The photo convinced the man.'
 b. ??De man overtuigde de foto.
 the man convinced the photo
 'The photo convinced the man.'
 c. De man werd overtuigd door de foto.
 the man became convinced by the photo
 'The man got convinced by the photo.'

(25) a. De foto beviel de man.
 the photo pleased the man
 'The photo pleased the man.'
 b. De man beviel de foto.
 the man pleased the photo
 'The photo pleased the man.'
 c. *De man werd bevallen door de foto.
 the man became pleased by the photo
 'The man got pleased by the photo.'

Because speakers of Dutch do not have the possibility to produce a passive form in the case of an unaccusative psych verb, fronting the animate object is the only option to start the sentence with the animate argument if it is the topic of the sentence.

Tableau 15 below shows that while in principle both object-fronting and passivization are possible with causative psych verbs, the passive structure is the optimal form used to express the interpretation in which the Patient (or rather, Experiencer) is the topic. This leaves the interpretation in which the man convinced the photo, hence satisfying PRECEDENCE but crucially violating SELECTION, for sentence (24b) which would also explain the low score this order receives in the rating studies (Lamers 2001, 2007).

Tableau 15: Bidirectional optimization of causative psych verb in Dutch.

Dutch, examples (24)	SEL	PREC	*Su/Pat	PROM	MARK TOPIC
☙ 1. *photo convinced man*, convince' (photo, man); photo is topic			*		
2. *photo convinced man*, convince' (man, photo); photo is topic	*	*			
3. *photo convinced man*, convince' (photo, man); man is topic				*	*
4. *photo convinced man*, convince' (man, photo); man is topic	*	*			*
5. *man convinced photo*, convince' (photo, man); photo is topic		*		*	*
6. *man convinced photo*, convince' (man, photo); photo is topic	*				*
7. *man convinced photo*, convince' (photo, man); man is topic		*	*		
8. *man convinced photo*, convince' (man, photo); man is topic	*				
9 *man convinced by photo*, convince' (photo, man); photo is topic			*	*	*
☙ 10. *man convinced by photo*, convince' (photo, man); man is topic			*	*	

If we assume that unaccusative psych verbs in Dutch cannot passivize because they lack an Agent, then this form does not compete with the active forms. Tableau 16 shows how in that case object-fronting becomes the optimal expression of the interpretation in which the man is the topic.

Tableau 16: Bidirectional optimization of unaccusative psych verb in Dutch.

Dutch, examples (25)	SEL	PREC	*Su/PAT	PROM	MARK TOPIC
☞ 1. *photo pleased man*, please'(photo, man); photo is topic				*	
2. *photo pleased man*, please'(man, photo); photo is topic	*	*			
3. *photo pleased man*, please'(photo, man); man is topic				*	*
4. *photo pleased man*, please'(man, photo); man is topic	*	*			*
5. *man pleased photo*, please'(photo, man); photo is topic		*		*	*
6. *man pleased photo*, please'(man, photo); photo is topic	*				*
☞ 7. *man pleased photo*, please'(photo, man); man is topic		*	*		
8. *man pleased photo*, please'(man, photo); man is topic	*				

Lamers & de Hoop's (2014) explanation of the unexpected difference in rating between the two classes of psych verbs thus builds upon the fact that unaccusative psych verbs cannot passivize in Dutch. Hence, the only way in which the speaker who uses an unaccusative psych verb can satisfy MARK TOPIC when the Experiencer is the topic, is by object-fronting. In the case of causative psych verb, however, passivization is an alternative strategy and a better (superoptimal) option to promote the topic.

6 Conclusion

This chapter used bidirectional Optimality Theory to analyze the interplay between competing structures and competing interpretations pertaining to the prominence (topicality) of (in)animate arguments. Several rather unexpected or even counterintuitive patterns in different languages could be analyzed with a small set of independently motivated constraints that seem to hold across languages.

First, we analyzed the pattern in Kinyarwanda, in which object-fronting is allowed as long as the two arguments are distinguishable, but not if the object outranks the subject in animacy (Morimoto 2008). We showed that in the latter case bidirectional optimization over form-meaning pairs will lead the hearer to an infelicitous interpretation.

Second, we examined the puzzling pattern of passivization in Biak, where the subject of a passive has to be an inanimate Patient (van den Heuvel 2006). Usually, animate, or generally high-prominent, Patients are more likely than inanimate ones to end up as the subject in a passive sentence. We accounted for this by assuming that inanimate Patients are normally not interpreted as topics, but a speaker can mark their topicality by using a passive. By contrast, animate Patients can be interpreted as topics on the basis of other lexical or syntactic cues, and hence, they do not need (nor allow for) passivization.

Finally, based on Lamers & de Hoop (2014), we presented a bidirectional OT analysis of the interaction between the speaker's choice and the hearer's interpretation of object-fronting in case of Dutch Experiencer object verbs. We accounted for Lamers & de Hoop's (2014) finding that object-fronting is relatively frequent in case of unaccusative psych verbs, while causative psych verbs give rise to the use of more passive sentences. Because a speaker cannot use a passive in the case of an unaccusative psych verb (as these verbs do not allow passivization), object-fronting becomes the optimal structure in a context in which the animate object is to be interpreted as the topic.

Thus, we have formalized Lamers & de Hoop's (2014) insight that both the speaker's and the hearer's perspectives constrain object-fronting and passivization. Not only does the speaker take into account the hearer's perspective, taking into consideration the question whether the hearer will arrive at the intended interpretation on the basis of a given form, but the hearer takes into account the speaker's perspective as well, taking into consideration the structural options the speaker has at their disposal to express a certain interpretation.

References

Aissen, Judith. 1999. Markedness and subject choice in Optimality Theory. *Natural Language and Linguistic Theory* 17(4). 673–711. https://doi.org/10.1023/A: 1006335629372.

Beliën, Maaike. 2016. Dutch impersonal passives: Beyond volition and atelicity. *Linguistics in the Netherlands 2016*, 1–13. https://doi.org/10.1075/avt.33.01bel.

van Bergen, Geertje. 2011. *Who's first and what's next? Animacy and word order variation in Dutch language production*. Nijmegen: Radboud University Disseration.

van Bergen, Geertje & Helen de Hoop. 2009. Topics cross-linguistically. *The Linguistic Review* 26(2–3). 173–176. https://doi.org/10.1515/tlir.2009.006.

Bickel, Balthasar, Alena Witzlack-Makarevich, Kamal K. Choudhary, Matthias Schlesewsky & Ina Bornkessel-Schlesewsky. 2015. The neurophysiology of language processing shapes the evolution of grammar: Evidence from case marking. *PLoS ONE* 10(8) e0132819. https://doi.org/10.1371/journal.pone.0132819.

Blutner, Reinhard, Helen de Hoop & Petra Hendriks. 2006. *Optimal communication*. CSLI Lecture Notes (177). CSLI Publications, Stanford.

Bouma, Gerlof. 2008. *Starting a sentence in Dutch. A corpus study of subject- and object-fronting*. Groningen: University of Groningen dissertation.

Broadwell, George Aaron. 2006. Syntactic valence, information structure, and passive constructions in Kaqchikel. In Leonid Kulikov, Andrej L. Malchukov & Peter de Swart (eds.), *Case, valency, and transitivity*. 376–392. Amsterdam: Benjamins.

Brunetti, Lisa. 2009. On the semantic and contextual factors that determine topic selection in Italian and Spanish. *The Linguistic Review* 26(2–3). 261–289. https://doi.org/10.1515/tlir.2009.010.

Comrie, Bernard. 1989. *Language universals and linguistic typology*. Chicago, IL: University of Chicago Press.

Cornelis, Louise H. 1997. *Passive and perspective*. Amsterdam: Rodopi.

Dahl, Östen & Kari Fraurud. 1996. Animacy in grammar and discourse. In Thorstein Fretheim, Jeanette K. Gundel (eds.), *Reference and referent accessibility*, 47–64. Amsterdam: Benjamins.

Dryer, Matthew S. 2013. Order of subject, object and verb. In Matthew S. Dryer & Martin Haspelmath (eds.), *The World Atas of Language Structures Online*. Leipzig: Max Planck Institute of Evolutionary Anthropology. http://wals.info/chapter/81 (2018-14-12).

Fauconnier, Stefanie. 2011. Differential Agent marking and animacy. *Lingua* 121(3). 533–547. https://doi.org/10.1016/j.lingua.2010.10.014.

Givón, Talmy. 1984. *Syntax: A functional typological introduction*. Amsterdam: Benjamins.

van den Heuvel, Wilco. 2006. *Biak. Description of an Austronesian language of Papua*. PhD dissertation, Free University of Amsterdam. Utrecht: LOT.

Hoekstra, Teun. 1984. *Transitivity: Grammatical relations in Government-Binding theory*. Dordrecht: Foris. https://doi.org/10.1515/9783112327241.

de Hoop, Helen. 1999. Optimal case assignment. *Linguistics in the Netherlands 1999*, 97–109. https://doi.org/10.1075/avt.16.10hoo.

de Hoop, Helen & Monique J. A. Lamers. 2006. Incremental distinguishability of subject and object. In Leonid Kulikov, Andrej L. Malchukov & Peter de Swart (eds.), *Case, valency, and transitivity*, 269–287. Amsterdam: Benjamins.

de Hoop, Helen & Bhuvana Narasimhan. 2005. Differential case-marking in Hindi. Mengistu Amberber & Helen de Hoop (eds.), *Competition and variation in natural languages: The case for case*, 321–345. Amsterdam: Elsevier. https://doi.org/10.1016/B978-008044651-6/50015-X.

de Hoop, Helen & Andrej L. Malchukov. 2008. Case-marking strategies. *Linguistic Inquiry* 39 (4). 565–587. https://www.jstor.org/stable/40071453.

Lamers, Monique J.A. 2001. *Sentence processing: Using syntactic, semantic, and thematic information*. Groningen: University of Groningen dissertation.

Lamers, Monique J.A. 2007. Verb type, animacy and definiteness in grammatical function disambiguation. *Linguistics in the Netherlands 2007*, 125–137. https://doi.org/10.1075/avt.24.13lam.

Lamers, Monique J.A. & Helen de Hoop. 2014. Animate object-fronting in Dutch: A production study. In Brian MacWhinney, Andrej L. Malchukov & Edith Moravcsik (eds.), *Competing motivations in grammar and usage*, 42–53. Oxford: Oxford University Press.

Lee, Hanjung. 2003. Parallel optimization in case systems. In Miriam Butt & Tracy HollowayKing (eds.), *Nominals: Inside and out*. Stanford, CA: CSLI Publications.

Legendre, Géraldine, William Raymond & Paul Smolensky. 1993. An Optimality-Theoretic typology of case and grammatical voice systems. *Berkeley Linguistics Society (BLS)* 19. 464–478. https://doi.org/10.3765/bls.v19i1.1498.

Legendre, Géraldine, Michael T. Putnam, Henriëtte de Swart & Erin Zaroukian. 2016. Introduction. In Géraldine Legendre, Michael T. Putnam, Henriëtte de Swart, and Erin Zaroukian (eds.), *Optimality-Theoretic syntax, semantics, and pragmatics: From uni- to bidirectional optimization*, 1–31. Oxford: Oxford University Press.

Lestrade, Sander, Geertje van Bergen & Peter de Swart. 2016. On the origin of constraints. In Géraldine Legendre, Michael T. Putnam, Henriëtte de Swart & Erin Zaroukian (eds.), *Optimality-Theoretic syntax, semantics, and pragmatics: From uni- to bidirectional optimization*, 179–199. Oxford: Oxford University Press.

Malchukov, Andrej L. 2006. Transitivity parameters and transitivity alternations. Constraining co-variation. In Leonid Kulikov, Andrej L. Malchukov & Peter de Swart (eds.), *Case, valency, and transitivity*, 329–357. Amsterdam: Benjamins.

Morimoto, Yukiko. 2008. From topic to subject marking: Implications for a typology of subject marking. In Helen de Hoop & Peter de Swart (eds.), *Differential Subject Marking*, 199–221. Dordrecht: Springer.

Øvrelid, Lilja. 2004. Disambiguation of syntactic functions in Norwegian: Modeling variation in word order interpretations conditioned by animacy and definiteness. *Proceedings of the 20th Scandinavian Conference of Linguistics*, Helsinki.

Perlmutter, David M. 1978. Impersonal passives and the unaccusativity hypothesis. *Proceedings of the Annual Meeting of the Berkeley Linguistics Society* 38. 157–189.

Primus, Beatrice. 1999. *Cases and thematic roles: Ergative, accusative and active*. Tübingen: Niemeyer. https://doi.org/10.1515/9783110912463.

Primus, Beatrice. 2012. Animacy, generalized semantic roles, and differential object marking. In Monique J.A. Lamers & Peter de Swart (eds.), *Case, word order and prominence: Interacting cues in language production and comprehension*, 65–90. Dordrecht: Springer.

Rissman, Lilia & Kyle Rawlins. 2017. Ingredients of instrumental meaning. *Journal of Semantics* 34(3). 507–537. https://doi.org/10.1093/jos/ffx003

Smolensky, Paul & Géraldine Legendre. 2006. *The harmonic mind: From neural computation to Optimality-Theoretic grammar*. Cambridge, MA: MIT Press.

de Swart, Peter. 2007. *Cross-linguistic variation in object marking*. PhD dissertation, Radboud University Nijmegen. Utrecht: LOT.

de Swart, Peter & Helen de Hoop. 2007. Semantic aspects of differential object marking. In Estela Puig-Waldmüller (ed.), *Sinn und Bedeutung* 11, 598–611. Barcelona: Universitat Pompeu Fabra.

de Swart, Peter & Helen de Hoop. 2018. Shifting animacy. *Theoretical Linguistics* 44(1–2). 1–23. https://doi.org/10.1515/tl-2018-0001.

Verhoeven, Elisabeth. 2014. Thematic prominence and animacy asymmetries. Evidence from a cross-linguistic production study. *Lingua* 143. 129–161. https://doi.org/10.1016/j.lingua.2014.02.002.

Zaenen, Annie. 1993. Unaccusativity in Dutch: Integrating syntax and lexical semantics. In James Pustejovski (ed.), *Semantics and the Lexicon*, 129–161. Dordrecht: Kluwer.

Zeevat, Henk. 2006. Freezing and Marking. *Linguistics* 44(5). 1095–1111. https://doi.org/10.1515/LING.2006.035.

Jeannique Darby, Artemis Alexiadou, Giorgos Spathas, Michael Walsh

Interpretability, aspectual coercion, and event structure in Object-Experiencer verbs: An acceptability study

Abstract: In this paper, we discuss an experimental, processing-based approach to English Object-Experiencer verbs. We argue that any investigation of the event structure properties of these verbs must crucially take into account not only considerations on the level of the verb, but also the influence of processes which take place when a verb is interpreted in context. We pay particular attention to the role of aspectual coercion, and its interaction with processing in judgments of acceptability. Our results support an analysis of Object-Experiencer verbs as comprising two sub-classes which differ in their event structure: one consisting of verbs which readily allow eventive and/or agentive readings, and the other containing essentially stative verbs, which may be more or less coerced into such readings. However, this latter group of states also behave differently from stative Subject-Experiencer verbs, in line with the causative nature of the former.

Keywords: object experiencer verbs, processing, aspectual coercion, stativity, agentivity

---

Acknowledgements: We are thankful to one anonymous reviewer and Elisabeth Verhoeven for their input. We started working on this paper a long time ago, when we were all members of the SFB 732 *Incremental Specification in Context* at the University of Stuttgart. The DFG support to that SFB as well as AL 554/8-1 (Alexiadou) are hereby acknowledged.

Jeannique Darby, Volda University College, Berte Kanutte-huset-216, 6103 Volda, Norway, e-mail: jeannique.anne.darby@hivolda.no
Artemis Alexiadou, Humboldt-Universität zu Berlin, Unter den Linden 6, 10099 Berlin, Germany, & Leibniz-Zentrum Allgemeine Sprachwissenschaft e-mail: artemis.alexiadou@hu-berlin.de
Giorgos Spathas, Leibniz-Zentrum Allgemeine Sprachwissenschaft, Schützenstraße 18, 10117 Berlin, Germany, e-mail: spathas@leibniz-zas.de
Michael Walsh, Australian National University, e-mail: michael.walsh@aiatsis.gov.au

https://doi.org/10.1515/9783110757255-006

1 Introduction

Psychological ('psych') verbs like *fear*, *frighten*, and *fascinate* describe the emotional state of an Experiencer argument. We focus on a sub-group of these verbs, the Object-Experiencer ('ObEx') verbs, which realize their Experiencer as a direct object (1a,b). Other verbs like *fear* in (1c) instead express the Experiencer in the subject position ('SubEx').[1]

(1)   a. The wolves frightened John.
        b. Wolves fascinate John.
        c. John fears wolves.

Which of these syntactic patterns a verb employs is thought to be connected to the verb's event structure, and the way in which the eventuality is conceptualized. Broadly, SubEx verbs like *fear* belong to the class of stative predicates, and they express an unbounded, static relation (Grimshaw 1990; Pustejovsky 1991; Rothmayr 2009; Landau 2010). ObEx verbs meanwhile describe a bounded situation that comes about due to a causal force (Dowty 1991; Croft 1993; Iwata 1995; Pesetsky 1995; Arad 1998; DiDesidero 1999; Biały 2005, *inter alia*). These kinds of aspectual differences have further implications for the expected syntactic behavior of these verbs more generally, as well as for theories of how the semantics of verbs and their arguments is mapped onto the syntax (Grimshaw 1990; Dowty 1991; Croft 1993; Levin & Rappaport Hovav 1995, 2005; Rappaport Hovav & Levin 1998, *inter alia*). However, while researchers generally agree regarding the stativity of SubEx verbs, the more precise aspectual properties of the ObEx class have been widely debated. Based on different verbs' potential for certain readings, many theories assume that ObEx verbs divide into at least two aspectual sub-types: i) verbs which are ambiguous between a stative and an eventive/agentive reading (e.g. *frighten*), and ii) verbs which are strictly stative/non-agentive (e.g. *fascinate*). The latter of these crucially give rise to characteristic 'psych' syntax. However, the distinction between these sub-classes is subtle, and there is disagreement as to whether they should be defined by their eventivity, agentivity, or both. In section 2 we turn to a detailed discussion of how these characteristics derive the various sub-classes of ObEx verbs. Analyses likewise differ concerning the aspectual class of the more restricted *fascinate*-verbs. Moreover, a

---

[1] We do not consider in depth those ObEx verbs which realize their Experiencer as a dative or indirect object (e.g. *appeal*: *The movie appeals to John*). For further discussion, see Belletti & Rizzi (1988).

recent experimental study (Grafmiller 2013) rejects the idea of aspectual subclasses altogether, as corpus and acceptability data suggest that these sub-groups do not have categorically different behavior in eventive/agentive contexts.

This paper investigates these conflicting claims within the context of a large-scale acceptability task. The goal of this task is to clarify whether and how any distinctions in eventivity and agentivity are manifested in the class of ObEx verbs. In particular, we focus on the behavior of the 'psych' *fascinate*-verbs, in order to contribute to a better understanding of how their aspectual features condition their syntactic behavior. We address the following questions:

(i) *Do ObEx verbs fall into two (or more) groups according to their potential for an agentive and/or eventive reading?*

   a. *If so, do these groups differ in eventivity, or only in agentivity*
   b. *Which aspectual class do the more restricted* fascinate-*verbs belong to?*

(ii) *To what extent might gradience between sub-classes of ObEx verbs be due to either aspectual coercion or comprehension factors? In other words, how does the behavior of ObEx verbs compare to that of other, more homogeneous verb classes with clearer aspectual properties?*

We therefore take issue with the claim that there is only one aspectual class of ObEx verbs, and report the results of an offline judgment study which takes factors like these into account. The results of our study are consistent with theories which assume that ObEx verbs consist of a sub-class of eventive/ambiguous verbs like *frighten*, and a sub-class of stative verbs like *fascinate* –specifically, a sub-class of 'causative states' (Arad 1998; Pylkkänen 2000). Although the distinctions between the two groups are indeed gradient rather than categorical, we argue that our results are best interpreted in light of the potential for aspectual coercion, and the way in which this mechanism interacts with comprehension and acceptability. In particular, we propose that ObEx causative states may allow for 'additive coercion' (van Lambalgen & Hamm 2005; Bott 2010; Bott 2015). This type of coercion functions as a repair mechanism that allows a stative verb to be (re-)interpreted as referring to a more complex eventuality, via a pragmatic operation in which missing elements are 'added' by the reader/hearer on the basis of world knowledge and contextual inference. We propose that this operation leads to greater difficulty in the processing of stative ObEx verbs in eventive/agentive contexts – thereby decreasing acceptability – but that successful completion of the repair ultimately results in degraded acceptability, rather than outright ungrammaticality.

The structure of the paper is as follows. Section 2 outlines three general claims made regarding the agentivity and eventivity of ObEx verbs, which will form the basis for our investigation. In Section 3 we discuss the potential influences of aspectual coercion and comprehension, and sketch predictions for how these factors might affect the acceptability of ObEx verbs in agentive/eventive contexts. The methods and results of our judgment task are described in Section 4, followed by a discussion of the theoretical implications of these results in Section 5. Section 6 concludes.

2 Aspectual sub-classes of ObEx verbs

The debate regarding the event structure of ObEx verbs stems in part from their aspectual ambiguity, with many of them giving rise to both eventive and stative readings (Grimshaw 1990; Pesetsky 1995; Arad 1998; Landau 2010, *inter alia*). Acceptability in contexts like purpose clauses, the progressive (2), or the imperative is usually used to disentangle these, often subtly different, readings:

(2) a. **Eventive:** Nina is frightening Laura.
b. **Stative:** *Nuclear war is frightening Laura.

The aspectual differences between the readings are paralleled in their syntactic behavior: in readings like (2a), psych verbs behave like typical causative, transitive verbs. In contrast, stative readings like (2b) seem to be associated with unique 'psych' syntactic properties, such as restrictions on extraction from the object and differences in forward and backward binding patterns (Belletti & Rizzi 1988; Arad 1998; Landau 2010; but cf. Grafmiller 2013).

Crucially, some ObEx verbs like *depress*, *concern*, and *disgust* seem to only permit these stative readings, and may therefore sound odd with purpose clauses/ the progressive:

(3) a. Nina depressed Laura (*to make her go away)./??Odd noises were continually depressing Sue.
b. Nina concerned Laura (*to make her go away)./*The news is concerning us.
c. Nina disgusted Laura (*to make her go away)./*Nina is disgusting Laura.
(Grimshaw 1990; Pesetsky 1995; Arad 1998)

Thus, unlike stative SubEx verbs, ObEx verbs seem to fall into two aspectual sub-types: those which allow eventive readings, and those which do not.

A number of theoretical approaches have aimed to answer such questions, and it is generally agreed that the syntax of eventive readings like (2a) is due to the fact that their event structure is similar to that of other causative verbs: aspectually causative, and change-of-state (i.e. from a state of 'not frightened' to 'frightened'). What is less clear are the exact properties which distinguish such readings from the 'psych' readings, and the *depress*-verbs from those like *frighten*. Below we outline two prevalent theoretical analyses of these aspectual contrasts, as well as a recent approach which argues against both analyses on the basis of further empirical data.

2.1 Eventive vs. stative causation

One common view is that it is the stativity of the verb or reading in itself which predicts psych behavior – more specifically, whether the verb describes a static eventuality as opposed to a *change* of state (Pesetsky 1995; Arad 1998; Alexiadou & Iordăchioaia 2014). Based on this, we can identify two classes of ObEx verbs: i) eventive/ambiguous verbs, which on their eventive readings describe a change-of-state and have typical transitive causative syntax; and ii) stative verbs like *depress/concern/disgust*, which do not allow eventive change-of-state readings, and thus exhibit psych behavior. However, in line with their distinct syntax, these stative ObEx verbs are thought to have a different conceptualization from simple, unbounded states like SubEx *fear*. Instead, they denote complex 'causative states', which consist of two causally-related sub-eventualities: the perception of a stimulus subject (e.g. *blood sausage* in (4)), and the mental state triggered by this stimulus (e.g. *disgust*; illustrated in (4) following Arad 1998 and Pylkkänen 2000; see also Croft 1993; DiDesidero 1999; Kratzer 2000; Biały 2005, *inter alia*).

(4) Blood sausage disgusts Nina.

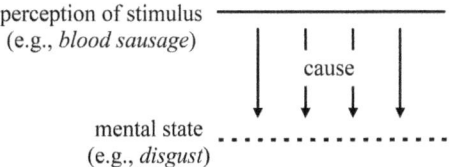

(adapted from Arad 1998)

The physical or mental perception of the stimulus is co-temporal with the mental state, and hence bounds it: as long as (and only when) the subject is perceived or thought about, it causes the mental state to hold.[2]

Under this analysis, there are two key properties which distinguish causative ObEx states from the eventive readings of *frighten*-verbs. Firstly, although the beginning and end of a causative state are bounded by perception of the stimulus, there is no *change*-of-state (e.g. from 'not disgusted' to 'disgusted' or vice versa) directly encoded in the meaning of the verb; rather, there is simply a relation that holds between the stimulus and the Experiencer during the time the stimulus is perceived. The second distinction is that, unlike eventive ObEx verbs, the causal relationship as in (4) requires neither action nor intent on the part of the (possibly inanimate) stimulus subject. As Arad (1998) describes it, the stimulus is not 'doing' anything (whether intentionally or not), but rather "[i]t is something *about* it which triggers the mental state." Causative states thus parallel other stative verbs in that their subject is not an Agent; *unlike* typical states, however, this subject does share with Agents its status as the initiator of a "causal chain" (see, e.g., Croft 1993; Grimshaw 1990; García-Pardo 2018) – it is what Pesetsky (1995) calls a "Causer".[3] In sum, this analysis argues that there is sub-class of stative ObEx verbs which is aspectually distinct – not only from eventive/ambiguous ObEx verbs, but from SubEx verbs as well.

2.2 Agentive vs. non-agentive events

While the above analyses focus mainly on the aspectual class of the verb, others suggest that the thematic role of the subject is of greater importance in determining psych behavior. Thus, although *Nuclear war frightened Laura* may indeed have a stative interpretation (made more salient in the simple present *Nuclear war frightens Laura*), many have argued that it is not stativity *per se* which conditions this reading's psych syntax, but rather the associated lack of an Agent argument (Grimshaw 1990; DiDesidero 1999; Landau 2010). Accordingly, it is only those readings/verbs which are non-agentive which give rise to psych effects. Any non-agentive readings like (5a,b) should therefore pattern

---

[2] This is argued by Pylkkänen (2000) to be indicative of its status as a stage-level rather than individual-level state (see Carlson 1977).
[3] This is distinct from the use of the term "Causer" in Arad (1998) and Alexiadou & Iordăchioaia (2014). We will follow Pesetsky (1995) here in using it to refer to the subjects of both stative and eventive non-agentive causatives (see section 2.2 below).

with stative readings, even if they are interpreted as involving an event (e.g. something happens which causes Laura to become frightened):

(5) a. Nina frightened Laura unintentionally/accidentally.
    b. The explosion/the noise/the thunderstorm frightened Laura.
       (Arad 1998)

The potential for an agentive reading is also seen as the most relevant property separating verbs like *depress/concern/disgust* from verbs like *frighten*, with the former being strictly 'non-agentive'. This is suggested not only by their incompatibility with purpose clauses as in (3), but also by their oddness with adverbs of intent or the imperative, even when the subject is animate (Arad 1998; DiDesidero 1999; Landau 2010):

(6) a. Nina (deliberately) frightened Laura./Frighten the birds!
    b. Nina (*deliberately) concerned Laura./*Depress Laura!

In terms of event structure, Landau (2010) argues that the agentive/non-agentive distinction is also associated with important aspectual differences. Agentive change-of-state readings like (2a, 6a) are claimed to be durative, telic accomplishments in the sense of Vendler (1957) – that is, they involve a process (e.g. of Nina doing something which will frighten Laura) and a natural endpoint (e.g. Laura becomes frightened), with an accompanying change of the Experiencer's mental state. In contrast, non-agentive readings and verbs are either states or, more likely, achievements. According to Landau (2010: 129), "relatively few" ObEx verbs are strictly stative (among them, *concern* and *depress*); rather, most of the ones that disallow agentive readings are instantaneous, eventive achievements, with the Experiencer in these cases describing a place "where a mental state . . . appears" (Landau 2010: 131). Together with (non-)agentivity, an ObEx verb's syntax is thus argued to be tied to its aspectual sub-classification as either i) a non-agentive achievement or state; or ii) an agentive accomplishment. From this perspective, the key differences between these sub-classes are that the eventualities expressed by the former group of verbs involve neither a process nor an Agent, in contrast to the latter. However, aside from the few states like *concern/depress*, all ObEx verbs are argued to be eventive.[4]

---

[4] There is a third recent approach by Marin & McNally (2011), who argue on the basis of Spanish data that psychological verbs marked with reflexive morphology are inchoative. For these

2.3 Gradient agentivity/eventivity

Many theoretical analyses like the above have argued in favour of sub-dividing ObEx verbs according to the features of their event structure; however, it is still not clear precisely what these features are. A recent study by Grafmiller (2013) thus takes a more experimental approach to distinguishing these sub-classes, and notes that part of this lack of consensus is due to disagreement over what the data look like in the first place.

In an effort to clarify this subtle data, Grafmiller (2013) uses an acceptability task to investigate the naturalness of 20 ObEx verbs in several agentive diagnostic contexts (e.g. with an agentive adverb like *deliberately*).[5] In this task, it was found that speakers rated agentive sentences as significantly more acceptable on average when they contained verbs characterized as agentive/eventive in the literature (e.g. *frighten*, *scare*), as compared to typical "non-agentive/stative" verbs (e.g. *depress*, *concern*, *fascinate*). However, when looking at the mean rating of each verb individually, the results revealed a continuous, gradient distribution with extensive variation in both hypothesized sub-classes, along with several verbs which were much more or less acceptable than expected. Moreover, the two sub-groups did not simply cluster on opposite ends of the acceptability scale; rather, their distributions displayed substantial overlap, such that there was no clear point of division between them. These results – combined with corpus examples of typical purportedly stative/non-agentive verbs in 'disallowed' contexts (7a/b below) – lead Grafmiller to conclude that English ObEx verbs do *not* form coherent sub-classes based on their potential for agentivity/eventivity. Instead, they belong to a single aspectual type, and any of them can be used to describe a dynamic and/or agentive event, to a greater or lesser extent. The gradient differences between different verbs, and the relative unnaturalness of verbs like *depress* and *concern* in these contexts are instead attributed to conceptual characteristics of the emotion they describe, combined with surrounding discourse context and pragmatic inferences.

(7)   a. The human race is constantly depressing me...
       b. I'm going to purposely bore you with this tip, but it TOTALLY WORKS.
       (Google; Grafmiller 2013: 114; 225)

---

authors, inchoativity is very different from telicity. Our results seem to suggest that this approach cannot be extended to English.

5 See also Verhoeven (2010) for a study which indicates cross-linguistic differences in the agentivity and eventivity of ObEx verbs.

Grafmiller argues that there are no clear sub-classes, but instead a completely continuous gradient distribution, where differences between verbs are due to world knowledge, likelihood of scenario, discourse context, etc. He also rejects coercion under the assumption that the non-agentive verbs could not appear in agentive/eventive contexts if they needed to be coerced. The main place where we disagree is that 1) we do think there will be clearer (though gradient) sub-classes and 2) argue that coercion has observable effects, i.e. not by completely restricting the contexts for these verbs, but by allowing them only with increased difficulty. That said, the same pragmatic/discourse factors he discusses likely also affect coercion.

Grafmiller's results suggest that introspection alone does not reveal the whole picture, as it will not necessarily capture potentially informative fine-grained patterns of variation. The corpus data also provide evidence that, regardless of how we analyze "stative/non-agentive" verbs, their use in eventive/agentive contexts is not outright prohibited. However, this non-categorical data does not necessarily require us to conclude that there are no aspectually distinct sub-classes of ObEx verbs. Firstly, there is little discussion of how the patterns found in this class compare to those of other, aspectually clearer verbs in the same diagnostic contexts.[6] Such comparison could provide an indication of the degree of gradience in acceptability which might be *independent* of verb type, and may also further clarify exactly which aspectual features ObEx verbs share with other verb classes. Furthermore, while Grafmiller (2013) notes that pragmatic and discourse factors can influence acceptability, he fails to account for the possibility that these and other linguistic and extra-linguistic factors – specifically sentence complexity, interpretability, and aspectual coercion – can in fact influence judgments in such a way that they *obscure* distinctions that are more clearly delineated in the underlying grammar. In particular, aspectual coercion can serve to increase the flexibility of a verb in terms of the contexts it can appear in, which may lead to more "fuzzy" aspectual distinctions – though, as we will argue, certain patterns can still be observed.

---

[6] Grafmiller (2013) in fact includes such verbs in the acceptability task, but does not report on their behavior in detail.

3 Interpretability, aspectual coercion, and gradient acceptability

Acceptability judgments are not solely a reflection of grammaticality (Miller & Chomsky 1963; Gerken & Bever 1986; Haider 2007; Sprouse et al. 2011, *inter alia*). Rather, in order to judge the acceptability of a sentence, speakers must at least partially read, parse, and interpret the sentence to be judged. As these procedures are part of sentence processing and comprehension, they are affected by performance factors such as linguistic ability, attention, semantic or structural ambiguity, and processing difficulty. The operations taking place during processing are of course many and complex, and single-point, offline judgments cannot capture all of the steps involved in arriving at a final response. However, such judgments have been found to broadly correlate with more general effects observed in online processing studies, such as the relative difficulty of parsing or interpreting a sentence (Bader & Meng 1999; Keller 2000; Fanselow and Frisch 2006; Alexopoulou and Keller 2007; Bornkessel-Schlesewsky & Schlesewsky 2007; Hofmeister et al. 2007; Sprouse 2008, *inter alia*). All other things being equal, the relationship between interpretability and acceptability is one in which sentences which require more effort to interpret are in turn judged as less acceptable, while less difficult sentences are judged more favorably. For example, Bornkessel-Schlesewsky and Schlesewsky (2007) report ERP evidence that temporary argument structure ambiguities in German are more difficult to process when the object precedes the subject rather than vice versa, although both are grammatical. The additional difficulty found for these sentences was also paralleled by lower acceptability ratings, both in speeded and offline tasks. Similar patterns are found in other studies: e.g. Hofmeister et al. (2007). Similarly, ungrammatical sentences which differ in relative interpretability may likewise differ in acceptability. For instance, although (8) and (9) are both ungrammatical, the former is easier to interpret, and would therefore likely be judged as comparatively more acceptable (or less unacceptable).

(8) *This be not a good sentence.

(9) *Sentence good not a be this.
 (Haider 2007: 390)

As Haider (2007) notes, this difference is related to how easy it is to repair the incorrect sentence: the easier the repair (e.g. replace the infinitive in 8 with a finite verb), the easier the sentence is to interpret, and vice versa (Featherston 2007; Haider 2007). Although these judgments represent a fairly coarse-grained reflection of processing, there is evidence that the relative acceptability of particular structures can provide an indication of underlying difficulties in interpretation and repair. As such, acceptability judgments may be subject to some of the same factors that affect sentence processing and comprehension. Importantly, such processing factors like interpretability and repair are continuous rather than categorical, with no clearly defined boundary between e.g. "easy to interpret" and "difficult". Their influence on acceptability may therefore result in greater variation even among sentences which should be similar in (un-)grammaticality; this, in turn, may make the boundaries of some distinctions less clear.

Although not all cases of gradient acceptability can be reduced to such processing factors (Keller 2000; Fanselow et al. 2006; Featherston 2007 and replies; Sprouse 2007; Schütze & Sprouse 2013, *inter alia*), there is reason to believe that interpretability and ease of repair are directly relevant to the assessment of event structure in ObEx verbs, due to the potential for a particular type of repair strategy known as *aspectual coercion*. Aspectual coercion involves a meaning shift or enrichment, which may be used as a means of resolving an aspectual conflict between the lexical aspect of a verb and its surrounding context – for instance, any strictly stative/non-agentive ObEx verbs in contexts that select for eventive/agentive verbs (Moens & Steedman 1988; Pustejovsky 1995; Jackendoff 1997; De Swart 1998; Zucchi 1998; Michaelis 2004; Bott 2010; Brennan & Pylkkänen 2010; Lauwers & Williams 2011; Bott 2015, *inter alia*). If the meaning of the sentence is taken at face value, the conflict may initially yield an uninterpretable sentence; however, in changing the meaning via coercion, the sentence may be "repaired", allowing a listener to arrive at a more reasonable interpretation. For instance, the verb *reach* as in *Harry reached the top of the mountain* describes an instantaneous change from not being at the top to being at the top (i.e. an achievement; Rothstein 2004). The progressive, in contrast, selects for eventualities that contain an ongoing process (Moens & Steedman 1988). When the two are combined in *Harry is reaching the top*, the result is difficult to interpret at face value, given that the instantaneous duration of *reach* is at odds with the interpretation that there is an extended, ongoing process of *reaching the top*. In order to resolve this conflict and repair the sentence, listeners may enrich the meaning of *reach* in this context by assuming that there is some other unspecified process that is ongoing, and which should eventually culminate in "reaching the top of the mountain". Barring additional context, world knowledge suggests that this process is 'climbing'. This results in the repaired interpretation of *Harry is reaching the top of the mountain* as "Harry is in the process of *climbing* to the top of the mountain" – despite the fact that "climbing" is neither overtly expressed, nor encoded in the meaning of the verb *reach* (Moens & Steedman 1988; Steedman 2005; Bott 2010). This type of enrichment falls under what Hamm and van Lambalgen (2005) refer to as *additive coercion*, as it involves the "adding in" of an element of meaning (e.g. 'climbing') that is not encoded in the verb's semantics (see also Bott 2010, 2015).[7] As this element is not overtly expressed, listeners must themselves employ world knowledge and discourse context in order to select the most plausible meaning that will make the sentence interpretable.

In line with this, sentences which involve aspectual coercion have also been associated with increased processing costs in online comprehension tasks, as compared to cases where the verb and its context match (Piñango et al. 1999; Todorova et al. 2000; Husband et al. 2006; Brennan & Pylkkänen 2008, 2010; Bott 2010, 2015; though cf. Pickering et al. 2006). Coerced sentences thus lead to slower reading times in self-paced reading (Todorova et al. 2000; Brennan & Pylkkänen 2008, 2010; Bott 2010), as well as increased processing load and/or semantic mismatch effects as measured via MEG/EEG (Brennan & Pylkkänen 2008, 2010; Bott 2015). This suggests that sentences involving aspectual coercion are comparatively more difficult to process, potentially as a result of the additional operation(s) a listener has to perform in order to interpret the sentence. In terms of acceptability, the increased difficulty in interpreting these coerced sentences predicts lower relative acceptability as compared to cases with no aspectual mismatch (and hence no need for coercion). This proposal is supported by the results of "makes sense" judgments included with the self-paced reading and neurological measures in several studies (Brennan & Pylkkänen 2010; Bott 2010, 2015). When participants were given 4–5 seconds to judge sentences as sensible or nonsensical, sentences with coercion received significantly fewer "yes, makes sense" judgments as compared to non-mismatch controls (but cf. Brennan & Pylkkänen 2008).[8]

Nevertheless, we do not necessarily predict that sentences like *Harry is reaching the top* should be as unacceptable as sentences which are clearly ungrammatical, like **Sentence good not a be this*. If we understand coercion as a

---

[7] They also discuss other types of aspectual coercion (see also Bott 2010, 2015); however, additive coercion is the most relevant for the purposes of this paper (see also section Discussion/predictions). Strictly speaking, the progressive also requires the removal or defocusing of the culmination of the eventuality (e.g. the moment of 'reaching'); however, see Bott & Hamm (2014).

[8] Similar patterns have been found in studies of "complement coercion" (e.g. *begin the book* where one must infer an unexpressed activity such as *reading* or *writing*), where coercion elicits increased difficulty in online processing and decreased acceptability (McElree et al. 2001; Pylkkänen & McElree 2007, *inter alia*).

repair mechanism, then successful completion of the coercion operation should result in a reasonable 'repaired' interpretation. Sentences which may be repaired via aspectual coercion should thus be more acceptable than those where repair is more difficult or unavailable, thereby partially mitigating the effects of increased difficulty. The availability of coercion may therefore be responsible for the occurrence in natural language of apparently "disallowed" aspectual combinations, such as *I'm going to purposely bore you with this tip* (Grafmiller 2013: 225). The positive influence of successful coercion is further supported by the 'makes sense' judgments for coerced sentences in Bott (2010, 2015) – although these sentences were judged as sensible less often than the control sentences, participants were still significantly more likely to say they made sense as compared to mismatch cases where resolution was not possible (e.g. **For two hours the ranger discovered the trap/the climber reached the top*). Whether or not a reasonable repair is available will of course depend on verb- and context-specific factors to some extent, as whether or not a plausible additional meaning can be located will vary according to the situation the sentence describes (Moens & Steedman 1988; Bott 2010). The success of coercion may itself thus also vary on a verb-by-verb basis, resulting in a more continuous spread of ratings.

In what follows we therefore take a view of aspectual coercion as a repair mechanism which may be triggered in cases of aspectual mismatch, and whose processes – though undoubtedly more complex than described here – may be broadly reflected in judgments of acceptability. In the case of additive coercion, we expect lower acceptability relative to non-mismatch controls. Conversely, we also expect that successfully coerced sentences will be more acceptable than cases where a reasonable repair is unavailable. The competing influences of increased difficulty and successful repair thus predict that sentences with aspectual coercion will elicit ratings which are *intermediate* between "fully acceptable" and "fully unacceptable". As coercion, like processing in general, may be affected by non-categorical factors, we therefore argue that the discovery of gradient acceptability in ObEx verbs does not *in itself* entail that the grammatical constraints underlying them are gradient as well (Chomsky 1965; Newmeyer 2007; Sprouse 2007, *inter alia*). Rather, the behavior of ObEx verbs (and other verbs) within agentive/eventive contexts will reflect these influences, which will in turn affect how these patterns should be analyzed and interpreted.

4 An acceptability study of agentivity and eventivity in ObEx verbs

This task investigated the relative acceptability of four types of verbs in agentive and/or eventive contexts:
1) purported "agentive/eventive" ObEx verbs (*'**ObExAgentive**'*)
2) purported "non-agentive" or "stative" ObEx verbs (*'**ObExNon-Agentive**'*)
3) non-agentive/stative SubEx verbs (*'**SubEx**'*)
4) agentive/eventive verbs (*'**Event**'*)

ObEx verbs were sorted according to their most common labels in the literature (see section 4.1/stimuli). Each verb was tested in three different sentence contexts: i) an agentive context, ii) an eventive context with an animate subject, and iii) an eventive context with an inanimate subject in order to check whether there are non-agentive eventive verbs. The acceptability of these sentences was assessed using an offline judgement task, in which speakers rated isolated sentences according to how natural they sounded (see Grafmiller 2013; Verhoeven 2010).

The primary goal was to test the extent to which ObEx verbs form aspectually distinct sub-classes such as the ones proposed above. However, we also probe beyond these groups, to address the question of where and on what basis such distinctions should be made – if at all. Importantly, the behavior of the ObEx verbs – both individually, and in terms of their distribution – is directly compared to that of other stative/non-agentive (SubEx) and eventive/agentive verbs (Event) in the same contexts. This comparison has two purposes: first, it will help to clarify the extent to which any gradience between aspectual (sub-)classes might be the result of coercion and/or general word knowledge factors. Second, it will help determine whether any potential sub-groups of ObEx verbs behave more like states, or more like eventive/agentive verbs – or whether they tend to be intermediate, suggesting some degree of coercion. This will further help to identify any sub-classes of aspectually more restricted ObEx verbs, as well as assess whether such verbs are primarily stative or simply non-agentive.

To investigate these issues, our study employs three different approaches to analyzing the acceptability ratings:
(1) A standard **linear mixed effects model (LME)** with Verb Type (4 groups: ObExAgentive, ObExNon-Agentive, SubEx, and Event) as the fixed effect of interest, as well as random effects for participants and verbs;
(2) A **qualitative scatterplot assessment** of how the individual verbs in each group are distributed, based on the mean rating for each verb;

(3) An **agglomerative hierarchical cluster analysis**, using the mean rating for each verb. This method starts with each verb's mean treated as a separate cluster, and at each step joins two increasingly larger clusters until all verbs belong to a single cluster. The more similar two clusters are, the earlier they will be joined.

The focus of the first analysis is on how acceptable each verb group is as a whole, and how it compares to the other three groups. The **LME** will compare overall ratings for each Verb Type, and test whether there are significant, consistent differences in acceptability between the four types, once verb-specific variation is accounted for. As discussed in section 2.3, however, this analysis may not give a complete picture: even if the overall means of two groups are distinct, the boundaries between them may not be. Additionally, the LME will not tell us whether any verbs behave more like members of a different group, or whether any groups might contain further potential sub-divisions.

The **scatterplot** and **cluster analyses** thus focus on these more fine-grained patterns of behavior. The data are broken down into the mean ratings for each individual verb, in order to assess how different verbs are distributed with respect to members of their own group and others. The scatterplot of these means will allow us to further examine the boundaries between the groups, and assess their degree of distinctness or overlap, as well as the amount of variability each group displays. It will also enable us to identify whether there are any natural divisions either within or across the groups, and whether these coincide with the initial Verb Type divisions that are based on the literature.

The **cluster analysis** of the verb means will serve to further quantify these impressions, as it will group verbs based solely on the means, with no assumptions about the number or structure of groups. The resulting dendrogram will be assessed with respect to where divisions are made; which verbs cluster together and how tightly; and how late particular clusters are joined, as a measure of their distinctiveness.

4.1 Methods

4.1.1 Participants

There were 152 participants in total, recruited via the internet. Participants were self-reported native speakers of any dialect of English and were between the ages of 17 and 60 (mean 27.6).

4.1.2 Materials and design

The task contained 72 verbs: 36 ObEx verbs, and 36 comparison verbs (18 SubEx verbs and 18 agentive/eventive 'Event' verbs). The ObEx verbs were drawn from previous studies (Pesetsky 1995; Verhoeven 2010; Grafmiller 2013; Alexiadou & Iordăchioaia 2014), and comprised 19 verbs claimed to allow agentive/eventive readings (ObExAgentive), and 17 verbs typically said to be stative/non-agentive (ObExNon-Agentive). The 36 comparison verbs were drawn from databases and dictionaries of English (the British National Corpus, CIT; CELEX, Baayen et al. 1993; *Merriam-Webster's Collegiate Dictionary*), and consisted of transitive verbs which allowed both human subjects and human objects. 18 of these were SubEx verbs, while 18 were eventive ('Event') verbs. All verbs in the latter group allowed (but did not require) Agents.

Each verb was embedded in a base sentence for use within the test contexts (see below). Base sentences for all contexts used a simple Subject-Verb-Object structure, with the verb in the past tense. The resulting sentences thus varied according to the factor of Verb Type, with four possible levels (ObExAgentive, ObExNon-Agentive, SubEx, or Event), illustrated in Table 1.[9]

Table 1: Number of verbs by Verb Type.

Verb Type	Number of verbs	Example base sentences
ObExAgentive	19	Michael *frightened* Laura.
ObExNon-Agentive	17	The hostess *charmed* the visitors.
SubEx	18	The shopkeeper *hated* the tourists.
Event	18	The nurse *tickled* the baby.

These 72 verbs within their base sentences were tested in three diagnostic contexts: i) an agentive context ii) an eventive context with an animate subject; and iii) an eventive context with an inanimate subject. The contexts are summarized and exemplified in Table 2 below.

---

[9] A full list of the verbs and their ratings on all conditions is included in the Appendix. All verbs were tested in the three diagnostic contexts in Table 2, which provides an example sentence for each context.

Table 2: Diagnostic contexts.

Context	Diagnostic	Example
Agentive	Agentive adverb (*deliberately, intentionally, on purpose*)	Michael intentionally *frightened* Laura.
Eventive + animate subject	*What happened was* . . . + animate subject	What happened was the reporter *surprised* the politician.
Eventive + inanimate subject	*What happened was* . . . + inanimate subject	What happened was the breeze *annoyed* the jogger.

The **agentive context** consisted of modification by agentive adverbs which "relate solely to degree of intent": *deliberately, intentionally,* and *on purpose* (Grafmiller 2013: 223; see also Verhoeven 2010).[10] Each verb was presented with one of the three selected adverbs as in (10) below.[11] All other things being equal, these adverbs should be acceptable only with verbs that allow an agentive reading.

(10) a. **ObExAgentive:** The boy deliberately upset Carol.
   b. **ObExNon-Agentive:** Isobel intentionally fascinated Alex.
   c. **SubEx:** The shopkeeper deliberately hated the tourists.
   d. **Event:** The nurse deliberately tickled the baby.

The second context tested the availability of an **eventive + animate subject** reading, using the *What happened was* . . . frame (Jackendoff 1983).[12] This frame selects for all verbs with eventive readings, regardless of either their aspectual sub-type or whether they allow an agentive subject.

---

[10] Other alternative diagnostics (e.g. the imperative, adverbs like *patiently*, and embedding under control verbs) are either not restricted to agentive uses, or are restricted to only a subset of agentive verbs. For more details regarding the problems with several typical agentivity diagnostics, see Grafmiller (2013: 227ff) and Verhoeven (2010).

[11] Speakers deemed the alternative *purposely* to be "unusual" during a pilot of this study. The phrasal form *on purpose* was presented sentence-finally.

[12] The more commonly used progressive in fact only permits predicates which have duration, and is thus odd with eventive achievements. Other eventivity tests are problematic for different reasons, with many actually diagnosing agentivity (see e.g. Lakoff 1966; Carlson 1977; Dowty 1979; Rothstein 2004; Grafmiller 2013, *inter alia*).

(11) a. **ObExAgentive:** What happened was Michael frightened Laura.
　　b. **ObExNon-Agentive:** What happened was George disgusted Karen.
　　c. **SubEx:** What happened was Thomas loved his grandfather.
　　d. **Event:** What happened was David hit his friend.

The final test context was the ***eventive + inanimate subject*** context, which investigated whether each verb allowed an eventive reading when there was no agentive interpretation available – i.e. a non-agentive eventive reading. Each ObEx and Event verb thus also appeared with an inanimate subject in the *What happened was . . .* frame. In principle, this context should be acceptable only for those verbs that allow an eventive reading without an Agent.[13]

(12) a. **ObExAgentive:** What happened was the thunder startled the baby.
　　b. **ObExNon-Agentive:** What happened was the book fascinated Alex.
　　c. **Event:** What happened was the rock hit the car.

There were therefore 198 test sentences across the three contexts. Additionally, each verb was also presented in its base sentence form as a filler. In total there were 270 sentences: 4 each for the 36 ObEx and 18 Event verbs, and 3 for the 18 SubEx verbs. These sentences were divided and counterbalanced over four questionnaire versions, such that each verb appeared only once (i.e. in a single context) within each version.[14] This design served to minimize any attenuation of relative difficulty or unacceptability that might result from stimulus repetition (Hofmeister et al. 2013).[15]

4.1.3 Procedure

The four 72-sentence questionnaires were presented online via Qualtrics (www.qualtrics.com). Each version of the questionnaire was given to 38 participants (152 in total); each participant completed only one version. Participants were instructed to provide a rating for each sentence according to how natural the sentence would sound in a conversation. Ratings were given on a 1–7 continuous

---

13 SubEx verbs were not presented in this context, as they require animate subjects; as such, the clear ungrammaticality of these sentences may have led to an artificial increase in the apparent acceptability of other sentence types (Haider 2007; Schütze & Sprouse 2013).
14 Each SubEx filler sentence appeared in two versions of the questionnaire.
15 Repetition within multiple agentive contexts may partially account for the lack of a clearer division in Grafmiller's (2013) results.

sliding scale, with 7 indicating 'perfectly natural'. Each questionnaire began with two filler sentences, followed by the rest of the sentences presented in a different random order for each participant. Questionnaires were completed in 15.75 minutes on average.

4.2 Results

Responses from two participants who finished the questionnaire in less than five minutes were removed (cf. Grafmiller 2013), as were those from four participants who provided the same rating for more than 70 % of their responses (well outside two standard deviations from the mean across participants). Raw ratings were z-score normalized by participant to correct for participant-specific scale bias or compression (cf. Schütze & Sprouse 2013).

Normalized ratings were further analyzed separately for each diagnostic context.[16] To correct for the possible influence of factors like participant attention or error, outlying ratings for individual verbs in a particular context (>2 standard deviations from the verb's mean rating in that context) were removed (4.9 % of the data).[17] The influence of verb frequency was then minimized by residualizing the remaining ratings using log surface frequency of the past tense form. The residualized ratings were used as input to all further analyses; more positive scores indicate higher acceptability.

The LME analyses were conducted in R (version 3.3.2) using the *lme4* package (Bates et al. 2012), and were structured in the same way for all three contexts. Residualized ratings were analyzed as the dependent variable, with Verb Type (4 levels: Event, ObExAgentive, ObExNon-Agentive, and SubEx) as a fixed effect. Levels of Verb Type were dummy coded using Event as the reference level. Random effects included intercepts for participants and verbs, and by-participant slopes for the effect of Verb Type. For the fixed effect tests, all *t*-values with an absolute value greater than 2 were considered significant (following Baayen 2008). Parameter estimates (Est.) and standard errors (SE) are reported below. For the cluster analyses, we report the results of Ward's method. This method is akin to

---

[16] The fact that the SubEx verbs do not appear in the inanimate subject condition precludes a larger analysis of the combined data. Additionally, combining the different diagnostics could obscure potential (sub-)patterns if the diagnostics differ in terms of either baseline acceptability, or the degree to which they induce coercion (Moens & Steedman 1988; Bott 2010, 2015).

[17] These data points were only outliers in terms of the verb means used in the scatterplot and cluster analyses; they were excluded from the LME analyses for consistency. We also conducted LMEs which included these outliers, and patterns of significance did not differ.

an analysis of variance, and at each joining step tries to minimize the variance within clusters based on the error sum of squares that results from the join.[18]

4.2.1 Agentive context

The LME revealed significant effects for Verb Type at the levels of ObExNon-Agentive (Est. = −0.93, SE = 0.14, t = −6.49) and SubEx (Est. = −1.71, SE = 0.14, t = −11.97); there was no significant effect at the level of ObExAgentive (Est. = −0.004, SE = 0.14, t = −0.03). Least squares means and standard errors output by the model for each of the four groups are summarized in Table 3. To further assess the overall differences between each group, we conducted planned pairwise comparisons using Bonferroni-adjusted t-tests of least squares mean differences; groups which are significantly different from one another are assigned different letters in Table 3.

Table 3: Least-squares means and standard errors of ratings by Verb Type (Agentive condition).

Verb Type	Least-squares mean	SE	Letter
Event	0.649	0.099	A
ObExAgentive	0.645	0.097	A
ObExNon-Agentive	−0.279	0.105	B
SubEx	−1.060	0.106	C

These analyses indicate a clear difference between Event verbs and SubEx verbs in the predicted direction: Event verbs are, on average, judged to be significantly more acceptable in an agentive, eventive context, while SubEx verbs are rated on the less acceptable end of the scale. The two groups of ObEx verbs pattern somewhat differently: on the one hand, ObExAgentive verbs are equally as acceptable as Event verbs in this context, and are rated significantly higher than the ObExNon-Agentive group. However, the latter are still overall significantly *better* in this context than stative SubEx verbs, and their ratings average around the middle of the distribution.

---

18 Results using other hierarchical clustering algorithms (average, centroid, complete linkage) did not differ substantially. For more details regarding clustering methods as applied to linguistic data, see, among others, Schulte im Walde (2003).

A somewhat more complex picture emerges when we examine how the individual verbs in each group are distributed. As expected, there is a degree of gradience and variability within all four groups. However, the Event and SubEx verbs cluster consistently on the opposing ends of the scale, and there is a fairly clear division between the two groups of verbs (apart from a low-rated Event outlier *rinse* at −0.39 and a higher rated SubEx outlier *worship* at −0.54, see Figure 1 plus full list in the Appendix). The same cannot be said for the two groups of ObEx verbs, however. While the ObExAgentive verbs are judged much like the Event ones, there is no clear division between the former group and the purportedly Non-Agentive verbs; indeed, at least five "Non-Agentive" verbs (*offend, demoralize, bore, horrify, and disgust*) behave inconsistently with their labels, and are judged to be just as acceptable in this agentive context as either ObExAgentive or Event verbs.

However, although the results do not show a clear division between "Agentive" and "Non-agentive" ObEx verbs as we have labelled them, we find that the distribution of these verbs as a whole is also not as even or continuous as Grafmiller's (2013: 252–53) analysis might predict. Instead, the ObEx verbs seem to primarily cluster around two or three areas, with some degree of separation between them (contra Grafmiller's findings with the same test context). The most acceptable of these clusters is distributed much like the Event verbs, grouping in a region of higher acceptability (here around 0.75–1.0) and diminishing to a tail (containing e.g. ObExAgentive *disappoint*; similar to Event *twirl*). This group contains most of the ObExAgentive verbs, as well as five higher rated "Non-Agentive" verbs (*offend, demoralize, bore, horrify,* and *disgust*). On the less acceptable end are three ObExNon-Agentive verbs (*interest, concern, fascinate*) whose behaviour most closely resembles that of the SubEx verbs. Finally, in an "intermediate" area falling roughly between most Event and SubEx verbs (range −0.65 to −0.14), we find a group of 2 ObExAgentive (*encourage, amuse*) and 9 ObExNon-Agentive verbs (*amaze, astonish, captivate, charm, puzzle, please, worry, invigorate, depress*).

The cluster analysis illustrated in Figure 2 seems to confirm these impressions. At the top of the figure are the least acceptable verbs; the first 20 of these (most of the SubEx verbs, along with ObExNon-Agentive *fascinate, concern,* and *interest*) belong to their own cluster. These verbs form the most coherent and distinct group, as they are joined to the other major cluster (52 verbs) only at the last step of the analysis. The Event verbs and the remainder of the ObEx verbs then belong to the other, more acceptable major cluster. In general, the Event verbs and most of the ObEx verbs (particularly ObExAgentive) are mostly mixed in with one another on the more acceptable end (the bottom of the dendrogram), without any clear patterns. However, the noted "intermediate" group of ObEx verbs (the 2 Agentive, e.g. *encourage* and 9 Non-Agentive, e.g. *depress*) forms its own distinct sub-cluster between the majority of the SubEx and Event verbs (aside from the furthest outliers of the latter groups, *rinse* and *worship*).[19] This simultaneously suggests that the verbs in this sub-cluster behave similarly to one another with regards to their acceptability with agentive adverbs, while also to some degree distinct from the other (sub-)groups of verbs.

Taken together, the results of this test suggest that this agentivity diagnostic not only makes the expected distinction between Event and SubEx verbs, but also may differentiate between two or three potential sub-groups of ObEx verbs. In the latter case, there is a clear tendency for some verbs to be more acceptable while others are rated on the lower end, as well as for a third group to receive ratings in an intermediate range between that of either Event or SubEx verbs.

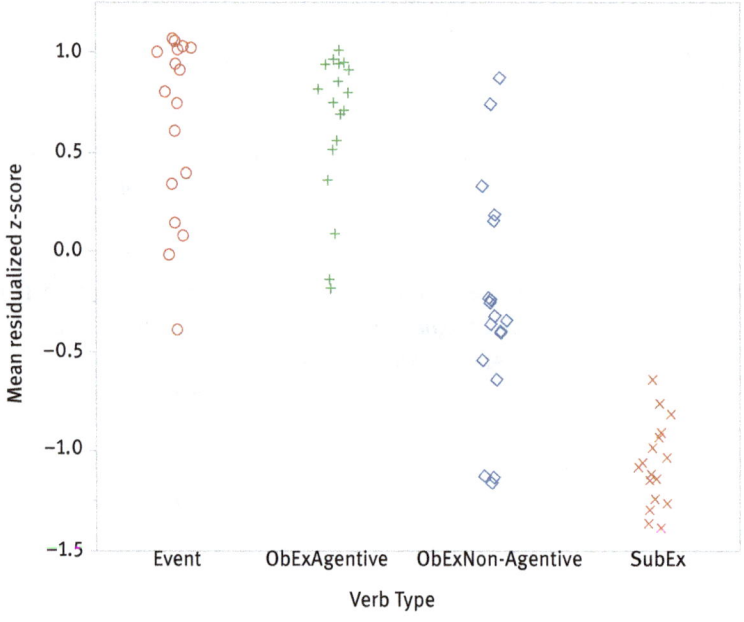

Figure 1: Mean ratings for each verb, by Verb Type (Agentive condition).

4.2.2 Eventive + animate subject context

The *What happened was . . .* frame was judged by many speakers to be relatively marked; thus, regardless of subject animacy, the sentences with this frame were,

---

19 The behavior of these two items suggests that there are some additional pragmatic or lexical factors at play.

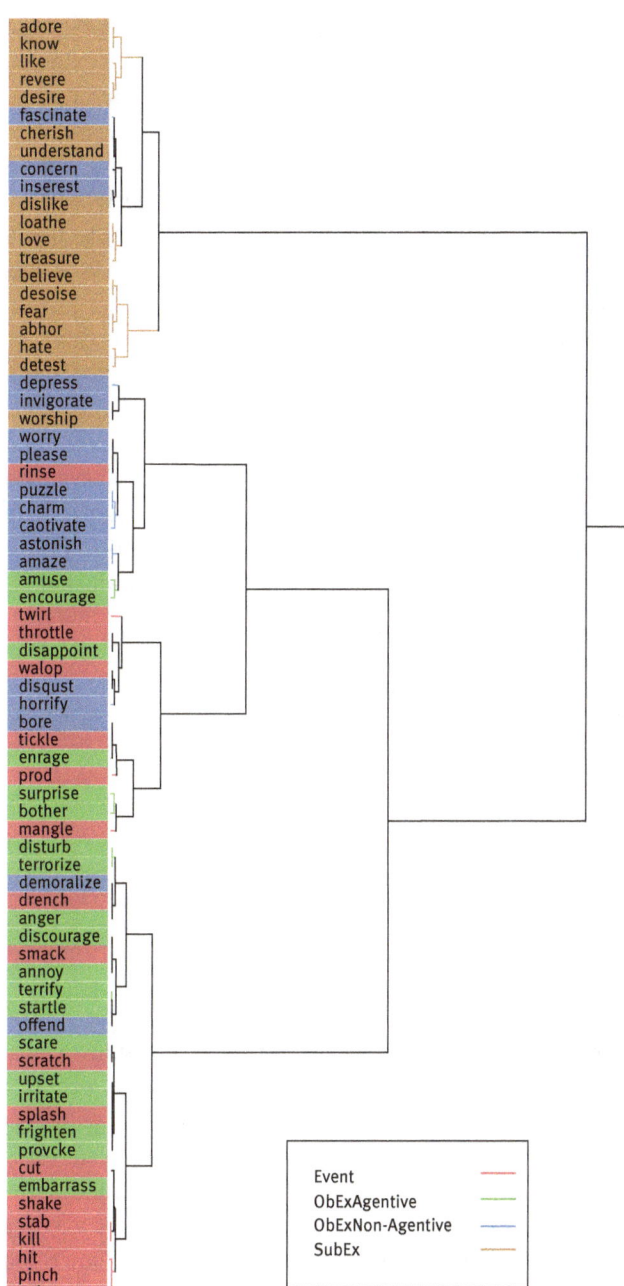

Figure 2: Hierarchical clustering of mean residualized ratings (Agentive condition).

on average, less acceptable than those with an agentive adverb (agentive mean raw rating: 4.7; *What happened was* . . . mean raw rating: 3.7). For a significant number of participants (43 out of 152; 28.3 %) the frame was virtually ungrammatical, with all *What happened was* . . . sentences eliciting a mean raw rating of less than 2 (where 1 is "completely unnatural"). As this unacceptability renders the diagnostic invalid for these participants, their responses to the *What happened was* . . . sentences (including those with an inanimate subject) were excluded from further analysis. After removing outlier ratings as described above, this left 22–27 ratings for each verb in each condition.

The LME for this test again revealed significant effects for Verb Type at the levels of ObExNon-Agentive (Est. = −0.31, SE = 0.07, t = −4.38) and SubEx (Est. = −0.55, SE = 0.08, t = −6.74); there was no significant effect at the level of ObExAgentive (Est. = −0.07, SE = 0.07, t = −0.99). Least squares means and standard errors output by the model are summarized in Table 4. Pairwise planned comparisons using Bonferroni-adjusted t-tests revealed the same pattern as in the Agentive context. All groups were significantly different from all other groups with the exception of Event and ObExAgentive, which did not significantly differ from one another.

Table 4: Least-squares means and standard errors of ratings by Verb Type (Eventive + animate subject condition).

Verb Type	Least-squares mean	SE	Letter
Event	0.232	0.061	A
ObExAgentive	0.166	0.052	A
ObExNon-Agentive	−0.076	0.051	B
SubEx	−0.316	0.055	C

These results again accord with the predictions made for Event and SubEx verbs, in that the former are significantly more acceptable than the latter in a context which should select for eventive verbs. As before, we also find a slightly different pattern for the ObEx verbs: ObExAgentive verbs are as acceptable as Event verbs in the *What happened was frame* . . ., and are significantly better than the ObExNon-Agentive group. Again, however, the Non-Agentive verb ratings average somewhere between the Event verbs and the stative SubEx ones, and are rated significantly better than the SubEx group.

However, although the pattern of mean differences is similar to that of the agentive adverb condition, the way the individual verbs are distributed within each group is somewhat different (Figure 3). While there is again some gradience and variability found within all of the groups, all of the verbs also fall within a much more restricted range as compared to the agentive context (range of 1.09 vs. 2.46 respectively), in line with the overall lower acceptability of the *What happened was . . .* sentences. Furthermore, although the Event and SubEx verbs in this condition still mostly cluster on either end of the distribution (apart from Event outlier *rinse* at –0.33 and SubEx outlier *believe* at 0.22), there is less separation between the inner tails of these groups (difference of 0.55 vs. 1.71 in the agentive condition, barring outliers). As for the ObEx verbs, there is a fairly even distribution of ratings across the generally more acceptable ObExAgentive verbs and the less acceptable ObExNon-Agentive ones, with no division between them. At least six of the latter verbs also behave more similarly to the ObExAgentive and Event verbs than might be expected (*offend, bore, charm, demoralize, horrify, and captivate*).

In contrast to the agentive condition, the ObEx verbs as a whole exhibit less of a clustering pattern here in the eventive frame. The majority of ObEx (23 verbs: 17 Agentive and 6 Non-Agentive) appear to fall roughly in the same range as most of the Event verbs, while the others (13 verbs: 11 Non-Agentive and 2 Agentive) seem more similar to the SubEx verbs; still, there is no clear point at which one proposed sub-group might be said to diverge from another. Instead, there is mostly a continuous distribution of more acceptable verbs to less acceptable ones.

The cluster analysis mirrors these general patterns (Figure 4). Rather than the two largest clusters simply consisting of mainly SubEx verbs on the one hand, and the remainder of the verbs on the other, the clustering suggests a more even division, roughly down the middle. Notably, the lower rated cluster (top half of the dendrogram) contains relatively more ObEx verbs in this condition – 13 out of 36 ObEx verbs were relatively less acceptable in this context, as compared to 3 with an agentive adverb. We also find that the purportedly non-agentive/stative verb *offend* is highly acceptable with the *What happened was . . .* diagnostic, being rated more favorably than any other verb in the task; given its similarly high mean rating with an agentive adverb, we may suggest that (minimally) this verb has previously been misclassified. However, there is one striking similarity between Figure 4 and the agentive dendrogram, in that there is a small sub-cluster consisting of mostly ObEx verbs, located at the lower end of the "eventive" cluster. It is here that we find 10 ObEx verbs – *encourage, terrify, disappoint, annoy, captivate, horrify, enrage, demoralize, discourage,* and *amuse* – all with ratings which fall between those of most of the SubEx and Event verbs, in an area of intermediate acceptability (*z-score* 0.01–0.12).

Overall, the results of this condition are less clear-cut than in the case of the agentive adverbs. On the one hand, the diagnostic for the most part functions as predicted, and the Event verbs are indeed generally more acceptable in this eventive context than the stative SubEx verbs. However, the boundaries between these two groups are not as clear, such that similar intermediate ratings do not necessarily indicate membership of the same aspectual class. While the lower acceptability of *What happened was* . . . sentences may partially account for these effects, the outlying verbs of the two control classes (*believe* and *rinse*) also suggest additional factors at play. That this is the case seems to be further confirmed by the behavior of the ObEx verbs. Although the ObEx verbs behave in line with Grafmiller's (2013) analysis – i.e. more or less as a single group with no clear point of division – the behavior of this group somewhat differs from that of the Event and SubEx verbs. Rather than most ObEx verbs being rated towards the higher or lower ends of the acceptability scale, many instead fall in an intermediate area. Given the location of this intermediate sub-cluster at the lower end of the Event range, we suggest that the judgments speakers have provided here are affected by the same factors conditioning the intermediate ratings in the agentivity test – potentially involving coercion – in combination with any considerations specific to this particular diagnostic.

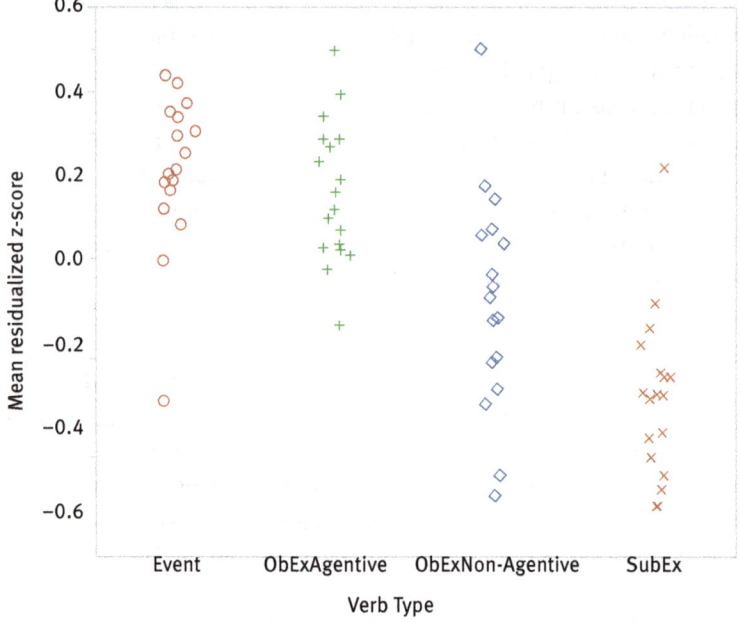

Figure 3: Mean ratings for each verb, by Verb Type (Eventive + animate subject condition).

Interpretability, aspectual coercion, and event structure — 163

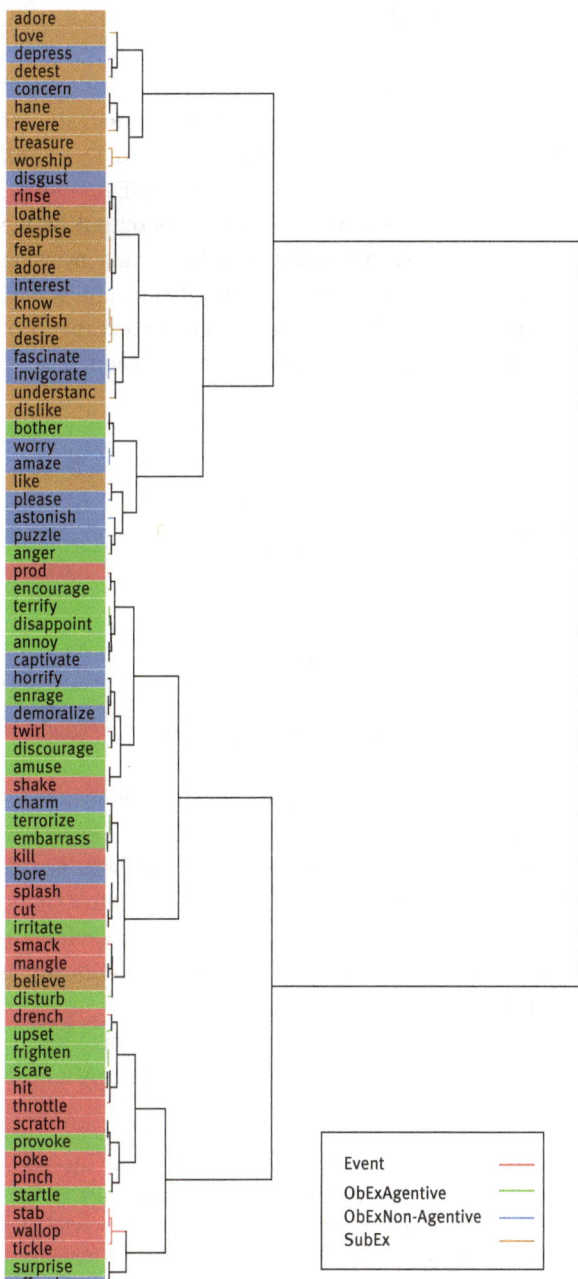

Figure 4: Hierarchical clustering of mean residualized ratings (Eventive + animate subject condition).

4.2.3 Eventive + inanimate subject context

As there were no ratings for SubEx verbs in this condition, the SubEx ratings from the previous context were included for comparison. The LME revealed significant effects for Verb Type at all levels: ObExAgentive (Est. = −0.16, SE = 0.06, t = −2.68), ObExNon-Agentive (Est. = −0.34, SE = 0.06, t = −5.23), and SubEx (Est. = −0.51, SE = 0.07, t = −6.94).[20] Least squares means and standard errors output by the model are summarized in Table 5.[21] However, pairwise planned comparisons using Bonferroni-adjusted t-tests revealed the same pattern as in the other conditions: all groups were significantly different from all other groups with the exception of Event and ObExAgentive, which did not significantly differ from one another.[22]

Table 5: Least-squares means and standard errors of ratings by Verb Type (Eventive + inanimate subject condition).

Verb Type	Least-squares mean	SE	Letter
Event	0.261	0.051	A
ObExAgentive	0.099	0.049	A
ObExNon-Agentive	−0.077	0.049	B
SubEx	−0.250	0.052	(B) C

The LME results show largely the same pattern as in previous conditions. Event verbs are more acceptable in this eventive context than SubEx verbs, as expected. The purportedly eventive ObExAgentive verbs behave most like the Event group, and are likewise significantly more acceptable than the purportedly stative ObEx-Non-Agentive verbs. However, as before, the latter group is still somewhat more acceptable on average than the SubEx group, though the difference here with an inanimate subject is not as statistically robust.

Turning to the scatterplot, the test sentences in this condition seem to lead to rather different within-class distributions of verbs (Figure 5 scatterplot). Although

---

20 It was not possible to compare this model to one with outliers included, as the latter failed to converge; instead, a model which included outliers but not random slopes was run. The pattern of results was largely the same, aside from a lack of significant difference between ObEx-Non-Agentive and SubEx. The difference we report should thus be viewed only as a trend.
21 The SubEx verb ratings here differ slightly from the animate subject condition as a result of within-condition frequency residualization.
22 The Bonferroni-corrected p-value for Event vs. ObExAgentive neared significance at t (79.97) = 2.67, p =.055. We have reported the most conservative interpretation here.

the Event verbs were on the whole the most acceptable, this acceptability appears to be highly dependent on the individual verb being judged. Furthermore, there are no clear outliers among this group; rather, the verbs are fairly evenly spread. Crucially, the range of these Event verbs also clearly overlaps with that of the SubEx verbs with animate subjects, and the division between these groups is not as well defined.

The ObEx verbs, meanwhile, are again evenly distributed across both the more acceptable ObExAgentive verbs and the less acceptable ObExNon-Agentive ones, with no clear point of division between them. However, apart from three verbs (*horrify*, *captivate*, *offend*), the ObExNon-Agentive verbs as a group fall more consistently in an area of lower acceptability when combined with inanimate subjects, at least as compared to the ObExAgentive and Event verbs. Still, for the ObEx verbs overall, there are no obvious areas where verbs tend to cluster in this *Eventive + inanimate subject* condition, nor any clear gaps in their distribution.

This relatively even spread of verbs across the four groups seems further supported by the dendrogram (Figure 6). More than half of the verbs (39, including 3 Event verbs) are grouped together in the same major cluster, towards the less acceptable end (top of the dendrogram). There also do not seem to be any substantial sub-clusters of ObEx verbs; instead, they are generally mixed in with Event or SubEx verbs, or else grouped into separate, distantly connected clusters.

Overall, if there are any distinctions between different verb types which may be found in these results, they may be obscured by other factors. This diagnostic does not provide a clear indication of a point at which we might divide ObEx verbs into semantically distinct sub-groups, nor is there the same intermediate "peak" of ObEx verbs that was found in the previous condition. Importantly, the lack of a defined separation between the Event and SubEx verbs also suggests that the ratings in this condition are subject to additional, unexpected influences.

For example, as a larger number of ObEx verbs were rated similarly to SubEx verbs in this condition, one might argue that the problem is that ObEx verbs are more likely to be read statively with an inanimate subject. However, seven Event verbs were also less acceptable in this condition, with three items even being clustered with the majority of the SubEx verbs. Rather than indicating a greater likelihood of stative readings, the lower ratings in this condition may therefore be affected by baseline differences in individual verbs' naturalness with inanimate subjects; such differences would need to be filtered out in order to have a clearer understanding of these results.

A related issue concerns the types of inanimate subjects which were chosen, and whether they can be understood as direct or indirect participants un the eventuality (Wolff 2003; Sichel 2010; Schäfer 2012; Alexiadou et al. 2013; Martin & Schäfer 2013). Thus, when the subject is only indirectly involved, a stative reading

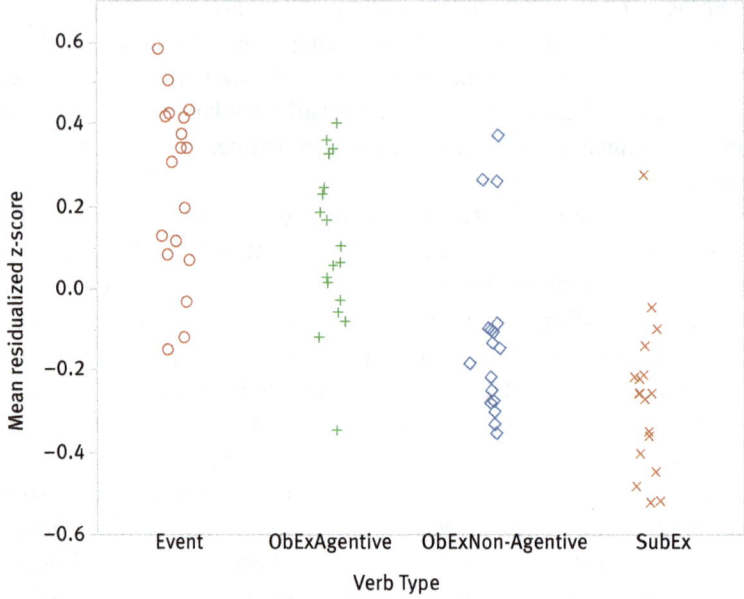

Figure 5: Mean ratings for each verb, by Verb Type (Eventive + inanimate subject condition).

is triggered (13a), even if the verb allows an eventive reading (13b); however, if the same subject can be viewed as directly causing the eventuality, it can trigger an eventive reading (13c) rather than a stative one (13d).

(13) a. *What happened was *the hurricane* justified the evacuation of the city.
 b. What happened was *the mayor* justified the evacuation of the city.
 c. What happened was *the hurricane* separated the family.
 d. *What happened was *the wall* separated the family.

Although both *justify* and *separate* allow eventive and stative readings, the availability of these readings does not strictly depend on the *animacy* of the subject, but on whether the subject can be viewed as a direct participant.[23] As the inanimate subjects in our study were not selected with this in mind, the ratings obtained in this condition may have been influenced by this factor in an unsystematic way.

Along with the possible influence of a baseline animacy preference, suchconsiderations suggest that further investigation is needed to more clearly assess the

---

[23] Note that all sentences in (13) are grammatical in the absence of *What happened was*.

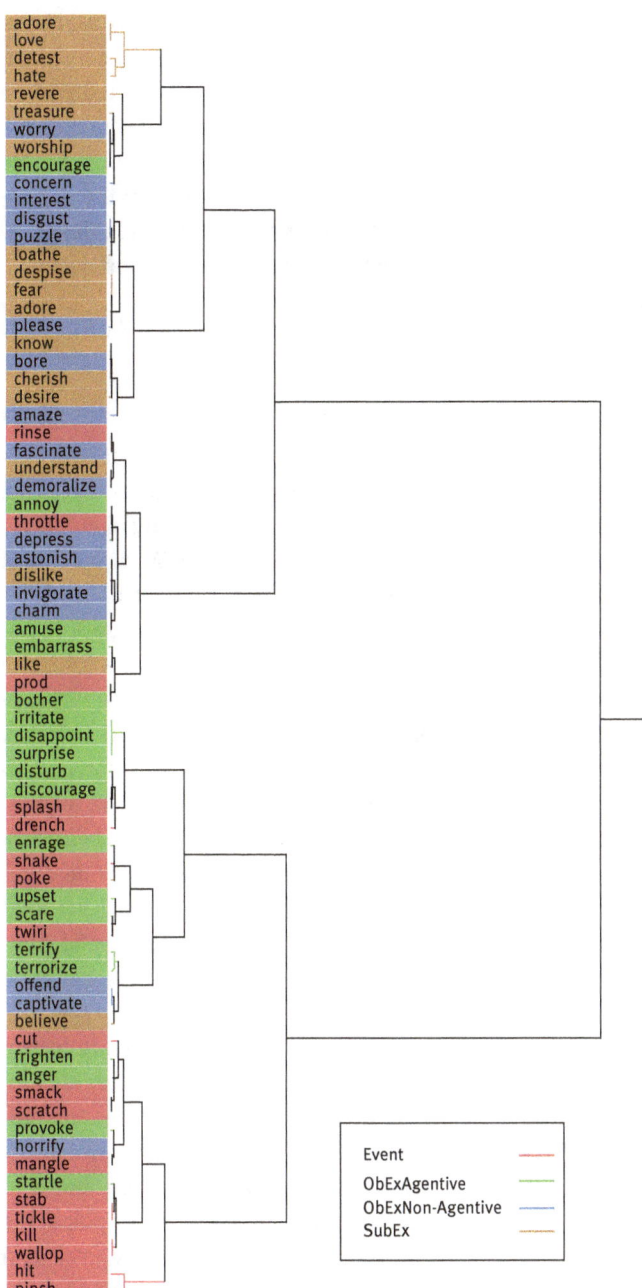

Figure 6: Hierarchical clustering of mean residualized ratings (Eventive + inanimate subject condition).

aspectual behavior of ObEx verbs in this context. However, regardless of the issues surrounding this test, the other conditions are not subject to the same considerations: as the animate subjects are all human, they all have the propensity to be directly involved in the eventuality described. Furthermore, as the sentences in these two conditions contain precisely the same subjects, verbs, and objects, the ratings obtained in the first two contexts are directly comparable. In the discussion below, we will focus on the previous two conditions, setting aside the questions which remain concerning the use of ObEx verbs with inanimate subjects.

5 General Discussion

The results reported in the previous sections are consistent with theories which assume that ObEx verbs consist of a sub-class of eventive/ambiguous verbs like *frighten*, and a sub-class of stative verbs like *fascinate* – specifically, a sub-class of "causative states" (for instance Arad 1998; Pylkkänen 2000). What we saw is that the distinctions between the two groups are indeed gradient rather than categorical. However, we argued that this is best interpreted in light of the potential for aspectual coercion, and the way in which this mechanism interacts with comprehension and acceptability. In particular, ObEx causative states may allow for 'additive coercion' (van Lambalgen & Hamm 2005; Bott 2010, 2015). This type of coercion functions as a repair mechanism that allows a stative verb to be (re-)interpreted as referring to a more complex eventuality, via a pragmatic operation in which missing elements are "added" by the reader/hearer on the basis of world knowledge and contextual inference. Precisely, this operation leads to greater difficulty in the processing of stative ObEx verbs in eventive/agentive contexts – thereby decreasing acceptability – but that successful completion of the repair ultimately results in degraded acceptability, rather than outright ungrammaticality.

We still cannot fully rule out the possibility that all ObEx verbs are in fact lexically specified as such causative states, and that they differ in ease of coercion simply because some have more conventionalized/entrenched coercion processes. However, the clustering at least in the agentive, and the relative consistency of which verbs are/are not so conventionalized is suggestive. More work needs to be done to fully account for their properties. Moreover, it is important to look at the behavior of individual verbs – as not all behave as labelled in literature, see also Verhoeven (2017). Our study highlights the importance of considerations of interpretability/processing when assessing grammaticality using acceptability, especially with subtle characteristics like aspect.

6 Conclusion

In this paper we presented an experimental, processing-based approach to the widely-discussed issue of lexical aspect in English Object-Experiencer verbs. We argued that any investigation of the event structure properties of these verbs must crucially take into account not only considerations on the level of the verb, but also the influence of processes which take place when a verb is interpreted in context. We drew particular attention to the role of aspectual coercion, and its interaction with processing in judgments of acceptability. Integrating these considerations into the design and analysis of our acceptability task, our results support an analysis of ObEx verbs as comprising two sub-classes which differ in their event structure: one consisting of verbs which readily allow eventive and/or agentive readings, and the other containing essentially stative verbs, which may be more or less coerced into such readings, see also Verhoeven (2017). However, this latter group of states also behave differently from stative SubEx verbs, in line with the causative nature of the former. Overall, the results presented here indicate that although the nature of both lexical aspect and acceptability may lead to highly complex, gradient patterns, taking this nature into consideration may help us to uncover important differences in the types of eventualities denoted by ObEx verbs – both within this class itself, and as compared to other psych verbs more generally. With respect to the theoretical approaches outlined in the section 2, our results provide further support for the class of stative causative verbs as a class distinct from that of stative experiencer verbs.

Appendix

Table A.1: Mean ratings and standard errors for each verb, by Verb Type (Agentive condition).

Verb	Verb Type	Mean	SE
poke	Event	1.068239	0.046254
pinch	Event	1.060952	0.05683
hit	Event	1.051249	0.045365
kill	Event	1.031471	0.045426
stab	Event	1.02205	0.047707
shake	Event	1.012473	0.047887
cut	Event	0.999706	0.053936

Table A.1 (continued)

Verb	Verb Type	Mean	SE
splash	Event	0.9458	0.052199
scratch	Event	0.915808	0.062889
smack	Event	0.802405	0.068555
drench	Event	0.740735	0.089314
mangle	Event	0.611019	0.084861
prod	Event	0.394666	0.107407
tickle	Event	0.339653	0.107323
wallop	Event	0.145223	0.13824
throttle	Event	0.080048	0.130253
twirl	Event	−0.01964	0.135316
rinse	Event	−0.39115	0.132035
embarrass	ObExAgentive	1.007931	0.048246
provoke	ObExAgentive	0.959853	0.041692
frighten	ObExAgentive	0.949206	0.038501
irritate	ObExAgentive	0.943404	0.061299
upset	ObExAgentive	0.940851	0.040639
scare	ObExAgentive	0.910452	0.056637
startle	ObExAgentive	0.856347	0.049581
terrify	ObExAgentive	0.851224	0.071561
annoy	ObExAgentive	0.811697	0.058293
discourage	ObExAgentive	0.801042	0.05695
anger	ObExAgentive	0.748537	0.075356
terrorize	ObExAgentive	0.711664	0.074698
disturb	ObExAgentive	0.690111	0.08738
bother	ObExAgentive	0.558396	0.094035
surprise	ObExAgentive	0.515613	0.102362
enrage	ObExAgentive	0.358237	0.102521
disappoint	ObExAgentive	0.090659	0.120539
encourage	ObExAgentive	−0.14389	0.123918
amuse	ObExAgentive	−0.1824	0.13554
offend	ObExNon-Agentive	0.871216	0.065779
demoralize	ObExNon-Agentive	0.738898	0.064591
bore	ObExNon-Agentive	0.327766	0.108829
horrify	ObExNon-Agentive	0.180294	0.119794
disgust	ObExNon-Agentive	0.156803	0.125145
amaze	ObExNon-Agentive	−0.23439	0.113641
astonish	ObExNon-Agentive	−0.25199	0.097337
captivate	ObExNon-Agentive	−0.32422	0.136566
charm	ObExNon-Agentive	−0.34671	0.139456
puzzle	ObExNon-Agentive	−0.36167	0.13272
please	ObExNon-Agentive	−0.39691	0.130093
worry	ObExNon-Agentive	−0.411	0.156016
invigorate	ObExNon-Agentive	−0.54812	0.111953

Table A.1 (continued)

Verb	Verb Type	Mean	SE
depress	ObExNon-Agentive	−0.64609	0.100696
interest	ObExNon-Agentive	−1.12497	0.100769
concern	ObExNon-Agentive	−1.13538	0.108615
fascinate	ObExNon-Agentive	−1.15983	0.090428
worship	SubEx	−0.53871	0.151193
detest	SubEx	−0.7647	0.143738
hate	SubEx	−0.81797	0.125548
abhor	SubEx	−0.91261	0.11021
fear	SubEx	−0.93514	0.103603
despise	SubEx	−0.98487	0.087377
believe	SubEx	−0.98891	0.117825
treasure	SubEx	−1.02901	0.089326
love	SubEx	−1.05589	0.112441
loathe	SubEx	−1.08164	0.127344
dislike	SubEx	−1.1178	0.103134
understand	SubEx	−1.14247	0.095205
cherish	SubEx	−1.1491	0.08579
desire	SubEx	−1.24432	0.083161
revere	SubEx	−1.26801	0.105534
like	SubEx	−1.30063	0.110872
know	SubEx	−1.36387	0.122852
adore	SubEx	−1.38928	0.113455

Table A.2: Mean ratings and standard errors for each verb, by Verb Type (Eventive + animate subject condition).

Verb	Verb Type	Mean	SE
tickle	Event	0.436451	0.107865
wallop	Event	0.421257	0.151586
stab	Event	0.419618	0.117762
pinch	Event	0.3706	0.119113
poke	Event	0.35039	0.127507
scratch	Event	0.338175	0.10492
throttle	Event	0.303794	0.129547
hit	Event	0.292755	0.158969
drench	Event	0.253469	0.138446
mangle	Event	0.212909	0.136105
smack	Event	0.205124	0.12631
cut	Event	0.189978	0.098538
splash	Event	0.183202	0.137143
kill	Event	0.165264	0.139078
shake	Event	0.122071	0.114443

Table A.2 (continued)

Verb	Verb Type	Mean	SE
twirl	Event	0.084227	0.099936
prod	Event	−0.00274	0.104509
rinse	Event	−0.33435	0.133307
surprise	ObExAgentive	0.497304	0.112142
startle	ObExAgentive	0.392807	0.138175
provoke	ObExAgentive	0.341546	0.104035
scare	ObExAgentive	0.287414	0.073502
frighten	ObExAgentive	0.287079	0.116772
upset	ObExAgentive	0.269987	0.099099
disturb	ObExAgentive	0.232878	0.101541
irritate	ObExAgentive	0.191357	0.108134
embarrass	ObExAgentive	0.160106	0.104946
terrorize	ObExAgentive	0.158745	0.078836
amuse	ObExAgentive	0.119446	0.097227
discourage	ObExAgentive	0.09957	0.077426
enrage	ObExAgentive	0.069592	0.114928
annoy	ObExAgentive	0.035753	0.101218
disappoint	ObExAgentive	0.029712	0.047361
terrify	ObExAgentive	0.023409	0.084213
encourage	ObExAgentive	0.01209	0.107985
anger	ObExAgentive	−0.02527	0.076664
bother	ObExAgentive	−0.15627	0.079085
offend	ObExNon-Agentive	0.501442	0.133012
bore	ObExNon-Agentive	0.17544	0.105797
charm	ObExNon-Agentive	0.145562	0.087326
demoralize	ObExNon-Agentive	0.071136	0.089437
horrify	ObExNon-Agentive	0.060511	0.102794
captivate	ObExNon-Agentive	0.037231	0.05572
puzzle	ObExNon-Agentive	−0.03672	0.102012
astonish	ObExNon-Agentive	−0.06349	0.083396
please	ObExNon-Agentive	−0.08788	0.083967
amaze	ObExNon-Agentive	−0.13693	0.111252
worry	ObExNon-Agentive	−0.14358	0.107741
invigorate	ObExNon-Agentive	−0.23343	0.088929
fascinate	ObExNon-Agentive	−0.23873	0.098391
interest	ObExNon-Agentive	−0.30587	0.091204
disgust	ObExNon-Agentive	−0.34406	0.111101
concern	ObExNon-Agentive	−0.51258	0.105792
depress	ObExNon-Agentive	−0.55706	0.071868
believe	SubEx	0.218005	0.120541
like	SubEx	−0.10516	0.139553

Table A.2 (continued)

Verb	Verb Type	Mean	SE
dislike	SubEx	−0.16037	0.094475
understand	SubEx	−0.19932	0.154326
desire	SubEx	−0.26983	0.112745
cherish	SubEx	−0.27851	0.117652
know	SubEx	−0.27976	0.099862
adore	SubEx	−0.31558	0.077353
fear	SubEx	−0.31729	0.098003
despise	SubEx	−0.31896	0.107752
loathe	SubEx	−0.33103	0.088498
worship	SubEx	−0.40933	0.099752
treasure	SubEx	−0.42255	0.132584
revere	SubEx	−0.46491	0.112466
hate	SubEx	−0.50852	0.106877
detest	SubEx	−0.54399	0.065473
love	SubEx	−0.57985	0.083782
abhor	SubEx	−0.58766	0.094826

Table A.3: Mean ratings and standard errors for each verb, by Verb Type (Eventive + inanimate subject condition).

Verb	Verb Type	Mean	SE
pinch	Event	0.583916	0.150869
hit	Event	0.506537	0.117441
wallop	Event	0.433846	0.136184
kill	Event	0.427898	0.112033
tickle	Event	0.417753	0.122384
stab	Event	0.416367	0.096053
mangle	Event	0.375049	0.074969
scratch	Event	0.341606	0.116473
smack	Event	0.34128	0.124042
cut	Event	0.307635	0.104128
twirl	Event	0.195104	0.100474
poke	Event	0.127597	0.116282
shake	Event	0.115255	0.097293
drench	Event	0.083256	0.05268
splash	Event	0.068729	0.097444
prod	Event	−0.03317	0.099257
throttle	Event	−0.11905	0.114495
rinse	Event	−0.14967	0.133628

Table A.3 (continued)

Verb	Verb Type	Mean	SE
startle	ObExAgentive	0.40529	0.102982
provoke	ObExAgentive	0.361652	0.126135
anger	ObExAgentive	0.341081	0.107891
frighten	ObExAgentive	0.32746	0.128837
terrorize	ObExAgentive	0.245607	0.131434
terrify	ObExAgentive	0.229937	0.11525
scare	ObExAgentive	0.186158	0.099482
upset	ObExAgentive	0.16748	0.10052
enrage	ObExAgentive	0.103972	0.101321
discourage	ObExAgentive	0.063593	0.100629
disturb	ObExAgentive	0.056382	0.105816
surprise	ObExAgentive	0.026861	0.086396
disappoint	ObExAgentive	0.024122	0.102451
irritate	ObExAgentive	0.016709	0.098419
bother	ObExAgentive	−0.02957	0.107953
embarrass	ObExAgentive	−0.05866	0.081299
amuse	ObExAgentive	−0.07986	0.111709
annoy	ObExAgentive	−0.12003	0.069094
encourage	ObExAgentive	−0.34538	0.139249
horrify	ObExNon-Agentive	0.374277	0.11702
captivate	ObExNon-Agentive	0.265688	0.103882
offend	ObExNon-Agentive	0.260768	0.122814
charm	ObExNon-Agentive	−0.08538	0.106816
invigorate	ObExNon-Agentive	−0.09844	0.096718
astonish	ObExNon-Agentive	−0.10118	0.0865
depress	ObExNon-Agentive	−0.10945	0.098026
demoralize	ObExNon-Agentive	−0.13179	0.064759
fascinate	ObExNon-Agentive	−0.14802	0.1252
amaze	ObExNon-Agentive	−0.18422	0.077645
bore	ObExNon-Agentive	−0.21777	0.09873
please	ObExNon-Agentive	−0.24987	0.090453
puzzle	ObExNon-Agentive	−0.27887	0.068819
disgust	ObExNon-Agentive	−0.27913	0.074703
interest	ObExNon-Agentive	−0.29984	0.101209
concern	ObExNon-Agentive	−0.33261	0.123248
worry	ObExNon-Agentive	−0.35179	0.060069
believe	SubEx	0.276531	0.120541
like	SubEx	−0.04668	0.139553
dislike	SubEx	−0.1001	0.094475
understand	SubEx	−0.14057	0.154326
desire	SubEx	−0.20904	0.112745
cherish	SubEx	−0.21704	0.117652

Table A.3 (continued)

Verb	Verb Type	Mean	SE
know	SubEx	−0.22256	0.099862
adore	SubEx	−0.25486	0.077353
fear	SubEx	−0.25778	0.098003
despise	SubEx	−0.25833	0.107752
loathe	SubEx	−0.26961	0.088498
worship	SubEx	−0.34838	0.099752
treasure	SubEx	−0.36086	0.132584
revere	SubEx	−0.40332	0.112466
hate	SubEx	−0.44921	0.106877
detest	SubEx	−0.48257	0.065473
love	SubEx	−0.52118	0.083782
abhor	SubEx	−0.52515	0.094826

References

Alexiadou, Artemis & Gianina Iordăchioaia. 2014. The psych causative alternation. *Lingua* 148. 53–79. https://doi.org/10.1016/j.lingua.2014.05.010.

Alexiadou, Artemis, Gianina Iordăchioaia, Mariángeles Cano, Fabienne Martin & Florian Schäfer. 2013. The realization of external arguments in nominalizations. *Journal of Comparative German Linguistics* 16(2–3). 73–95. https://doi.org/10.1007/s10828-014-9062-x.

Alexopolou, Theodora & Frank Keller. 2007. Locality, cyclicity, and resumption. *Language* 83(1). 110–160.

Arad, Maya. 1998. *VP structure and the Syntax-Lexicon Interface*. London: University College London dissertation.

Ariel, Mira. 1990. *Accessing noun-phrase antecedents*. London: Routledge.

Ariel, Mira. 2001. Accessibility theory: An overview. In Ted J.M. Sanders, Joost Schilperoord & Wilbert Spooren (eds.), *Text representation: Linguistic and psycholinguistic aspects*, 29–87. Amsterdam: Benjamins.

Baayen, R. Harald. 2008. Analyzing Linguistic Data. A Practical Introduction to Statistics Using R. Cambridge University Press

Bach, Emmon. 1986. The algebra of events. *Linguistics and Philosophy* 9(1). 5–16.

Bader, Markus & Michael Meng. 1999. Subject-Object Ambiguities in German Embedded Clauses: An Across-the-Board Comparison. Journal of Psycholinguistic Research 28(2):121–143.

Bates, Douglas, Martin Maechler & Ben Bolker. 2012. lme4: Linear Mixed-Effects Models Using S4 Classes (R Package Version 0.999999-0).

Bayen, R. Harald, Richard Piepenbrock and Hedderik van Rijn. 1993. The CELEX lexical data base on CD-ROM. Philadelphia: Linguistic Data Consortium.

Belletti, Adriana & Luigi Rizzi. 1988. Psych-verbs and θ-theory. *Natural Language and Linguistic Theory* 6(3). 291–352. https://doi.org/10.1007/BF00133902.

Biały, Adam. 2005. *Polish Psychological Verbs at the Lexicon-Syntax Interface in Cross-linguistic Perspective*. Frankfurt am Main: Peter Lang Verlag.

Bornkessel-Schlesewsky, Ina & Matthias Schlesewsky. 2007. The wolf in sheep's clothing: Against a new judgment-driven imperialism. *Theoretical Linguistics* 33(3). 319–333. https://doi.org/10.1515/TL.2007.021.

Bott, Oliver. 2010. *The Processing of Events* (Linguistik Aktuell/Linguistics Today 162) Amsterdam: Benjamins. https://doi.org/10.1075/la.162.

Bott, Oliver. 2015. Can semantic theories be tested experimentally? The case of aspectual coercion. In Joanna Blaszczak, Dorota Klimek-Jankowska & Krzysztof Migdalski (eds.), *Mood, Aspect, Modality Revisited*. Chicago, IL: University of Chicago Press. https://doi.org/10.7208/9780226363660-011.

Bott, Oliver & Fritz Hamm. 2014. Cross-linguistic variation in the processing of aspect. In Barbara Hemforth, Barbara Mertins & Cathrine Fabricius-Hansen (eds.), *Psycholinguistic Approaches to Meaning and Understanding Across Languages*, 83–109. Dordrecht: Springer.

Brennan, Jonathan & Liina Pylkkanen. 2008. Processing events: Behavioral and neuromagnetic correlates of aspectual coercion. *Brain and Language* 106(2). 132–43. https://doi.org/10.1016/j.bandl.2008.04.003.

Brennan, Jonathan & Liina Pylkkanen. 2010. Processing psych verbs: Behavioural and MEG measures of two different types of semantic complexity. *Language and Cognitive Processes* 25(6). 777–807. https://doi.org/10.1080/01690961003616840.

Carlson, Gregory N. 1977. *Reference to Kinds in English*. Amherst, MA: University of Massachusetts dissertation.

Chomsky, Noam. 1965. *Aspects of the Theory of Syntax*. Cambridge, MA: MIT Press.

Croft, William. 1993. Case marking and the semantics of mental verbs. In James Pustejovsky (eds.), *Semantics and the Lexicon*, 55–72. Dordrecht: Kluwer. https://doi.org/10.1007/978-94-011-1972-6_5.

Croft, William. 2012. *Verbs: Aspect and Causal structure*. Oxford: Oxford University Press.

Cupples, Linda. 2002. The structural characteristics and on-line comprehension of experiencer-verb sentences. *Language and Cognitive Processes* 17(2). 125–62. https://doi.org/10.1080/01690960143000001.

De Swart, Henriëtte. 1998. Aspect shift and coercion. *Natural Language and Linguistic Theory* 16(2). 347–85. https://doi.org/10.1023/A:1005916004600.

DiDesidero, Linda. 1999. Psych Verbs: Acquisition, Lexical Semantics, and Event Structure. Evanston, IL: Northwestern University dissertation.

Dowty, David R. 1979. *Word Meaning and Montague Grammar*. Dordrecht: Reidel.

Dowty, David R. 1991. Thematic proto-roles and argument selection. *Language* 67(3). 547–619. https://doi.org/10.2307/415037.

Fanselow, Gisbert, Caroline Féry, Matthias Schlesewsky & Ralf Vogel (eds.). 2006. *Gradience in Grammar: Generative Perspectives*. Oxford: Oxford University Press.

Fanselow, Gisbert & Stefan Frisch. 2006. Effects of processing difficulty on judgments of acceptability. In Gisbert Fanselow, Caroline Féry, Ralf Vogel & Matthias Schlesewsky (eds.), *Gradience in Grammar: Generative Perspectives*, 291–316. Oxford: Oxford University Press.

Featherston, Sam. 2007. Data in Generative Grammar: The stick and the carrot. *Theoretical Linguistics* 33(3). 269–318. https://doi.org/10.1515/TL.2007.020.

Featherston, Sam. 2008. Relax, lean back, and be a linguist. *Zeitschrift für Sprachwissenschaft* 28(1). 127–32. https://doi.org/10.1515/ZFSW.2009.014.

García-Pardo, Alfredo. 2018. *The morphosyntax of states. Deriving aspect and event roles from argument structure.* Los Angeles, CA: University of Southern California dissertation.

Gennari, Silvia P. & Maryellen C. MacDonald. 2009. Linking production and comprehension processes: The case of relative clauses. *Cognition* 111(1). 1–23. https://doi.org/10.1016/j.cognition.2008.12.006.

Gerken, Louann & Thomas G. Bever. 1986. Linguistic intuitions are the result of interactions between perceptual processes and linguistic universals. *Cognitive Science* 10(4). 457–76. https://doi.org/10.1016/S0364-0213(86)80013-1.

Grafmiller, Jason. 2013. The Semantics of Syntactic Choice: An Analysis of English Emotion Verbs. Stanford, CA: Stanford University dissertation.

Grimshaw, Jane. 1990. Argument Structure. Cambridge, MA: MIT Press.

Haider, Hubert. 2007. As a matter of facts – comments on Featherston's sticks and carrots. *Theoretical Linguistics* 33(3). 381–94. https://doi.org/10.1515/TL.2007.025.

Hamm, Fritz & Michial van Lambalgen. 2005. *The Proper Treatment of Events.* Malden, MA: Blackwell.

Hartshorne, Joshua K., Timothy J. O'Donnell, Yasutada Sudo, Miseon Lee, Miki Uruwashi & Jesse Snedeker. Submitted. Linking meaning to language: Linguistic universals and variation.

Hofmeister, Philip, T. Florian Jaeger, Ivan A. Sag, Inbal Arnon, & Neal Snider. 2007. Locality and accessibility in wh-questions. Roots: Linguistics in Search of its Evidential Base, ed. by Sam Featherston & Wolfgang Sternefeld, 185–206. Berlin: Mouton de Gruyter.

Hofmeister, Philip, T. Florian Jaeger, Inbal Arnon, Ivan A. Sag & Neal Snider. 2013. The source ambiguity problem: Distinguishing the effects of grammar and processing on acceptability judgments. *Language and Cognitive Processes* 28(1–2). 48–87. https://doi.org/10.1080/01690965.2011.572401.

Husband, Edward M., Alan Beretta & Linaea Stockall. 2006. Aspectual computation: Evidence for immediate commitment. Talk given at AMLaP 2006, Nijmegen, The Netherlands.

Hirsch, Nils. 2018. German psych verbs: Insights from a decompositional perspective. Berlin: Humboldt Universität zu Berlin dissertation.

Iwata, Seizi. 1995. The distinctive character of psych-verbs as causatives. *Linguistic Analysis* 25. 95–120.

Jackendoff, Ray. 1983. *Semantics and Cognition.* Cambridge, MA: MIT Press.

Jackendoff, Ray. 1997. *The architecture of the language faculty.* Cambridge, MA: MIT Press.

Kearns, Kate. 2003. Durative achievements and individual-level predicates on events. *Linguistics and Philosophy* 26(5). 595–635. https://doi.org/10.1023/A:1025803912153.

Keller, Frank. 2000. *Gradience in grammar: Experimental and computational aspects of degrees of grammaticality.* Edinburgh: University of Edinburgh dissertation.

Kratzer, Angelika. 2000. Building statives. In Lisa J. Conathan, Jeff Good, Darya Kavitskaya, Alyssa B. Wulf & Alan C. L. Yu (eds.), *Berkeley Linguistics Society (BLS): General Session and Parasession on Aspect* 26, 385–99.

Lakoff, George. 1966. Stative adjectives and verbs in English. In Anthony G. Oettinger (ed.), *Mathematical Linguistics and Automatic Translation*, I1-I16. Report NSF-17, The Computation Laboratory. Cambridge, MA: Harvard University.

Landau, Idan. 2010. *The locative syntax of experiencers.* Cambridge, MA: MIT Press.

Lauwers, Peter & Dominique Willems. 2011. Coercion: Definition and challenges, current approaches, and new trends. *Linguistics* 49(6). 1219–35. https://doi.org/10.1515/ling.2011.034.

Levin, Beth. 1993. *English Verb Classes and Alternations*. Chicago, IL: University of Chicago Press.

Levin, Beth and Malka Rappaport Hovav. 1995. *Unaccusativity: At the Syntax-Lexical Semantics Interface*. Cambridge, MA: MIT Press.

Levin, Beth and Malka Rappaport Hovav. 2005. *Argument Realization*. Cambridge: Cambridge University Press.

Manoulidou, Christina, Roberto G. de Almeida, George Schwartz & Vasavan Nair. 2009. Thematic roles in Alzheimer's disease: Hierarchy violations in psychological predicates. *Journal of Neurolinguistics* 22(2). 167–86. https://doi.org/10.1016/j.jneuroling.2008.10.002.

Marín, Rafael & Louise McNally. 2011. Inchoativity, change of state, and telicity: Evidence from Spanish reflexive psychological verbs. *Natural Language and Linguistic Theory* 29(2). 467–502. https://doi.org/10.1007/s11049-011-9127-3.

Martin, Fabienne and Schäfer, Florian. 2013. "On the Argument Structure of Verbs with Bi- and Mono-Eventive Uses." In Proceedings of the 42nd annual meeting of the North East Linguistic Society (NELS 42), Stefan Keine and Shayne Sloggett (eds), 297–308. Amherst: GLSA Publications.

McElree Brian, Martin Pickering, Rachel Seely, Ray Jackendoff. 2001. Reading time evidence for enriched composition. Cognition. 78: B17–25.

Michaelis, Laura A. 2004. Type shifting in construction grammar: An integrated approach to aspectual coercion. *Cognitive Linguistics* 15(1). 1–67. https://doi.org/10.1515/cogl.2004.001.

Miller, G. A. & Noam Chomsky. 1963. Finitary models of language users. In Duncan R. Luce, Robert Bush & Eugene Galanter (eds.), *Handbook of Mathematical Psychology*, vol. 2, 419–493. New York: Wiley.

Moens, Marc & Mark Steedman. 1988. Temporal ontology and temporal reference. *Computational Linguistics* 14(2). 15–28.

Newmeyer, Frederick J. 2007. Commentary on Sam Featherston, 'Data in generative grammar: The stick and the carrot'. *Theoretical Linguistics* 33(3). 395–399. https://doi.org/10.1515/TL.2007.026.

Pesetsky, David. 1995. *Zero Syntax: Experiencers and Cascades*. Cambridge, MA: MIT Press.

Pickering, Martin, Brian McElree, Steven Frisson, Lillian Chen, & Matthew Traxler. 2006. Underspecification and aspectual coercion. Discourse Processes, 42(2), 131–155.

Piñango, Maria M., Edgar Zurif & Ray Jackendoff. 1999. Real-time processing implications of enriched composition and the syntax-semantics interface. *Journal of Psycholinguistic Research* 28(4). 395–414. https://doi.org/10.1023/A:1023241115818.

Piñon, Cristopher. 1997. Achievements in an event semantics. In Aaron Lawson (ed.), *Semantics and Linguistic Theory (SALT) 7*, 276–293. Ithaca, NY: CLC Publications. https://doi.org/10.3765/salt.v7i0.2781.

Prince, Ellen F. 1978. A comparison of *wh*-clefts and *it*-clefts in discourse. *Language* 54(4). 883–906. https://doi.org/10.2307/413238.

Pustejovsky, James 1991. The syntax of event structure. *Cognition* 41(1–3). 47–81. https://doi.org/10.1016/0010-0277(91)90032-Y.

Pustejovsky, James. 1995. *The generative lexicon*. Cambridge, MA: MIT Press.

Pylkkanen, Liina. 2000. On stativity and causation. In Carol L. Tenny & James Pustejovsky (eds.), *Events as Grammatical Objects: The Converging Perspectives of Lexical Semantics and Syntax*, 417–42. Standford, CA: CSLI Publications.

Pylkkänen, Liina and Brian McElree. 2007. An MEG study of silent meaning Journal of Cognitive Neuroscience 19(11):1905–21.

Rappaport Hovav, Malka & Beth Levin. 1998. Building verb meanings. In Miriam Butt & Wilhelm Geuder (eds.), *The Projection of Arguments: Lexical and Compositional Factors*. Stanford, CA: CSLI Publications.

Roehm, Dietmar, Antonella Sorace & Ina Bornkessel-Schlesewsky. 2012. Processing flexible form-to-meaning mappings: Evidence for enriched composition as opposed to indeterminacy. *Language and Cognitive Processes* 28(8). 1244–74. https://doi.org/10.1080/01690965.2012.712143.

Rothmayr, Antonia. 2009. *The structure of stative verbs*. Amsterdam: Benjamins.

Rothstein, Susan. 2004. *Structuring events: A study in the semantics of lexical aspect*. Oxford: Blackwell.

Schäfer, Florian. 2012. Two types of external argument licensing – The case of causers. *Studia Linguistica* 66(2). 1–53. https://doi.org/10.1111/j.1467-9582.2012.01192.x.

Martin, Fabienne & Florian Schäfer. 2013. On the argument structure of verbs with bi- and mono-eventive uses. In Stefan Keine & Shayne Sloggett (eds.), *North East Linguistic Society (NELS) 42*, vol. 2, 297–308.

Schulte im Walde, Sabine. 2003. *Experiments on the automatic induction of German semantic verb classes*. Stuttgart: Institut für Maschinelle Sprachverarbeitung, Universität Stuttgart dissertation.

Schütze, Carson T. & Jon Sprouse. 2013. Judgment data. In Robert J. Podesva & Devyani Sharma (eds.), *Research Methods in Linguistics*, 27–50. Cambridge, UK: Cambridge University Press.

Sichel, Ivy. 2010. Event structure constraints in nominalization. In Artemis Alexiadou & Monika Rathert (eds.), *The syntax of nominalizations across languages and frameworks*, 151–90. Berlin & New York: Mouton de Gruyter. https://doi.org/10.1515/9783110245875.159.

Smith, Carlota S. 1991. *The Parameter of Aspect*. Dordrecht: Kluwer.

Sorace, Antonella & Frank Keller. 2005. Gradience in linguistic data. *Lingua* 115(11). 1497–1524. https://doi.org/10.1016/j.lingua.2004.07.002.

Sprouse, Jon. 2007. Continuous acceptability, categorical grammaticality, and experimental syntax. *Biolinguistics* 1. 123–134.

Sprouse, Jon. 2008. The differential sensitivity of acceptability judgments to processing effects. *Linguistic Inquiry* 39(4). 686–94. https://doi.org/10.1162/ling.2008.39.4.686.

Sprouse, Jon, Shin Fukuda, Hajime Ono, & Robert Kluender. 2011. Reverse island effects and the backward search for a licensor in multiple wh-questions. Syntax 14(2):179–203.

Sprouse, Jon. and Almeida, D. 2012. Assessing the reliability of textbook data in syntax: Adger's *Core Syntax*. *Journal of Linguistics* 48(3). 609–52. https://doi.org/10.1017/S0022226712000011.

Steedman, Mark. 2005. *The productions of time*. Unpublished Ms.

Todorova, Marina, Kathy Straub, William Badecker & Robert Frank. 2000. Aspectual coercion and the online computation of sentential aspect. Cognitive Science Society (CSS).

Van Voorst, Jan. 1992. The aspectual semantics of psychological verbs. *Linguistics and Philosophy* 15(1). 65–92. https://doi.org/10.1007/BF00635833.

Verhoeven, Elisabeth. 2010. Agentivity and stativity in experiencer verbs: Implications for a typology of verb classes. *Linguistic Typology* 14(2–3). 213–251. https://doi.org/10.1515/lity.2010.009.

Verhoeven, Elisabeth. 2017. Scalar or features in verb meaning? *Belgian Journal of Linguistics* 31(1). 164–193. https://doi.org/10.1075/bjl.00007.ver.

Wolff, Phillip. 2003. Direct causation in the linguistic coding and individuation of causal events. *Cognition* 88(1). 1–48. https://doi.org/10.1016/S0010-0277(03)00004-0.

Zucchi, Sandro. 1998. Aspect shift. In Susan Rothstein (ed.), *Events and grammar*, 349–70. Dordrecht: Kluwer.

Patricia Irwin
Discourse and unaccusativity
Quantitative effects of a structural phenomenon

Abstract: This paper brings together syntactic analysis with corpus results to argue that a subset of unaccusative verb phrases, those with verbs that typically denote motion or manner of motion (e.g. *arrive*, *walk in*) share a discourse property with *there* BE sentences – that of establishing a new discourse referent. The theoretical motivation for the corpus experiment is an analysis in which verbs like *arrive* and *walk in* occur in an "existential unaccusative" structure, a structure in which part of the denotation of the VP is McNally's (1992, 1997) function INSTANTIATE, which triggers the establishment of a discourse referent in existential sentences (see also McCloskey 2014). Results from a corpus experiment are presented in which the ratio of indefinite/definite subjects of existential unaccusative sentences is compared to that of unergative sentences. The comparison of these ratios was found to be statistically significant, where the comparatively greater number of indefinite subjects of existential unaccusative sentences was not the result of chance. The utility and limits of corpus experiments for syntactic theory is discussed. It is argued that corpus data can inform syntactic theory, though the limits of corpus data for supporting or refuting specific syntactic models is acknowledged.

Keywords: experimental syntax, argument structure, discourse referents, unaccusativity, existential verbs, corpus study

1 Introduction

One of the goals of this paper is to show how corpus data can be used to inform syntactic theory. The relevant question in syntactic theory is the structure of unaccusative verb phrases. The domain of interest is the information structural effects of a subtype of unaccusative sentence, a type called the "existential unaccusative" subtype (Irwin 2018), illustrated in (1)–(2) with the verbs *arrive* and *walk (in)*:

Patricia Irwin, Swarthmore College, Department of Linguistics, 500 College Ave., Swarthmore, PA, USA, e-mail: pirwin1@swarthmore.edu

https://doi.org/10.1515/9783110757255-007

(1) A hippie arrived.

(2) Some hippies walked in.

Many researchers have proposed more than one way for a verb phrase to be unaccusative (Kural 2002; Alexiadou & Anagnostopoulou 2004; Embick 2004; Alexiadou & Schäfer 2011; Irwin 2012, among others); on the analysis advocated here (Irwin 2018), existential sentences like (1) and (2) share parts of the structure and meaning of "existential" *there* BE sentences as in (3):

(3) There's a hippie at the door.

Irwin's (2018) analysis of sentences like (1) and (2) builds on work in which a core property of *there* BE sentences is the establishment (or re-establishment) of a discourse referent (McNally 1992, 1997). This analysis thus predicts that existential unaccusative sentences should have discourse referent establishment as one of their discourse properties. This paper presents a small corpus experiment that tests this prediction about shared discourse function.[1] The prediction is tested by comparing the frequency of discourse new subjects of existential unaccusative sentences versus those of unergative sentences – where unergative sentences are those with verbs like *laugh*, typically analyzed as having subjects that are "true" external arguments. The results of the corpus experiment support the hypothesis that existential unaccusative sentences establish discourse referents for their subjects more than unergative sentences do.

The results are interpreted to suggest that the discourse function of existential unaccusative sentences is a desirable property of any theoretical analysis of them, just as the discourse function of *there* BE sentences is a core property of their analysis. Irwin (2018) presents one such analysis of existential unaccusatives, but it is noted that the corpus results support other theoretical analyses that encode this discourse property. In this way, we see both the utility of corpus experiments for syntactic theory – in confirming a key property in our syntactic models – and the limits of corpus experiments – since the corpus study does not speak to specific details of the proposed theoretical model.

---

[1] Because of the experimental methodology employed, the term "corpus experiment" (rather than corpus "study" or "analysis", for example) is used throughout the paper. This terminological distinction is important in light of the broader methodological goal of contributing to discussion about the kinds of evidence that are relevant for syntactic theory (Chomsky 1986: 36ff).

The paper is structured as follows: the first section provides some background on unaccusativity, with a focus on English. This section presents an overview of key aspects of the shared structure and meaning that is proposed for the existential unaccusatives; this analysis predicts that existential unaccusative sentences like (1) and (2) share some of the discourse functions of *there* BE sentences like (3). Section 3 describes the method and results of a corpus experiment that tests this prediction; this part of the paper goes into some detail about how the components of a theoretical analysis are operationalized for the corpus experiment. Section 4 takes a qualitative approach by examining the data from the corpus experiment. This section compares the discourse function of the extracted corpus sentences with indefinite subjects of two representative verbs, *laugh* and *arrive*. Section 5 concludes with some directions for future research.

2 Background

The term "unaccusative" has been used in many different ways. The definition assumed in this paper is structural: an unaccusative verb phrase lacks an external argument and has at least one VP-internal argument (see Embick 2004; Irwin 2012). As Embick (2004) points out, this structural definition means that passive sentences count as unaccusative.[2] In this paper, however, the focus will be on one of the two standard types of unaccusative VPs.

Approaches to unaccusativity typically divide verbs into two classes based on semantic criteria: verbs that denote a change-of-state such as *break*, *freeze*, and *melt*, and those that denote motion or existence, such as *arrive*. Unaccusativity diagnostics in English are particularly sensitive to the semantic distinction between change-of-state and existence/motion; English lacks the robust unaccusativity diagnostics that other languages have – Italian has *ne*-cliticization for example (Burzio 1986). This sensitivity to different unaccusativity diagnostics has led to some puzzles about what unaccusativity diagnostics are truly diagnosing.

Many verbs that denote changes of state undergo the causative/inchoative alternation, shown in (4)–(5) with *break*:

(4)   The kids broke the vase.

---

[2] This is not the case if one assumes an analysis of the passive in which an external argument is structurally represented, as in Chomsky (1957); Baker, Johnson & Roberts (1989); Collins (2005).

(5) The vase broke.

(6) The vase broke <the vase>.

The inchoative alternant (5) is typically analyzed as unaccusative, as shown schematically in (6) – as diagnosed by this alternation and by diagnostics such as the direct object restriction on resultatives (see Levin & Rappaport Hovav 1995).

Verbs that denote existence/motion, on the other hand, tend not to undergo the causative/inchoative alternation, as illustrated for *arrive* in (7)–(8).

(7) A group of boisterous kids arrived.

(8) *The bus arrived a group of boisterous kids.

And yet verbs like *arrive* are suspected to be unaccusative: their counterparts in other languages pass unaccusativity tests that cut across semantically-defined classes of verbs, and in English, verbs like *arrive* pass a different proposed unaccusativity test, *there*-insertion, as shown in (9). But the *there*-insertion diagnostic fails for change-of-state verbs like *break*, as shown in (10):

(9) There arrived a group of boisterous kids.

(10) *There broke several vases yesterday.

The fact that no single syntactic diagnostic works for all semantic classes of verbs in English has been seen as a problem, and the fact that a diagnostic like *there*-insertion works for *arrive* but not for *break* has been called an "unaccusative mismatch" (L. Levin 1986).[3] Even more problematic is the fact that some verbs that are typically seen as agentive can allow *there*-insertion. For example, Levin (1993) points out that if a manner of motion verb like *run* or *dart* is given a direction (with a PP such as *into the room*), then *there*-insertion is acceptable (11):

(11) There darted into the room a little boy. (Levin 1993: 89)

---

3 See Levin & Rappaport Hovav (1995) for a more nuanced discussion of unaccusativity mismatches than the cursory discussion provided here.

The theoretical approach in this paper brings together the structural definition of unaccusativity, referenced at the beginning of this section, with recent approaches to argument structure in which syntactic structure is distinct from verbal identity (Marantz 2013). On this approach, the semantic properties of a verb do not solely determine the syntactic environment that the verb can occur in. In other words, a given verb (or verbal root, on this approach) might be compatible with more than one syntactic structure. The central role of syntactic structure in the approach of this paper allows us to consider the possibility that verbs that at first sight seem quite different – e.g. *dart* and *arrive* – might occur in similar structures and with similar meanings.

From this perspective of "syntacticized event structure" (Marantz 2013), the occurrence of *dart* in a *there*-insertion sentence like (11) comes about when the root √DART occurs in an extended VP that allows *there*-insertion. On this type of analysis, what has been seen as an unaccusativity mismatch is analyzed as the ability of certain roots to occur in different syntactic structures. Change-of-state verbs like *break* and *freeze* typically occur in a syntactic structure that does not allow *there*-insertion, and it is this structure that allows for the causative/inchoative alternations that we see in (4)–(5).

Irwin (2012) proposes two basic syntactic structures for unaccusative VPs, one associated with "change of state" verbs like *break*, *freeze*, *melt*, and the other associated with verbs like *arrive*, *come in*, etc. Irwin (2018) proposes that the *arrive*-type structure shares elements of the structure and meaning of existential *there* BE sentences. This analysis extends to predicates like *dart in* as in (11), so that sentences like (12) with *arrive*, (13) with *dart in*, and even (14) with *break* have a very similar syntactic analysis – one that predicts they should also share some discourse functions with *there*-insertion sentences like (11).

(12) A little boy arrived.

(13) A little boy darted in.

(14) A thief broke in.

More concretely, Irwin (2018) proposes that shared structure and meaning allows *arrive*-type sentences to serve one of the discourse functions of *there* BE sentences, that of establishing a new discourse referent. The following sections briefly review this theoretical proposal and then describe a corpus experiment designed to test this prediction.

2.1 *There* BE sentences

The example in (15) shows an existential *there* BE sentence in English, where the standard terms for the parts of an existential sentence are identified.

(15) There is   [some tea] [in the cupboard].
           BE PIVOT   CODA

The structure assumed for English *there* BE sentences builds on McCloskey's (2014) analysis of Irish existentials. In McCloskey (2014), existential sentences in Irish such as (16) are analyzed as a SC, consisting of subject nominal (the pivot) and the word *ann* 'in it', which in this use is an existential predicate.[4]

(16) Tá   fion   ann.   (Irish, McCloskey 2014: 374, ex. 79)
       is   wine   in.it
       'There's wine'

The denotation of the existential predicate *ann* 'in it' in McCloskey's analysis incorporates two key properties of existential sentences: the establishment of a discourse referent, accomplished through McNally's (1992, 1997) predicate INSTANTIATE, and the insight from Francez (2007) that existential sentences have as part of their core meaning a contextually determined location – where this location is not equivalent to what is termed the "coda" in existential sentences. The denotation of *ann* 'in it' is beyond the scope of this overview, but as McCloskey writes, the key to its meaning is that it combines "McNally's fundamental semantics for existentials with Francez's theory of the context-dependence of existential propositions" (2014: 374). The proposal in Irwin (2018) explicates McCloskey's analysis and adapts it to English *there* BE and existential unaccusative sentences.

It is important to note that on both McCloskey's analysis and the adaptation in Irwin (2018), the contextually-determined locational element that is part of the denotation of *ann* 'in it' is not identical to the coda. The contextually-determined locational element is always silent; informally, it can be thought of as the "at here" function, where "here" is a "definite null anaphor" (McCloskey 2014: 358). The term "LOC" is used for this part of an existential predication. In addition, analyses like these that build on McNally (1992, 1997) analyze the coda as an optional element, semantically a modifier and syntactically an adjunct. The schematization in (17) illustrates these concepts.

---

4 *Ann* is translated as 'in-it' for historical reasons (McCloskey 2014: 347).

(17) There is [some tea] e (in the cupboard).
　　　 BE　PIVOT　　 LOC CODA

The structure in (18), shows the structure assumed for *there* BE sentences in English, where the verb takes a headed small clause complement (PredP), and the complement of the small clause is the DP pivot (Hazout 2004, 2008). The Pred head is labeled Pred$_{exist}$ since it is a specialized existential predicate, like *ann* on McCloskey's analysis, and with roughly the same denotation as *ann*. The specifier of the PredP is the contextually-determined element LOC, implemented as a PlaceP. This is the position where the expletive *there* originates in Williams (1994) and following analyses (e.g. Hazout 2004, 2008; Myler 2016). The structure in (18) is compatible with such an analysis, but the many issues of *there* must be set aside here (see Deal 2009 for discussion).

(18) Structure of an English *there* BE sentence (Irwin 2018: 10)

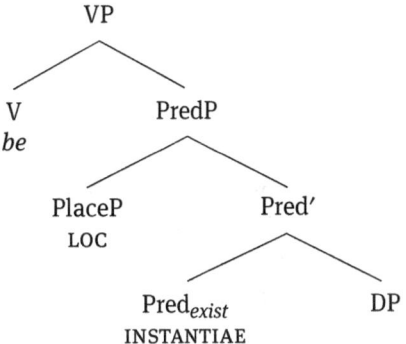

2.2 Existential unaccusative sentences

The analysis in the previous section forms the foundation for the analysis from Irwin (2018) of existential unaccusative sentences. As noted above, this analysis builds on the idea that there is more than one way for a verb phrase to be structurally unaccusative. On this analysis, which is in the spirit of Hoekstra & Mulder (1990), verbs like *arrive* and *walk in*, can occur in the Pred$_{exist}$P structure (19).

(19) Existential unaccusative structure (Irwin 2018)

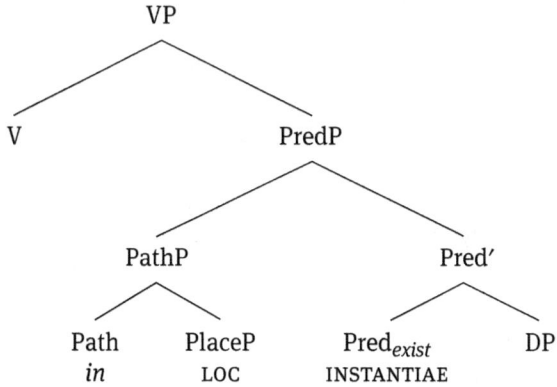

The difference between the *there* BE structure in (18) and the existential unaccusative structure in (19) lies in the specifier of the PredP: the existential unaccusative structure requires Spec,PredP to be interpreted as a Path, a Path to the contextually-determined LOC. The Path head in the existential unaccusative structure must be overt and is often a particle-like preposition such as *in*. In a sentence with a verb like *arrive*, a Path element (*a-* in the case of *arrive*) is incorporated into the verb, as proposed by Moro (1997: 291, fn. 19).

This paper will not present all of the arguments in favor of the analysis in (19) (see Irwin 2012, 2018 for those details). For the purposes here, what is important is the proposal that existential *there* BE and existential unaccusative sentences have shared elements of structure and meaning. One of those shared elements is the function INSTANTIATE, which triggers the establishment of a discourse referent. On this analysis, English has two relevant structures that are particularly well-suited for establishing new discourse referents – the existential *there* BE structure and the existential unaccusative structure. The use of *there* BE sentences for the (re-)establishment of new discourse referents is well-known; if existential unaccusatives also establish discourse referents by means of INSTANTIATE, then this predicts that speakers would make use of this structure – all other things being equal – for discourse referent establishment too. This is what the corpus experiment below is designed to test.

3 Experiment

The motivating intuition behind the corpus experiment described in this section is the following: if existential unaccusatives and existential *there* BE sentences share the discourse referent establishing function INSTANTIATE, there should be evidence in usage for speakers' recruiting the existential unaccusative structure for this discourse function. The following subsections describe the corpus experiment: the operationalizing of the relevant notions from syntactic theory; the hypothesis formulation in terms of the operationalization; the collection of the data from the corpus, in which factors like sentence type and lexical frequency were controlled for.

3.1 Method

The hypothesis behind the experiment concerns the usage of a particular syntactic structure, but corpus data obviously does not contain speakers' analyses of the sentences they use. The first step in implementing the experiment is to operationalize syntactic structure. For this experiment, specific verbs serve as stand-ins for syntactic structures. For example, a sentence with the verb *arrive* is assumed to occur in the existential unaccusative structure – with a VP-internal argument that is part of an existential small clause. The verbs used as stand-ins for the existential unaccusative structure included *enter*, *arrive*, and *emerge*. These verbs were chosen because they were all judged by the author as acceptable in *there*-insertion sentences (see also Milsark 1974) – the class of *arrive*-type verbs in English is quite small if "particle verb" predicates like *walk in*, *dart in*, *come over*, etc. are excluded.[5] These verbs were also selected because unergative verbs matched in lexical frequency were found for them.

The existential unaccusative structure is contrasted with the unergative structure, one in which the single argument of the sentence is VP-external. Verbs that were stand-ins for the unergative structure, *laugh*, *smile*, and *sleep*, pass the cognate object diagnostic. For example, *smile* occurs productively in cognate object sentences like (20):

(20) The child smiled a wide smile.

---

[5] As discussed here and in Irwin (2018), sentences with indefinite subjects of predicates like *walk in* are assumed to have the *arrive*-type syntactic structure, but these "particle verb" predicates, though very productive, are much harder to search and control for in a corpus study.

Finally, the verbs chosen for comparison were matched for lexical frequency in the corpus, as discussed below.

The experiment also requires an operationalization of newness to the discourse; this discourse property is operationalized as indefiniteness. In other words, a DP of the form [a NP] like *a cat* is assumed to have the status discourse-new. This assumption is far from perfect, of course, since not all discourse-new entities are indefinite in form (for discussion, see Birner 1996, among others), and not all indefinites are new in their discourse status. For the purposes of this experiment, only indefinites of the form [a/an NP] were included; for comparison, only definite DPs of the form [the NP] were included.

Put in these operationalized terms, then, the prediction is as follows: relative to the frequency of definite subjects of these verb types respectively, we expect to find more indefinite subjects of existential unaccusative verbs than indefinite subjects of unergative verbs. It is worth noting at this point that this hypothesis does not speak directly for or against the specific syntactic decomposition proposed here and in Irwin (2018). But the results will be interpreted to suggest that any theoretical model should capture the asymmetry in the discourse function of existential unaccusative vs. unergative verbs; the decomposition proposed here is one such model that captures that asymmetry. The proposed analysis also predicts an asymmetry between subjects of unaccusative verbs of the *break/freeze* type versus those of the existential unaccusative type, since although the subject of the change-of-state verbs is analyzed as an underlying object, that argument is not part of an existential predication. As discussed further along, the testing of this hypothesis is set aside for future work.

3.1.1 Corpus, verbs, and lexical frequency

The Corpus of Contemporary American English (COCA) was used (Davies 2008) since it has the advantage of being large (450 million words at the time of the data collection), freely available, and containing a mix of genres, including spoken data (TV shows), novels, magazines, newspapers, film scripts, and more.[6] In order to use verbs matched for lexical frequency, the representatives for the existential unaccusative class were chosen first, since English has fewer of these that occur as single verbs, as noted above. These were chosen from the list of top

---

6 The size of the COCA has increased since this corpus study was conducted; as of 2021, the COCA now contains more than one billion words.

50,000 words in the corpus.[7] Unergative verbs that were closely matched for lexical frequency were then chosen. These verbs, along with lexical frequency and ranking in the COCA are given in Tables 1 and 2 below.

Table 1: Existential unaccusative verbs.

rank	verb	frequency
710	enter	54,479
813	arrive	47,435
1307	emerge	24,476

Table 2: Unergative verbs.

rank	verb	frequency
710	enter	54,479
813	arrive	47,435
1307	emerge	24,476

3.2 Procedure

For each verb, sentences of two types were extracted: those with indefinite subjects ("a/an NP") and those with definite subjects ("the NP"). Example search strings used in the COCA interface are given in (21)–(22):

(21) Example search string (for *smile*) for indefinite subjects
.|;|, a|an [n*] [smile].[v*]

(22) Example search string (for *smile*) for definite subjects
.|;|, the [n*] [smile].[v*]

---

[7] Available online at http://www.wordfrequency.info/intro.asp.

These search strings are such that the definite/indefinite NP would most likely be in subject position – that is what the punctuation separated by the "pipe" symbol captures.[8]

Further processing of the data returned by the searches was performed as follows: only sentences in which the target verb was the main verb were included; and only complete sentences were included (the search results included a few incomplete sentences such as *a baby smiling*). Finally, because the unergative verbs are strongly biased toward animate subjects, only sentences with animate subjects were included in the analysis.

3.3 Results

After processing the extracted sentences as described above, the total number of (existential) unaccusative sentences was 973, and the total number of unergative sentences was 925.[9] Tables 3 and 4 show the breakdown of the extracted sentences by verb type. Table 3 shows the number of (existential) unaccusatives broken down by verb, and Table 4 shows unergatives by verb. The verbs in each table are listed in order of COCA ranking from highest to lowest frequency.

Table 3: Sentences with unaccusative verbs (N=973).

Verb	N	ratio
enter	387	39.8 %
arrive	411	42.2 %
emerge	175	18.0 %
total	973	100 %

---

[8] This search string has the drawback of excluding all sentences in which the NP is modified (e.g. *a happy child*); it also excludes sentences with adjunct material between subject and verb (e.g. *a child slowly entered*). Finally, the search string only includes verbs in simple forms – i.e. simple present and simple past – so, for example, sentences with modals or in the progressive were not included. As an anonymous reviewer points out, it may be that these restrictions create a slight bias toward definite subjects, since adjectival modification might be more common with indefinite subjects in a presentational context.

[9] The word "unaccusative" rather than "existential unaccusative" is used here for brevity in this section.

Table 4: Sentences with unergative verbs (N=925).

Verb	N	ratio
laugh	413	44.7 %
smile	373	40.3 %
sleep	139	15.0 %
total	925	100 %

These tables show that the distribution of the verbs in the extracted sentences matches that of the ranking and lexical frequency for the corpus overall. Within the unaccusative and unergative groups, sentences with the two most frequent verbs (*enter* and *arrive* for the unaccusatives and *laugh* and *smile* for the unergatives) account for approximately 80 % of the data, and in both the unergative and unaccusative groups, the data is evenly distributed between these verbs.[10] The least frequent verbs in each category (*emerge* for the unaccusatives and *sleep* for the unergatives) account for 18 % and 15 % of the data in each of their categories respectively.

We turn now to the distribution of definite and indefinite subjects for the two sentence types, focusing specifically on the proportion of indefinite subjects within each sentence type. Table 5 shows that 25.3 % of the unaccusative sentences have indefinite subjects; Table 6 shows that 3.8 % of the unergative sentences have indefinite subjects.

Table 5: Unaccusative subjects.

Subject type	N	ratio
Definite	727	74.7 %
Indefinite	246	25.3 %
total	973	100 %

---

[10] There is likely some noise in the lexical frequency for *enter*; this may be because of this word's use in legal contexts, as in "the judge entered a plea of guilty". Extracted sentences with this type of usage were excluded from the analysis.

Table 6: Unergative subjects.

Subject type	N	ratio
Definite	890	96.2 %
Indefinite	35	3.8 %
total	925	100 %

Note that the low N for indefinite subjects of both sentence types is to be expected. Even though indefinite subjects are not categorically disallowed in English, corpus work has repeatedly found that English, like many languages, disfavors new information in subject position (Horn 1986; Prince 1981, 1992; Beaver et al. 2005, *inter alia*). To the extent that indefiniteness is correlated with discourse newness, then, the low N for indefinite subjects found in the data is unsurprising.

Let us return to the hypothesis about the distribution of indefinite subjects: if verb type does not make a difference for the establishment of new discourse referents in subject position, then the ratio of definite to indefinite subjects should be roughly the same in both sentence types – we expect the ratio of indefinite subjects of unaccusatives (25.3 %) and indefinite subjects of unergatives (3.8 %) to be very similar. These ratios are clearly not the same, and the difference is statistically significant. A Pearson's Chi-squared test shows that the distribution of indefinite/definite subject types between the unaccusative and unergative sentences is statistically significant (23).

(23) Pearson's Chi-squared test with Yates' continuity correction
Chi-squared = 172.07, df = 1, p-value < .001

To put this result differently – when the proportion of indefinite and definite subjects for each verb type is compared, the higher frequency of indefinite subjects in the unaccusative group is not the result of chance. This result supports the hypothesis that existential unaccusatives establish new discourse referents more than unergatives do. Future corpus work will determine if existential unaccusatives establish new discourse referents more than *break*-type unaccusatives do.

4 Further data exploration

The significance testing above confirms the hypothesis that verb type does matter for discourse referent establishment from subject indefinites. Because the data extracted from the corpus is small, the data can be explored further, qualitatively, for the discourse functions that the sentence types in question have. In particular, we can apply the litmus test for discourse referent establishment, subsequent reference. This descriptive section compares the sentences with indefinite subjects with *arrive* and *laugh*. In addition to comparing the degree to which each verb type establishes a persistent discourse referent, we will also explore some of the other uses that these indefinite subject sentences have. The results from this section support the claim that indefinite subjects of arrive establish persistent discourse referents more than indefinite subjects of *laugh*, but we will also see that *arrive*-type sentences have an interesting variety of other discourse functions.

The data for this comparison followed the same methods for searching the corpus and processing the extracted data as in original study, but because it was carried out in the spring of 2019, the number of sentences extracted is not the same as that of the original study (because the COCA has increased in size). The comparison here is between *laugh* and *arrive*. *Arrive* was selected because it is the prototypical verb of the existential unaccusative class (setting aside *come in*, etc.), and *laugh* was chosen because it matches *arrive* most closely in rank and lexical frequency in the COCA. After excluding non-animate subjects and processing the data as described above, the N's for indefinite subjects for the 2016 and 2019 searches are as shown in Table 7.

Table 7: Indefinite subjects extracted from 2016, 2019 searches.

Verb	N (2016)	N (2019)	% of data
laugh	13	16	~17 %
arrive	66	79	~83 %
totals	79	95	100 %

The extracted sentences from the both searches contain the same proportions of *laugh* and *arrive* sentences – in both data sets, subjects of *laugh* account for approximately 17 % of the indefinite subjects, and *arrive* sentences account for about 83 % of the data. The discussion in this section will focus on the data from the (2019) search, since this includes the data from the (2016) search.

One qualitative generalization that can be made about all of the discourse referents established by these indefinite subjects is that for the most part these are fairly transient discourse referents, even in the cases where the referent is subsequently referred to. This is likely a fact of most narratives – most stories only have a few main characters. The discourse referents that are most salient and referred to frequently over the course of a narrative tend to be established at the beginning of a narrative, early on. But even granted that the discourse referents established by indefinite subjects are fairly minor ones, we still find striking differences in subsequent reference between unergative and existential unaccusative sentences.

The most clear-cut diagnostic for discourse referent establishment is subsequent reference to the indefinite NP – using a definite NP, a pronominal, or a name – in one of the following sentences. Using this diagnostic, Table 8 shows that 6 % indefinite subjects of *laugh* were subsequently referred to, and 47 % of subjects of *arrive* were subsequently referred to.

Table 8: Discourse reference.

Verb	Subsequent reference definite/pronominal/name	None	Unclear
laugh	6 % (N=1)	93 % (N=15)	0 % (N=0)
arrive	47 % (N=37)	43 % (N=34)	10 % (N=8)

Table 8 also shows that the data for *arrive* included a number of unclear cases – in 10 % of the *arrive* sentences it was not clear from the context what the discourse status of the indefinite NP was.

The clearest pattern in the data from this exploration is the fact that, with one exception, subjects of *laugh* are not subsequently referred to.[11] The discourse referent that is most salient for the *laugh* sentences is an event – specifically, a sound event. These sentences might be called "scene-setting" since they add

---

11 The context of the exceptional unergative sentence is given in (i) below, with the two pronominal references underlined:

i. He sat midway forward, studying the passengers around him: their gestures, where they looked, whom they talked to and in what tones. They were all so transparent. **A woman laughed**, and he stared <u>her</u> down. "I'm not a freak," he snarled, and <u>she</u> couldn't muster a response. He turned away sullenly. "I'm better than you. I'm better than all of you."

descriptive information to the scene. In the case of *laugh*, they add auditory description to a scene. Examples (24) and (25) give two instances from the extracted sentences with *laugh*. Here we see that both sentences establish a discourse referent that is subsequently referred to by a pronoun or a definite NP, but the reference is to a sound event in both cases. In these examples, the target sentence is in boldface, and the discourse reference in the subsequent sentence is both underlined and in boldface.

(24) Directly below her, in the street, **a woman laughed**. **It** was a throaty, intimate sound.

(25) Around the bend, **a child laughs** # I start toward **the sound** as # I slowly begin to creep toward my

In the examples given below as (26)–(27), these unergative sentences do not establish any salient discourse referents – not even the sound event is referred to. These unergative sentences simply provide sensory, scene-setting details.

(26) In the echoing wings, **a girl laughed** somewhere, and a door slammed.

(27) Out in Kilindini Harbor, a hippo snorted. **A hyena laughed** somewhere in the night.

Subjects of *arrive* were more likely to be subsequently referred to than subjects of *laugh*. The selections in (28)–(30) give two examples of what the different types of subsequent reference to subjects of *arrive* look like.[12]

(28) **A guest arrives** through the festooned gate. A girl, something of a tomboy – flannel shirt and blue jeans, a red cowboy hat. **She** holds out a present wrapped in paper

(29) **A general arrives**; the trembling stationmaster gives **him** the last two troikas, including the one reserved for couriers. **The general** drives off

---

[12] Example (28) has the interesting distinction of presenting a new entity with two indefinites – first with "a guest", and then with "a girl". This is also the case with example (32).

(30) Just as I'm ready to leave for the morning's contest, **a man arrives**, his calm voice telling me, "We have her." I hired **this man** last night. In a rented hyperplane, **he** and some associates flew home, running an errand for me.

In some cases, *arrive* sentences do, in fact, serve to introduce salient discourse referents, though as noted above, most narratives only have a few main characters, so the rareness of these in the extracted sentences is not surprising. Some of these examples from the corpus are from plays, as in (31), where the script continues with the first lines from the character.

(31) **A woman arrives**, **MAGGIE**, Hawkins' producer.

Two other examples of non-trivial discourse referents established by *arrive* are given in (32) and (33):

(32) In season three, **an American arrives** on the scene, a real American here. I mean **Cora**, Lady Grantham, is an American

(33) After a day in the Pakistani capital, **a man arrived** and said **his** name was Akhtar. We would only ever know him as Akhtar

The qualitative analysis of indefinite subjects of *laugh* suggests that unergative sentences with indefinite subjects most often serve to add descriptive, scene-setting information. But it should be noted that sentences with *arrive* can also serve this function. This is especially the case with the 43 % of *arrive* sentences that are not followed up by a subsequent reference. Descriptively, what is the discourse function (or perhaps narrative function) of these sentences? In the typical case of this usage, a person arrives on the scene and to bring either information (e.g. news, a command, or a message) or an object (e.g. a menu or food). Examples (34)–(36) illustrate this usage; in these examples, the sentence with *arrive* is in boldface, and the item that the indefinite subject brings is underlined and in boldface.

(34) A few minutes later, **a maid arrived** bearing a tray with **a pot of tea and a cup** -- not two cups, but only a single one. Mother didn't seem to care.

(35) A few weeks later, Sally Ganz remembers, **a messenger arrived** to return **the pieces.** The Ganzes discovered that they now owned two damaged

(36) On the twenty-eighth, in the depths of the gray Lenten cold, **a messenger arrived** bearing **a letter**, not from Siegen but from the castle of the Count

5 Discussion and conclusion

In this paper it was hypothesized that a subtype of unaccusative sentence can serve one of the discourse functions of existential *there* BE sentences. The corpus study supports this hypothesis in showing that the greater proportion of indefinite subjects of existential unaccusatives vs. unergatives is not the result of chance. The experiment described here has the limitations noted above – small overall N, limited in tense – but it provides proof of concept that syntactic theory and corpus research can mutually inform each other. The corpus experiment supports the claim that a subset of unaccusative sentences serve the same discourse function as *there* BE sentences, but it does not support or refute the details of the syntactic analysis that generated the hypothesis. Finally, it was noted that the next step in this line of research would be a similar corpus experiment comparing existential unaccusative verbs with change-of-state intransitives like *break* and *freeze*, since the latter class are predicted to behave, in discourse, more like the unergatives.

There is one objection that might be raised with respect to the way in which existential unaccusativity was operationalized in this experiment: The stand-ins for the existential unaccusative structure included the verbs *enter*, *arrive*, and *emerge*. A reasonable objection might be that those verbs inherently denote coming on the scene. There are at least two replies to this objection. One reply is simply that in terms of Levin's (1993) verb classifications, only *emerge* is considered a "verb of appearance"; *arrive* and *enter* are listed as verbs of inherent motion.

Another reply is that on the syntactic analysis assumed here, *arrive*-type verbs occur in the existential unaccusative structure, but as a class, they are unusual since they are derived from Latin preposition + verb constructions. Irwin (2018) argues that a more familiar existential unaccusative sentence in English consists of a motion or manner of motion verb such as *come, run, walk, dart, dance* with a non-incorporated particle such as *in* or *up*. With an indefinite subject, then, we get existential unaccusative sentences such as those in (37)–(40):

(37) A lady walked in.

(38) A little boy darted into the room.

(39) A cab pulled up.

(40) A bird darted by with golden wings. (Guéron 1980: 653)

These are the types of sentences that Guéron (1980) described as "presentational" – as only interpretable on an LF in which the VP denotes "the appearance of the subject in the world of the discourse" (Guéron 1980: 653). And as Guéron points out, none of the verbs in these types of sentence has appearance as a core part of their meaning.[13]

On the analysis proposed here, the existential unaccusative structure itself is responsible for the meaning of appearance or coming-on-the-scene: it does this through the small clause structure and the function INSTANTIATE, part of the denotation of Pred$_{exist}$. The verbal root (*walk*, *dart*, etc.) simply adds additional information about the manner by which that coming-on-the-scene event occurs. Future corpus work will determine the extent to which this prediction holds in usage.

References

Alexiadou, Artemis & Elena Anagnostopoulou. 2004. Voice morphology in the causative-inchoative alternation: Evidence for a non-unified structural analysis of unaccusatives. In Artemis Alexiadou, Elena Anagnostopoulou & Martin Everaert (eds.), *The Unaccusativity Puzzle: Explorations of the Syntax-Lexicon Interface*, 114–136. Oxford: Oxford University Press.
Alexiadou, Artemis & Florian Schäfer. 2011. An unaccusativity diagnostic at the syntax-semantics interface: *There*-insertion, indefinites and restitutive *again*. In Ingo Reich, Eva Horch & Dennis Pauly (eds.), *Sinn & Bedeutung*, 15. 101–115.
Baker, Mark, Kyle Johnson & Ian Roberts. 1989. Passive arguments raised. *Linguistic inquiry* 20(2). 219–251. https://www.jstor.org/stable/4178625
Beaver, David, Itamar Francez & Dmitry Levinson. 2005. Bad subject: (Non-)canonicality and NP distribution in existentials. In Efthymia Georgala & Jonathan Howell (eds.), *Semantics and Linguistic Theory (SALT) 15*, 19–43. Ithaca, NY: CLC Publications. https://doi.org/10.3765/salt.v15i0.2920.
Birner, Betty J. 1996. *The discourse function of inversion in English*. London: Routledge.
Burzio, Luigi. 1986. *Italian syntax: A Government-Binding approach*. Dordrecht: Reidel.
Chomsky, Noam. 1957. Syntactic structures. The Hague: Mouton.

---

[13] On the manner of motion class, Levin (1993: 90) notes on that there are "potentially extended uses of certain verbs as verbs of existence."

Chomsky, Noam. 1986. *Knowledge of language: Its nature, origin, and use*. New York, NY: Praeger Publishers.
Collins, Chris. 2005. A smuggling approach to the passive in English. *Syntax* 8(2). 81–120. https://doi.org/10.1111/j.1467-9612.2005.00076.x
Davies, Mark. 2008. The Corpus of Contemporary American English: 450 million words, 1990–present. Available online at http://corpus.byu.edu/coca/. (2021-04-13).
Deal, Amy Rose. 2009. The origin and content of expletives: Evidence from "selection". *Syntax* 12(4). 285–323. https://doi.org/10.1111/j.1467-9612.2009.00127.x
Embick, David. 2004. Unaccusative syntax and verbal alternations. In Artemis Alexiadou, Elena Anagnostopoulou & Martin Everaert (eds.), *The unaccusativity puzzle: Explorations of the syntax-lexicon interface*, 137–158. Oxford: Oxford University Press. DOI: https://doi.org/10.1093/acprof:oso/9780199257652.003.0006
Francez, Itamar. 2007. Existential propositions. Stanford, CA: Stanford University dissertation.
Guéron, Jacqueline. 1980. On the syntax and semantics of PP extraposition. *Linguistic Inquiry* 11(4). 637–678. https://www.jstor.org/stable/4178188.
Hazout, Ilan. 2004. The syntax of existential constructions. *Linguistic Inquiry* 35(3). 393–430. https://doi.org/10.1162/0024389041402616
Hazout, Ilan. 2008. On the relation between expletive "there" and its associate: A reply to Williams. *Linguistic Inquiry* 39(1). 117–128. https://doi.org/10.1162/ling.2008.39.1.117
von Heusinger, Klaus. 2007. Referentially anchored indefinites. In Ileana Comorovski & Klaus von Heusinger (eds.), *Existence: Semantics and syntax*, 273–292. Springer.
Hoekstra, Teun & René Mulder. 1990. Unergatives as copular verbs: Locational and existential predication. *The Linguistic Review* 7. 1–79.
Horn, Laurence R. 1986. Presupposition, theme and variations. In Anne M. Farley, Peter T. Farley, Karl-Erik McCullough (eds.), *Chicago Linguistic Society* (CLS) 22, 168–192.
Irwin, Patricia. 2012. Unaccusativity at the interfaces. New York, NY: New York University dissertation.
Irwin, Patricia. 2018. Existential unaccusativity and new discourse referents. *Glossa: a journal of general linguistics* 3(1). 1–42. https://doi.org/10.5334/gjgl.283
Kural, Murat. 2002. A four-way classification of monadic verbs. In Artemis Alexiadou (ed.), *Theoretical approaches to universals*, 139–163. Amsterdam: Benjamins. https://doi.org/10.1075/la.49.07kur
Levin, Beth. 1993. *English verb classes and alternations: A preliminary investigation*. Chicago, IL: University of Chicago Press.
Levin, Beth, & Malka Rappaport Hovav. 1995. *Unaccusativity: At the syntax-lexical semantics interface*. Cambridge, MA: MIT Press.
Levin, Lorraine S. 1986. Operations on lexical forms: Unaccusative rules in Germanic languages. Cambridge, MA: MIT doctoral dissertation.
Marantz, Alec. 2013. Verbal argument structure: Events and participants. *Lingua* 130. 152–168. https://doi.org/10.1016/j.lingua.2012.10.012
McCloskey, James. 2014. Irish existentials in context. *Syntax* 17(4). 343–384.
McNally, Louise. 1992. An interpretation for the English existential construction. Santa Cruz: University of California at Santa Cruz dissertation.
McNally, Louise. 1997. *A semantics for the English existential construction*. New York, NY: Garland.
Milsark, Gary. 1974. *Existential sentences in English*. Cambridge, MA: Massachusetts Institute of Technology dissertation.

Moro, Andrea. 1997. *The raising of predicates: Predicative noun phrases and the theory of clause structure*. Cambridge, UK: Cambridge University Press.

Myler, Neil. 2014. Building and interpreting possession sentences. New York, NY: New York University dissertation.

Myler, Neil. 2016. *Building and interpreting possession sentences*. Cambridge, MA: MIT Press.

Prince, Ellen F. 1981. Toward a taxonomy of given-new information. In Peter Cole (ed.), *Radical pragmatics*, 223–256. New York, NY: Academic Press.

Prince, Ellen F. 1992. The ZPG letter: Subjects, definiteness, and information-status. In William C. Mann & Sandra A. Thompson (eds.), *Discourse description: Diverse analyses of a fund-raising text*, 295–325. Philadelphia, PA: Benjamins.

Williams, Edwin S. 1994. *Thematic structure in syntax*. Cambridge, MA: MIT Press.

Index

acceptability 2–6, 8, 129, 137–140, 144–151, 154, 157, 158, 161, 162, 165, 168, 169
adjective
– material adjective 14, 17
– privative adjective 13, 15–17, 29
agent 35, 36, 43, 44, 48, 54, 55, 72, 105, 106, 115, 120–123, 125, 128, 129, 132, 142
agentivity 2, 4, 5, 8, 138, 139, 140, 143, 144, 153, 158, 162
agreement 5, 6, 28, 36, 41, 79, 105, 108–111, 124
alternation constructions 35, 43, 47, 49, 51–53, 57, 58
animacy 2, 7, 8, 17, 43, 44, 69–75, 77, 78, 83, 86–90, 92–97, 105–113, 117, 118, 120–124, 128, 130, 133, 158, 166
animacy effect 8, 69, 72, 74, 75, 77, 78, 86, 87, 89, 92–97
animacy hierarchy 107, 124
animal-for-statue construction 13, 17, 29
applicative 34, 50–53, 54, 58, 59
argument hierarchy 1
argument realization 1
argument structure 1–7, 9, 13, 15, 17, 33, 34, 37, 38, 40, 41, 44–47, 49, 50–52, 58, 59, 146, 181, 185
aspectual coercion 8, 137, 139, 140, 145–149, 168, 169
asymmetry 13, 14, 18, 19, 190

benefactive 2, 7, 33–35, 46–54, 56–59

case
– accusative 2, 6, 7, 47, 53–57, 59, 70, 72, 76, 79, 80–83, 87, 88, 90–93, 95, 96, 108, 109
– ergative 6
– dative 1, 2, 7, 33–35, 38, 42, 43, 46–59, 69–73, 76, 79–83, 87, 88, 90–96, 138
case assignment 51, 76, 77
case marking 59, 69–79, 82, 83, 86, 89, 92–97
causative 8, 129–133, 137, 139–142, 168, 169, 183–185

causative alternation 1
change-of-state 141–143, 183–185, 190, 199
coercion 4, 8, 137, 139, 140, 145, 147–151, 155, 162, 168, 169
comparative 7, 13, 14, 18, 19–21
compositional 7, 14
constituent 5, 15, 36–39, 41, 50, 53, 75, 76, 108
Construction grammar 14
cross-linguistic 107, 121, 129, 144

dative alternation 1, 33, 38, 42, 43, 46, 47, 49, 51–57
degree particle 14, 17, 18, 28, 29
discourse context 40, 126, 144, 145, 148
discourse referent 8, 181, 182, 185, 186, 188, 189, 195–198
Dutch 8, 42, 76, 77, 105–109, 111, 120, 121, 127–133

EEG 23–25, 78, 84, 85, 90, 92, 95, 148
English 8, 9, 15, 18, 20, 36, 44, 46, 47, 49, 50, 51, 71, 115, 121, 128, 137, 144, 151, 152, 169, 183, 184, 186–190, 194, 199
ergativity 1, 2
ERP 2, 7, 16, 17, 23, 28, 69–71, 73, 74, 83, 85, 87, 90, 146
event structure 37, 137, 138, 140, 141, 143, 144, 169, 185
eventive 8, 137–145, 147, 149, 150, 152–154, 156, 158, 160–169, 171, 173
eventivity 2, 4, 8, 58, 138–140, 144, 153
experiencer 8, 72, 105, 129, 130, 132, 133, 137, 138, 142, 143, 169
– subject-experiencer (including SubEx etc) 137, 138, 142, 150–167, 169, 171, 173–175
– object-experiencer (including ObEx variants etc) 8, 137–145, 147, 149, 150, 152–155, 169–174

functional 7, 17, 34, 36, 41, 43, 45, 46
functional head 7, 34

Index

German 6, 7, 12, 14, 15, 19, 20, 22, 24, 25, 33, 34, 36, 39, 47, 49, 50, 51, 53, 54, 59, 69, 70–73, 75–77, 79, 80, 83, 89, 93–95, 109, 111, 146
gradable 18, 28

head noun 14, 17

inanimate 7, 8, 43, 44, 69–72, 74, 79, 80–84, 86–88, 90–95, 97, 105–107, 120–125, 133, 142, 150, 152–155, 160, 164–168, 173
incremental 7, 29, 34, 36, 37–41, 60
inference 42, 139, 139, 144, 168
inherent case 1

Japanese 6, 37, 40

Korean 6, 36, 37, 40, 50

lexical aspect 169, 147

mental lexicon 34, 76
modal 18, 20, 22

non-agentive 4, 5, 138, 142–145, 147, 150, 152–167, 170–174

optimality theory 106, 113, 114, 133

passive construction 8, 121–125, 129
passivization 4, 8, 76, 96, 105, 106, 120–126, 129, 130, 133
patient 8, 20, 35, 36, 43, 72, 106, 109, 114, 115, 120–125, 128–130, 133
pragmatic 3, 17, 22, 139, 144, 145, 158, 168
preposition 2, 17, 42, 46, 47, 49–51, 54, 58, 75, 76, 96, 188, 199
prepositional 17, 22, 30, 36, 38, 40, 43, 46–48, 51, 53, 54, 56

privative 7, 13–17, 19, 23, 29
prominence 113, 117–122, 124, 128, 129, 133, 106, 109–111
psych predicates 1. See also psych verbs
psych verb(s) 4, 5, 126, 129–133, 140
purpose clause 20, 21, 22, 26

radical incrementality 33, 34, 40, 45, 60
reflexivization 7, 13, 14, 17, 19, 20
role assignment 70, 72, 77, 79

standard of comparison 13, 14, 20–22, 28, 29
standardizer 21, 22, 28, 29, 30
stative 8, 121, 137–142, 143–145, 147, 150, 152, 156, 160–162, 164, 165, 166, 168, 169
structural case 1, 51, 72, 76, 96

thematic 7, 33, 35–38, 40, 41, 43–50, 53, 55, 58–60, 70–72, 74, 77, 78, 94, 95, 97, 129, 142
thematic role 7, 33, 34, 36–38, 40, 41, 43–49, 55, 59, 60, 70–72, 77, 78, 129, 142
topic 8, 35, 105–107, 109, 111, 113–120, 124–133
topicality 114, 116, 120, 124, 128, 133
transitive 1, 19, 46, 48, 58, 70–74, 76–78, 93, 97, 107–109, 120–123, 127–129, 140, 141, 152, 199
transitivity 72, 73

unaccusativity 1, 183–185, 199
unergative(s) 1, 2, 4, 9, 129, 181, 182, 189–194, 196–199

weak incrementality 34, 39, 40
word order 2, 4, 5, 8, 36, 37, 40, 51, 56, 70, 71, 74, 79, 105–108, 110, 111, 115, 117, 128

www.ingramcontent.com/pod-product-compliance
Lightning Source LLC
Chambersburg PA
CBHW050526170426
43201CB00013B/2098